IMAGES
*of America*

# THE POMO OF LAKE COUNTY

**On the Cover:** Wearing traditional regalia, Hudson Jack and his son from Big Valley Rancheria demonstrate age-old Pomo dances for audiences at the Lake County Fair in 1950. At the microphone, Bill Graves from Upper Lake Rancheria joins them since singer/musicians are increasingly rare. Graves's sister and daughter are also dancing the more sedate women's part. (Photograph by McCloud's Lakeport Photo Service, courtesy Lake County Historic Courthouse Museum.)

IMAGES
*of America*

# THE POMO OF LAKE COUNTY

K. C. Patrick

ARCADIA
PUBLISHING

ISBN 978-0-7385-5604-8

Published by Arcadia Publishing
Charleston, South Carolina

Printed in the United States of America

Library of Congress Catalog Card Number: 2007935819

For all general information contact Arcadia Publishing at:
Telephone 843-853-2070
Fax 843-853-0044
E-mail sales@arcadiapublishing.com
For customer service and orders:
Toll-Free 1-888-313-2665

Visit us on the Internet at www.arcadiapublishing.com

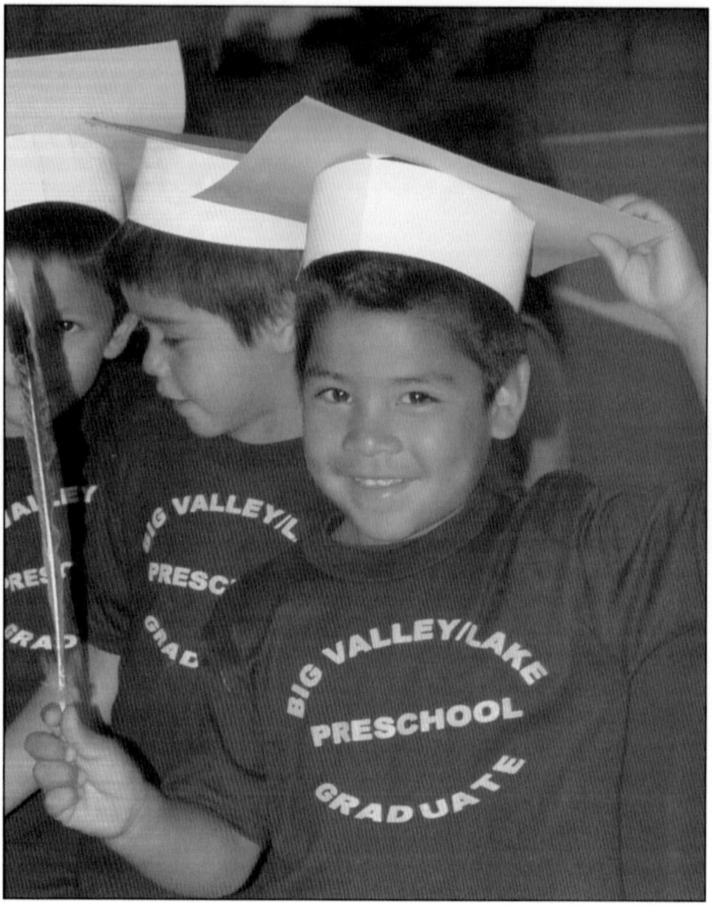


**DEDICATION.** To the Children. Tony Jack said to me, "Maybe if they know what has happened to us, they will understand that emptiness they feel when they reach a certain age." Beyond the emptiness, I hope they will feel pride in the endurance and gentle adaptability that is the survival skill and strength of the Lake County Pomo. Hope, they say, is a thing with feathers. (Photograph by Carol Dillenger, Big Valley Rancheria.)

# Contents

# ACKNOWLEDGMENTS

Thank you to everyone who helped make this book possible. I apologize for errors and omissions. Thanks to my Arcadia publisher and editors for their patience and perseverance; to the staffs at Lake County Historic Courthouse Museum and Lower Lake Historic Schoolhouse Museum for their support and resourcefulness, and especially Sunday afternoons with Donna Howard; to Sherri Smith-Ferri and Keith Whitewolf James at the Grace Hudson Museum in Ukiah for their time and warmth; to archivists at Field Museum in Chicago; to Trett Bishop and Robert Lee, who set aside their own considerable skill as photographers to restore the old work of others; to archaeologists John Parker and Maureen Carpenter for assisting me as if I were a colleague; to the Lake County Historical Society and Heyday Books for allowing me to use their published material; to Katie Whelchel for giving me her husband's *The Distant Bells of St. Turibius Mission*; to Dan Edmonson's as yet unpublished thesis; to the memory of Henry Mauldin for his generous foresight in writing down so much; and to Chris Mauldin for perspective. Unless otherwise stated, all maps are historian Henry Mauldin's.

Some people have boxes of photographs and some people have none; without a secure family home and storage, it is almost impossible to accumulate possessions and memorabilia. The Lake County Pomos have been refugees in their own country, afflicted by poverty and persecution. Add to that a non-graphic language culture whose familial relations are not like European lineages and a traditional reluctance to mention the dead lest they be dishonored. In that light, I am especially grateful to those who have been so generous with their memories: Jim and Gail Brown, Ignatius Elliott, JoJo Gomez, Tony Jack, John W. Johnson, Les Miller, Charlene Munoz, Betty Nitka, and Donna White. You raise me up.

I am also grateful to my family and friends near and far who never seem to lose faith: Stephen and Rebecca Coleman; Dan'l Coleman, the class of 1957; the memory of Marcus Anderson; and my friend from the beginning, Marcia Sanderson.

# INTRODUCTION

## THE POMO OF LAKE COUNTY: FROM CRADLE TO CASINO

They had no word for sad. They are now called Pomo, but the native people had no word for themselves, since there was no reason to say the obvious. Everyone understood they were not, for example, deer or fish; they were people. There were words in several languages for places, such as *Koi*, and the people who lived at that place, *Koi-en-fo*. There were no political subdivisions such as Napa and Lake County; people simply went where there was a comfortable place to live and eat and where no one else already lived. But settlers and scholars needed names, so they labeled the Pomo and their neighbors by the languages they spoke: Eastern Pomo, Southeastern Pomo, Northern Pomo, Central Pomo, and so forth. Each had a unique spoken language with specific vocabulary, verbal punctuation, and cultural context, not intelligible to the others. In the forests north of the Clear Lake Basin lived the unfriendly Yuki, an entirely different linguistic family, and to the east and south lived four or five other language groups. Little Clear Lake Basin may have been unique in its diversity, but the people had inhabited the region for so long they had worked it out.

The culture of the Native Americans here must have been incredibly mysterious to people arriving with their own babble of languages and thousands of years of European culture of war, poverty, and domination, overlaid with recent American experiences. When men used the word "tribe," for example, it evoked images of screaming Indians charging an invading wagon in an effort to protect their hunting grounds, or perhaps a memory of well-armed Mohawk soldiers in battles during the French and Indian War with English colonists. The Declaration of Independence labeled Native Americans "merciless Indian Savages whose known rule of warfare is an undistinguished destruction of all ages, sexes, and conditions." Lake County Pomo had no tribes in the sense that Europeans understood them; they were more like seven small Italian city-states—the people in Florence were different from the people in Venice, and the people near what became Middletown were different from the people in what became Lakeport. They were entirely independent tribelets and spoke different languages, so some neighbors had to be bi- or tri-lingual. Even thousands of years ago, there seems to have been plenty of travel, trade, and intermarriage, so people accommodated one another even if they didn't speak the language.

Similarly, there were no "chiefs" in the sense of Geronimo or Sitting Bull. In early accounts, the headman was often called captain, since he did not rule but led by example, negotiation, and consensus. He might have been called a preacher, since each day began with him or her exhorting the people to be moral and wise. The people of the Clear Lake Basin were singularly unwarlike. There were no war chiefs needed and no culture of triumph or killing. In one recorded skirmish, notable for its great numbers, outlanders attacked and killed six women who were gathering seeds. Men from villages near Kelseyville and Lakeport got together and attacked the camp of the killers, slaying 19. At that point, the two leaders called it even and everyone went home. Other reports indicate that battles over hunting or gathering territory usually ended when the first man was killed, and then the winning side paid the losers for their loss.

These Native Americans made little trash, did not built temples or make sacrifices, and did not accumulate wealth of silk or gold, so they were often thought of as lazy. They acknowledged that they had been given a bounteous world and they worked to keep it balanced and unchanged from their Creator's design.

Imagine their astonishment at the ways of the Spanish, the Russians, and the soon-to-be Americans.

Today's self-determining tribes have the same key challenges on their community agendas that trouble the rest of the world, such as immigration, an economy of scarcity, and tradition versus change. Who should be allowed to join the community and who should be forced to go somewhere else? Who decides and on what basis? Ancient Pomos would never have allowed anything to run out; there was a careful balance of consumption and restoration. But today is someone else's world, and there may not be enough food or dry and warm housing, and health may run out before life. Growth and decay are out of balance and the climate is changing. What will that mean? Will there be enough? Who decides where the resources are applied and on what basis? Tradition is secure and comfortable because the results are reliable and time-tested. There is little anxiety when the outcome is assured. There's no luck or accident. Change is exciting and imaginative, cultivating the new, and the outcome may be positive or not. There are unplanned challenges and mistakes. Sometimes it is impossible to go back because the old is gone. Who decides on the accommodation between reliable and risky?

Imagine the astonishment if the Lake County Pomo already had discovered some solutions to these challenges.

# One

# WHAT WERE THEY THINKING?

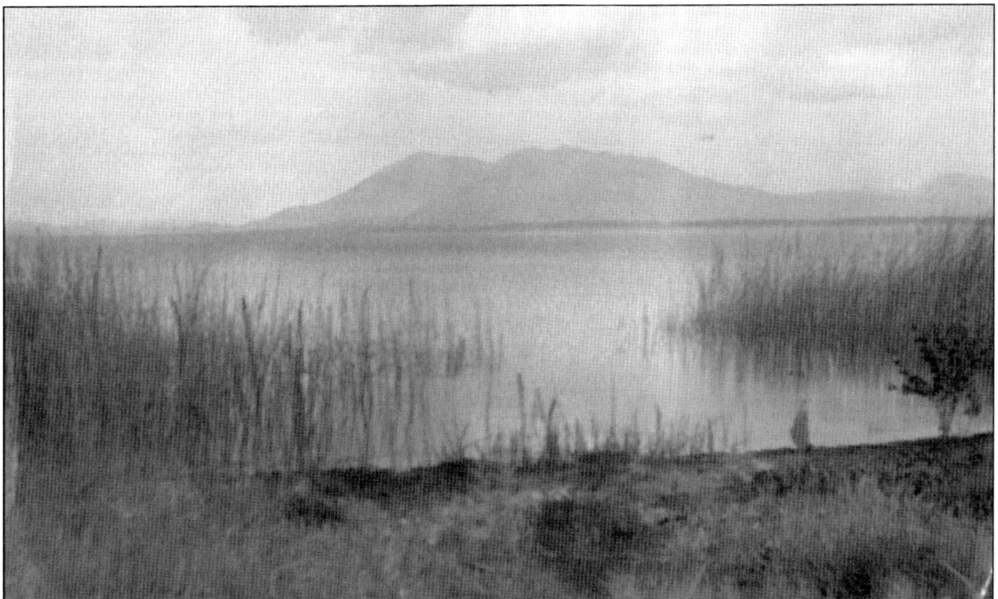

**AFTER DEVIL'S POST PILE AND SONORA PASS.** Clear Lake Basin must have looked like the Garden of Eden to trail-weary pioneers when they stopped and gazed down—the pure blue gem of the lake reflecting the same-color clear sky, set in golden hillsides dotted with shadowing oaks and purple-blue mountains all around. The meadows of grass grew as high as a horse's belly. Streams trickled down the hillside and here and there a spring was pumping out of the earth's heart. Perhaps there was even a welcoming column of smoke rising from what might be home. The Native Americans retreated to their forests. (Courtesy Lake County Historic Courthouse Museum.)

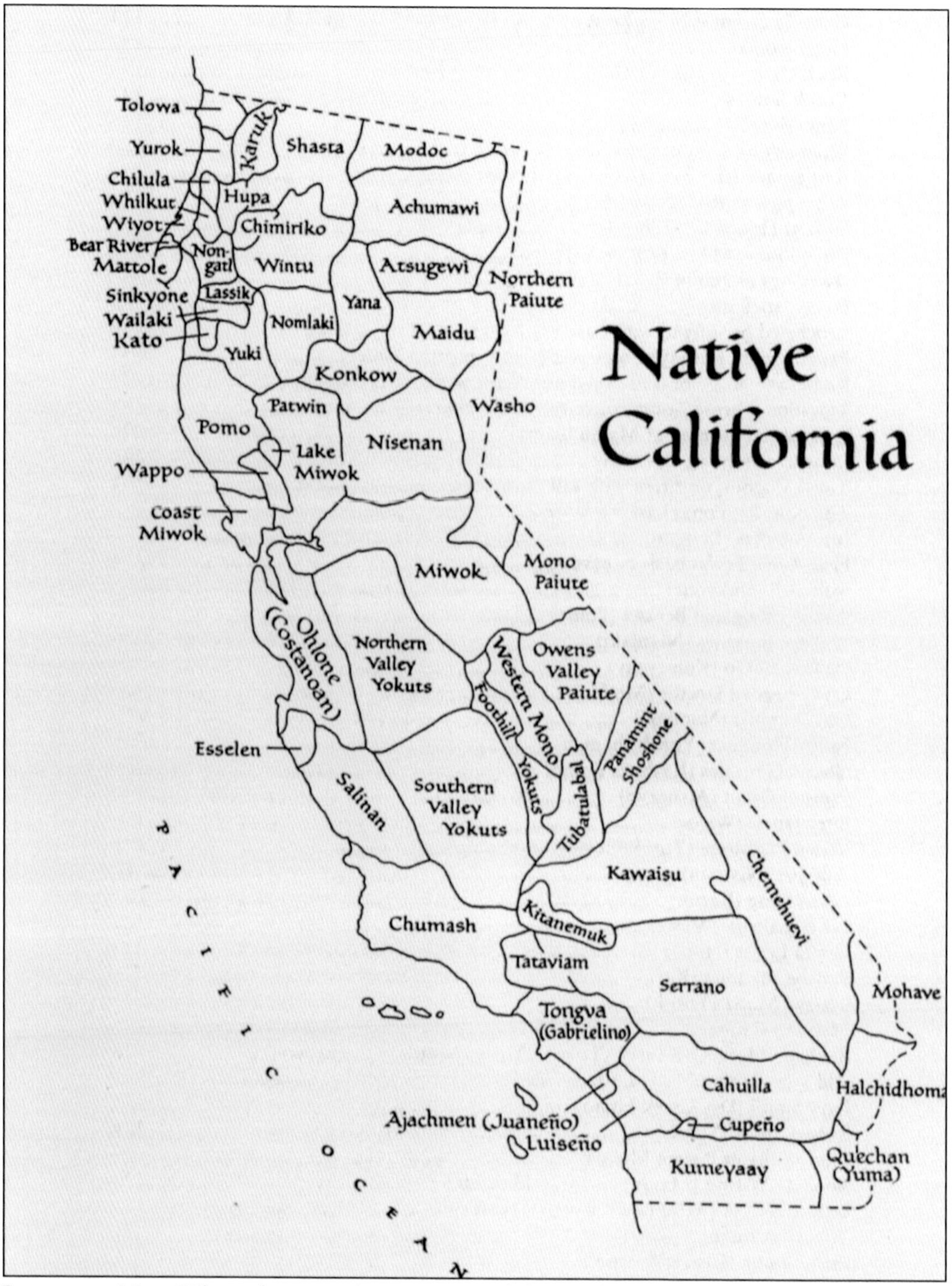


**LANGUAGE MAP.** When white men first came to California, they found more than 100 languages spoken, more than 70 percent of them mutually unintelligible. The population was estimated at about 310,000. The several dozen independent tribal groups labeled as Pomo spoke seven mutually incomprehensible languages. The Lake County area heard three Pomo languages, plus Yuki, Wappo, Lake Miwok, and Hill Patwin resident voices. By 1900, fewer than 20,000 Native Americans lived in all of California. (Map used with permission of M. Margolin, Heyday Books, Inc.)

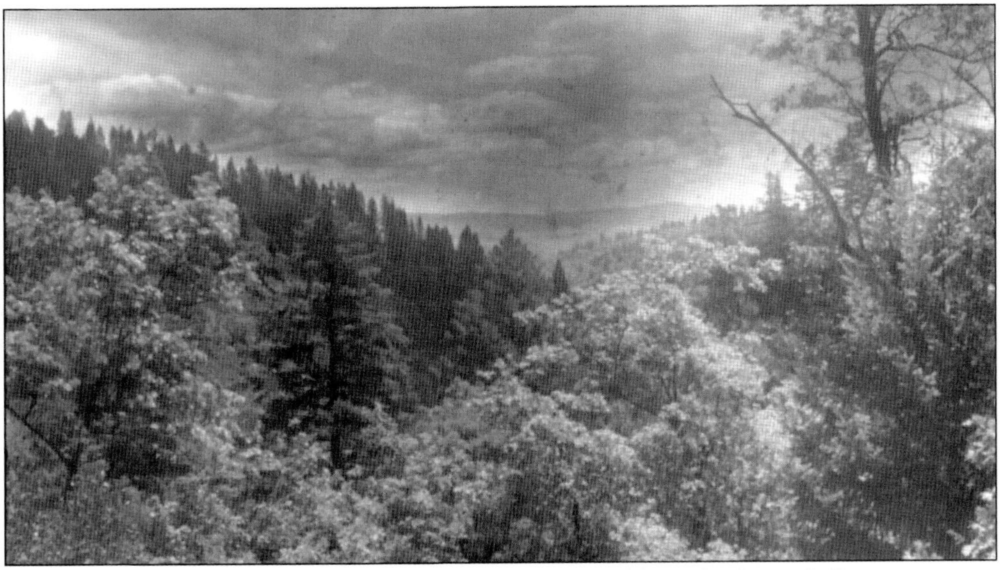

**A GREAT WHITE SNOW WILL COME.** Story tellers recited how the Spanish flew in on great white wings over the water and said this land was their chief's. They did not stay. English came to the bay where the people gathered seafood and salt. They sailed off but made it known that their queen claimed that place. Mountain men came, but finding no beaver or otter, they departed quickly, leaving articles of clothing for the naked people. By the time the padres came up from Mexico, half the people had departed from great barking coughs, a pox on the skin, and a mother's breath that could kill her child, and they did not go away. (Courtesy Lake County Historic Courthouse Museum.)

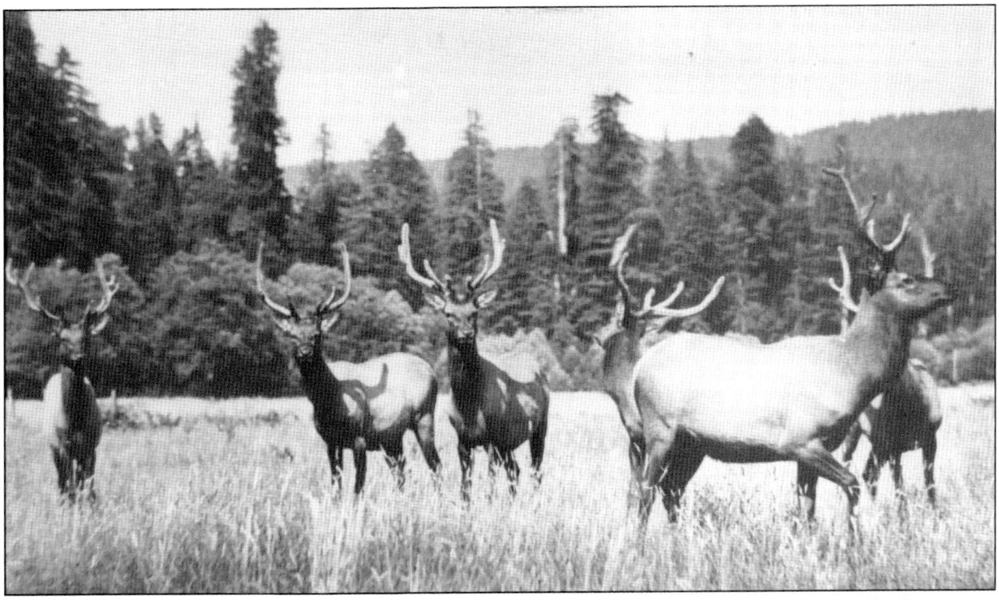

**NO NEED FOR GREED IN ALL THIS ABUNDANCE.** Looking down from Fishell's Hill, there may be 400 elk in the wallow. One mature male will make many meals: fresh-cooked, dried to mix with acorn mush to make a thick soup boiled in a basket. Nothing is waste: the bones, antlers, and teeth will be tools, the skin will be a wrap or sliced into straps and thongs, the testicles may be made into charms to hang over a boy's cradle. (Courtesy *Lake County Record-Bee.*)

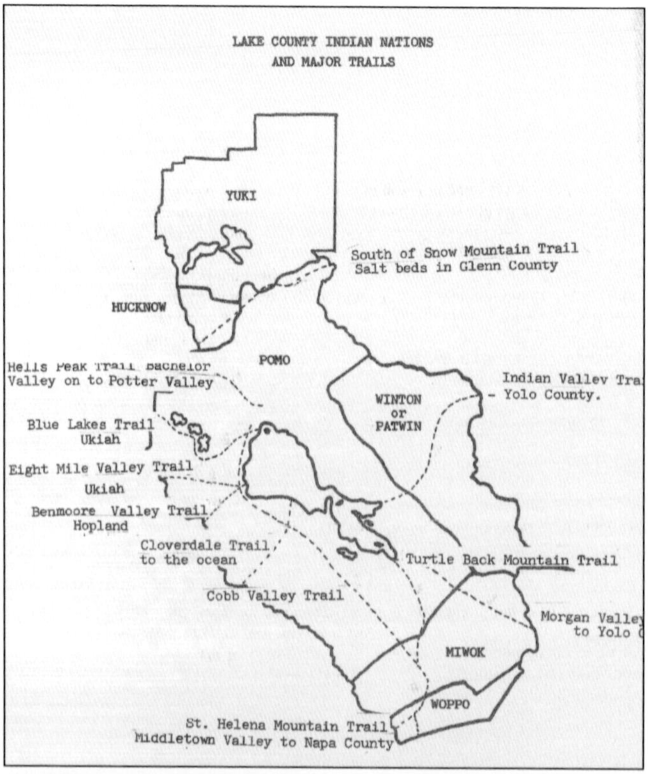


**MAKING INROADS.** There were no roads, and following a trail in single file took some effort. Based on well-worn animal tracks, Indian trails had been carefully maintained for centuries so that bare feet went uninjured and no roots or branches reached onto the trail. Every child learned to remember where there was water. The birds go silent as a runner approaches, virtually naked with his sling wrapped across his forehead holding back his dark glossy hair. Startled, he leaps off the trail into the brush. Up trail, the unflappable oxen continue to widen the beaten path. This Pomo has just discovered his first ox, wagon, and sunburned homesteader. (Courtesy Lake County Historic Society.)

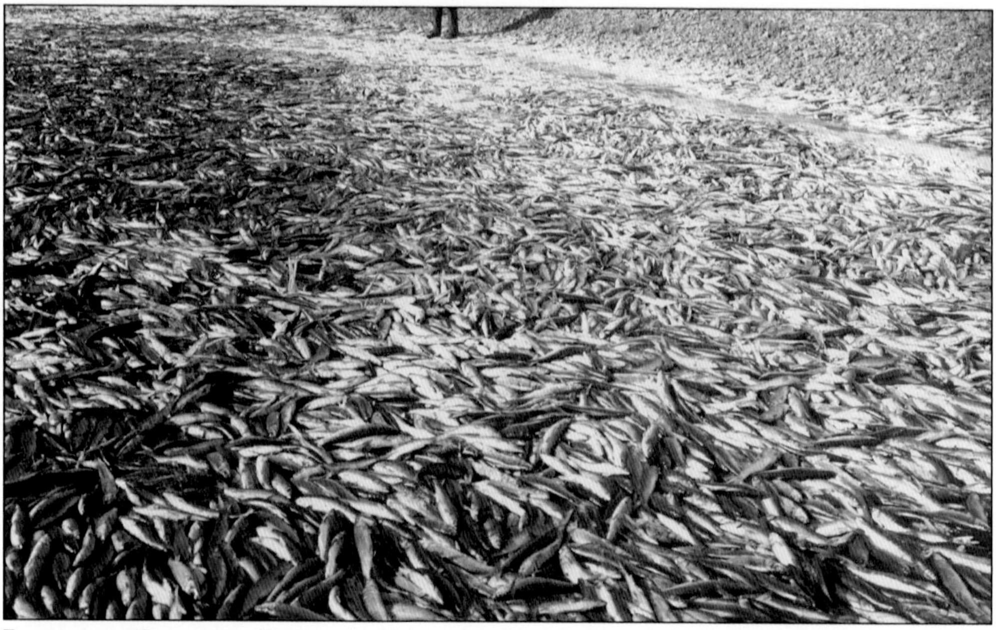

**PLENTY TO TRADE OR SHARE.** At Kelsey Creek, spawning fish are stranded upstream three to five feet deep. Wicker fish traps aren't needed at the lake to catch fish one at a time. This is a better-than-usual year for the tribelet that lives here. Just scoop up the fish and partially dry them, then split and clean them, and dry them the rest of the way for storage through the winter. (Photograph by O. E. Meddaugh, courtesy Lake County Historic Courthouse Museum.)

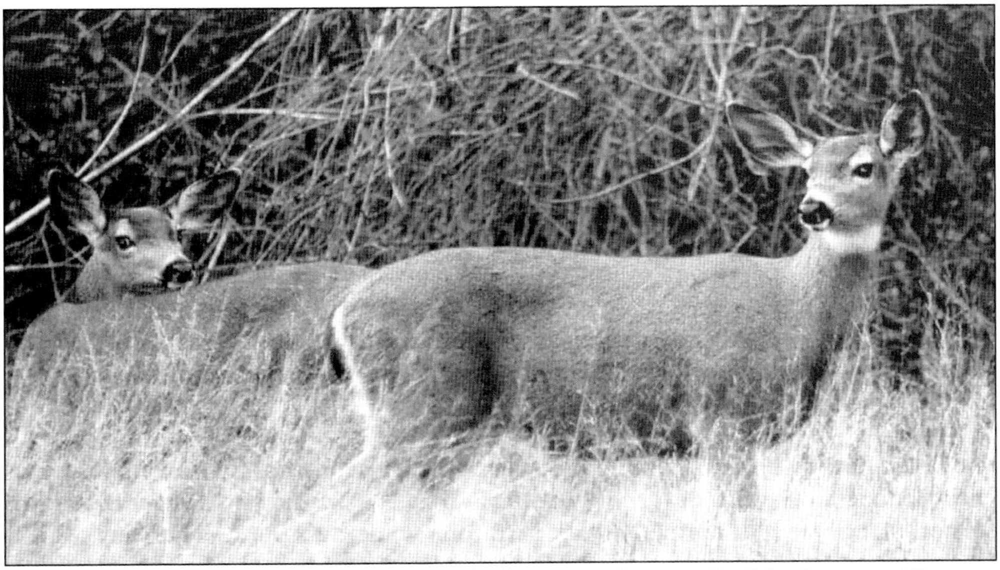

EACH CREATURE HAS ITS PLACE. The gentle deer come down to the lake for water. They are safe from hunters who are not hungry, but the mountain lions follow them. Here in the mud are bear prints—it's too hard to tell whether a black bear, brown bear, or grizzly. They all live here and come to dine on the fish too. They are bigger and faster than people and powerful in many ways. They may even be shamans in disguise.

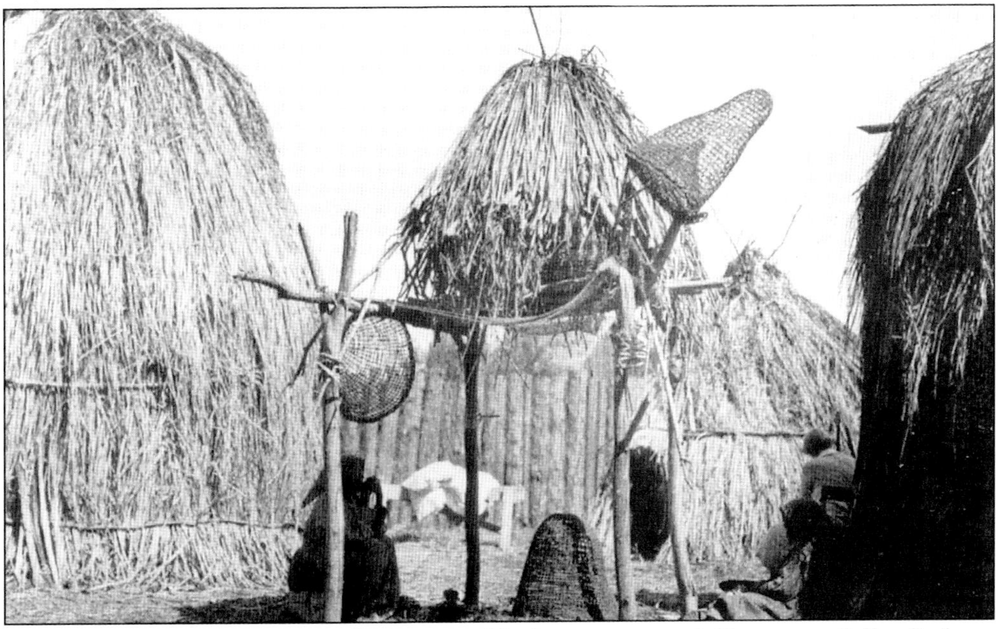

TULES ARE THE STAFF. Natives had no metal before contact with Europeans. Fallen limbs or still-tender tree branches were gathered, bent, and bound as supports for dwellings and storage. Sheaves of tules were harvested from the lakeshores and marshes, tied together, layered to shed rainwater, and secured to the forms. A smoke hole was left at the top and an entrance on the side. If the dwelling housed more than one family, it was easily expandable with additional entrances and smoke holes. Fish traps dry atop the acorn storage around 1900. (Photography by John Hudson, Robert Lee Collection, courtesy Lake County Historic Courthouse Museum.)

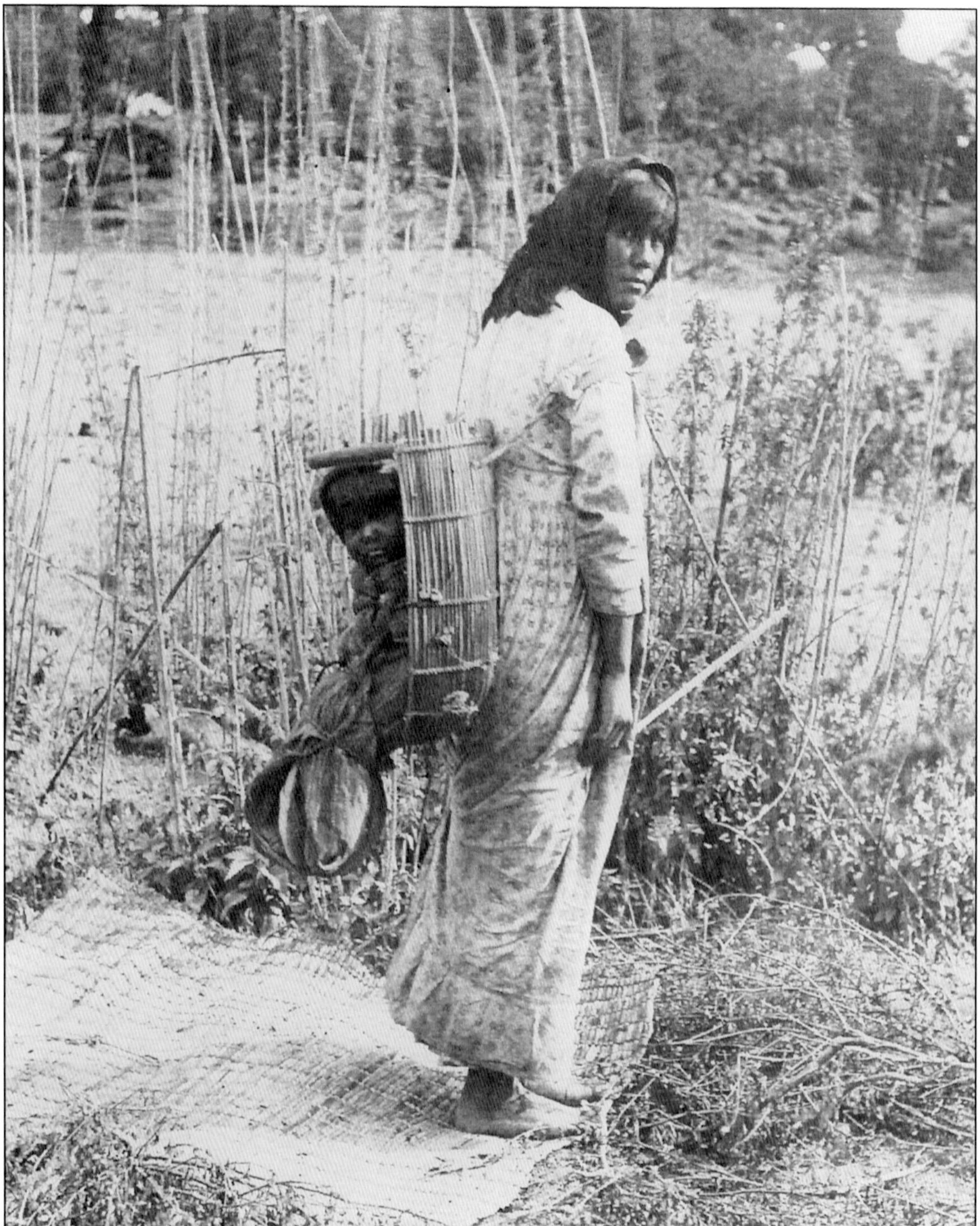

**A Plant for all Seasons.** Tule mats were woven to cover inside walls and packed-dirt floors. White manzanita was used for fires since it had few sparks. Tule houses were not saved from fires; new ones were built. Tule shoots could be eaten in the spring and again when they re-grew; they could be split, shredded and made into mantles, skirts, and diapers. Tule marshes trapped sediment, provided feeding and breeding ground for lake fish and waterfowl, and was a reliable resource. (Courtesy Lower Lake Historic Schoolhouse Museum.)

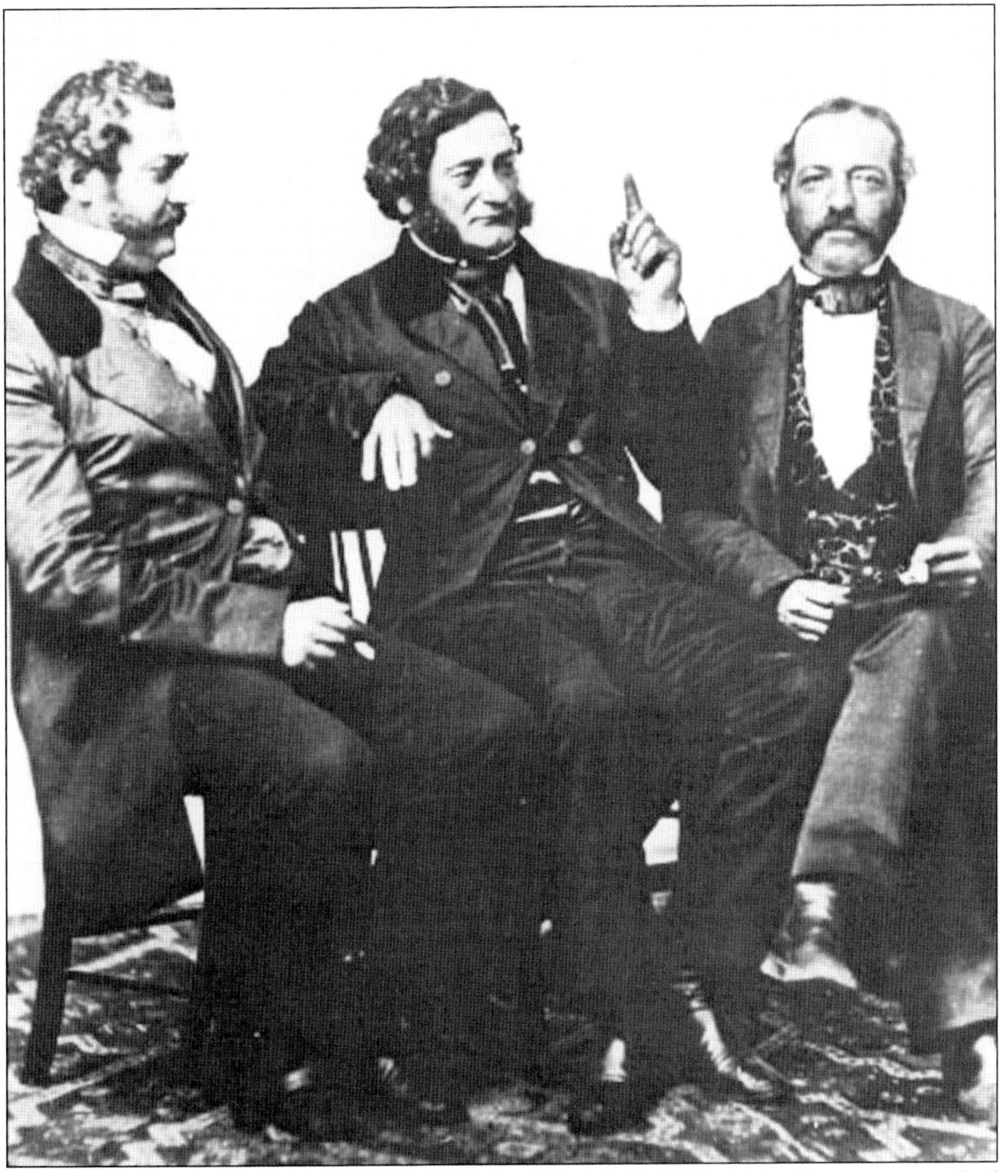

**Going With God.** The chain of Catholic missions founded by Fr. Junipero Serra never reached Clear Lake, but Spanish soldiers like Mariano Vallejo and his brother Salvador (center in the portrait above) raided the area to capture laborers and prospective neophytes. Salvador was said to be arrogant, hot tempered, and vengeful, and was apparently well schooled in intimidation and killing. He formed an alliance with Chief Solano, who often accompanied him on raids. On an island where the people claimed they would rather die than be separated from their homes, he arranged for that to happen. At another time, he invited leaders to an island to parlay, then sealed them in their dance house and incinerated them while Solano's warriors whooped in triumph. Salvador Vallejo claimed a huge land grant in Lake County and brought in long-horned cattle. He employed an Indian majordomo and several capable vaqueros in his absence. In 1848, he sold the 800 or so cattle and grazing rights to four men: Charles Stone, Andrew and Ben Kelsey, and Mr. Stirland. Salvador's grant was later disallowed by the Supreme Court. (Courtesy California Military Museum.)

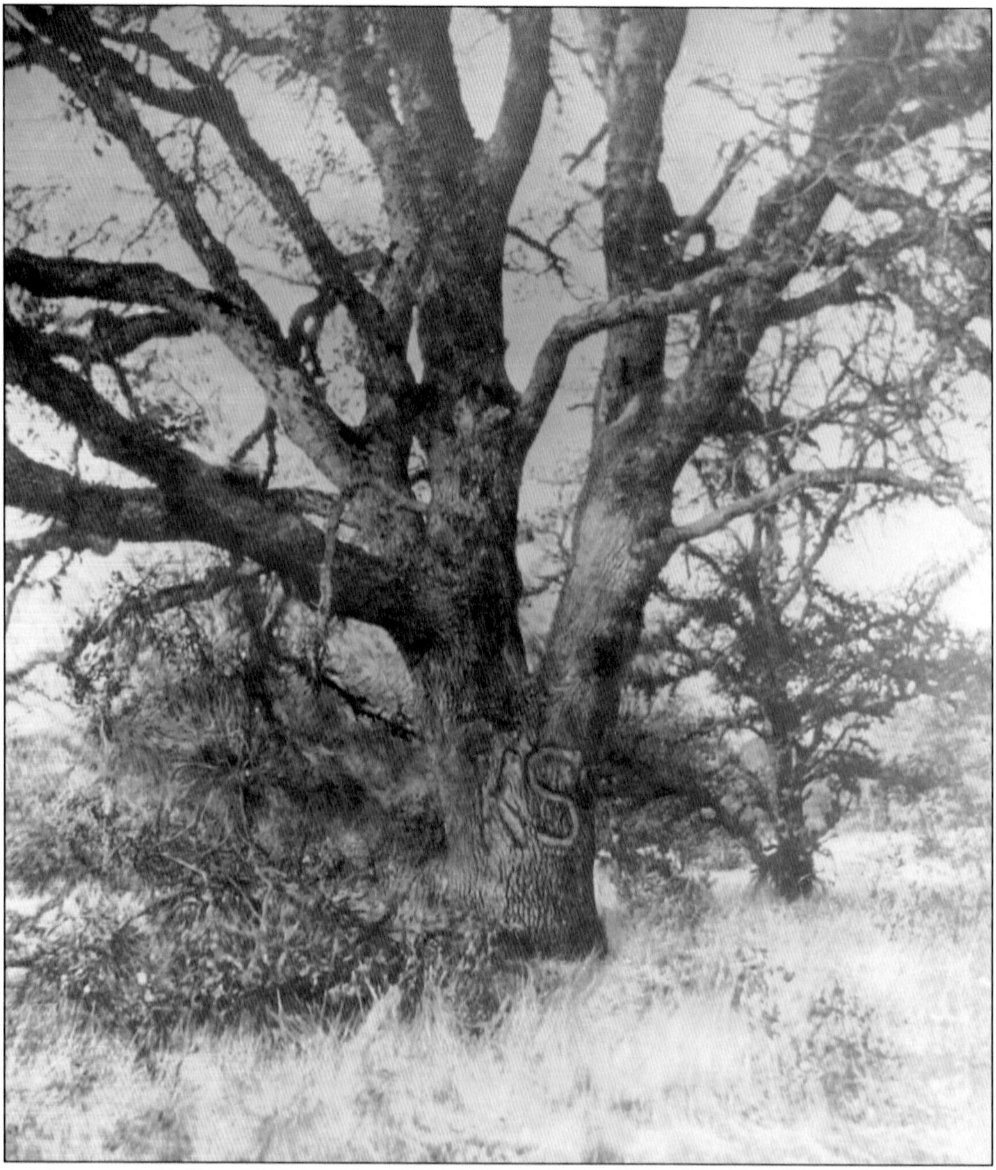

**A Massacre of Two.** Stone and Andy Kelsey started their lordly abuse immediately, forcing several hundred Li-Leeks, Habenapos, and Kulenapos to live in two camps on the creek and construct a large adobe house for them, issuing only starvation rations. They made good on their threats with humiliation, flogging, and sexual slavery. Guests were entertained with Indian target practice and their choice of young girls. When news came of James Marshall's discovery of gold at Sutter's Mill, they picked 50 young men to hurry with Ben Kelsey to the gold fields. Kelsey sold the group's supplies to miners and abandoned the young Indians. Ill and starving, they died trying to find a trail back. Only three returned. More elders died of starvation. When an attempt to steal a cow for food failed and Kelsey's favorite horse was lost, the Indians' fear and outrage exploded. Kelsey and Stone were murdered with one arrow and one rock. They were buried on a nearby hillside (above). Historian Robert Heizer assembled various versions, and this was the tale repeated by all sides. (Photograph from the Kelsey family, courtesy Lake County Historic Courthouse Museum.)

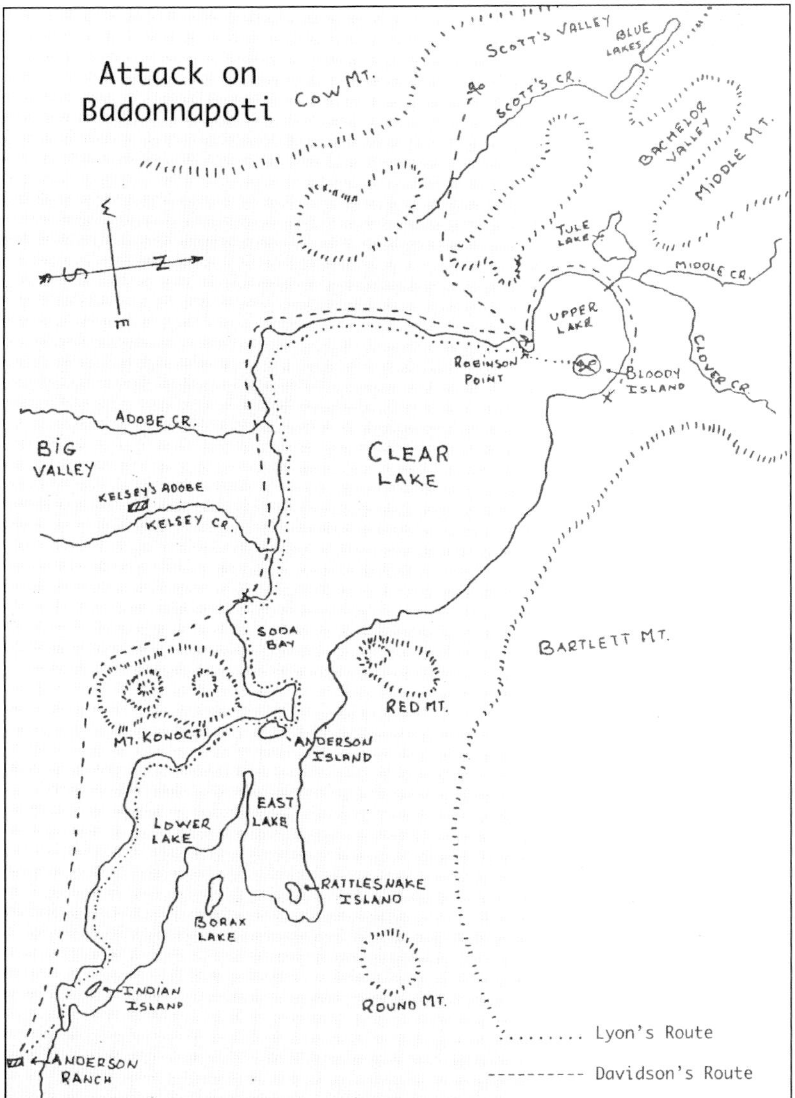


**A MASSACRE OF MANY.** When word of the killings reached the U.S. Army commander at Sonoma, he dispatched Lt. J. V. Davidson and Company C First Dragoons to reconnoiter, "ascertain positively the tribe that is guilty," and apprehend the guilty Indians. The lieutenant only located people on the fishing island of Badonnapoti. In April, Brevet Capt. Nathaniel Lyon was assigned as a replacement commander of Company C, its mountain howitzer and seven artillerists, three 15-man whaleboats and wagons, the First Dragoons, and citizen volunteers. Lyons's war-college tactics worked flawlessly, catching the natives in crossfire. No quarter was shown to man, woman, or child on land, and then the boats searched the tules to bayonet survivors. One old woman said it took five days to gather all the dead at what became known as Bloody Island. Captain Lyon continued toward Ukiah, encountering another group of innocent Indians near Bloody Rock and wiping them out. (Courtesy Lake County Historic Courthouse Museum.)

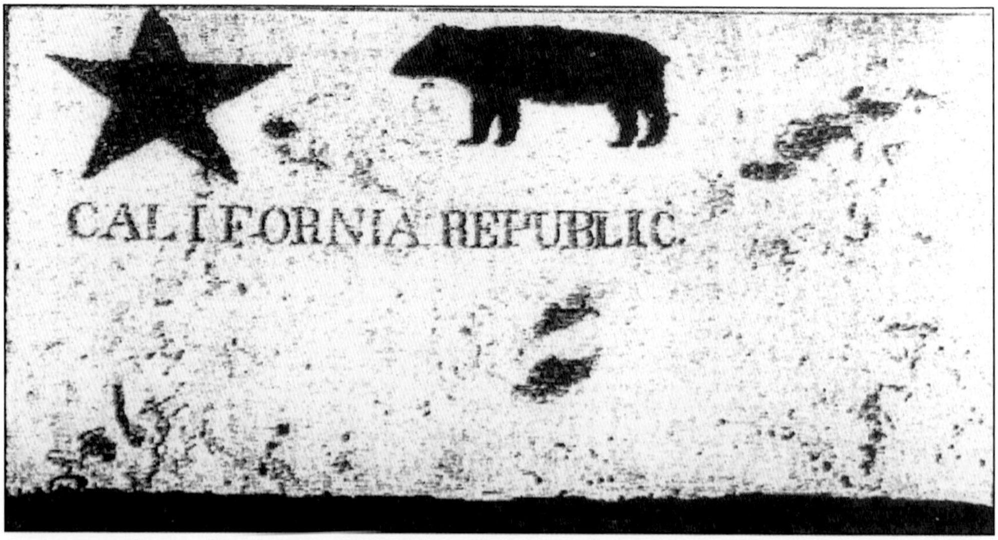


**CHANGING FLAGS.** The Treaty of Guadalupe-Hidalgo ended the war with Mexico, giving United States citizenship to anyone who had been a Mexican citizen, including Lake County's Indians. This Bear Flag, burned in the 1906 earthquake, is said to have been painted by William L. Todd when a few men seized territorial governor Mariano Vallejo in Sonoma and raised their revolutionary flag. Local lore tells that Upper Lake pioneers from the Grigsby-Ide party made the Bear Flag, and Celia Elliot Dewell contributed her red flannel. Although it looked like a run for independence, it was a move to push the United States into admitting California quickly as a non-slave state before the Civil War. (Courtesy California Historical Society.)

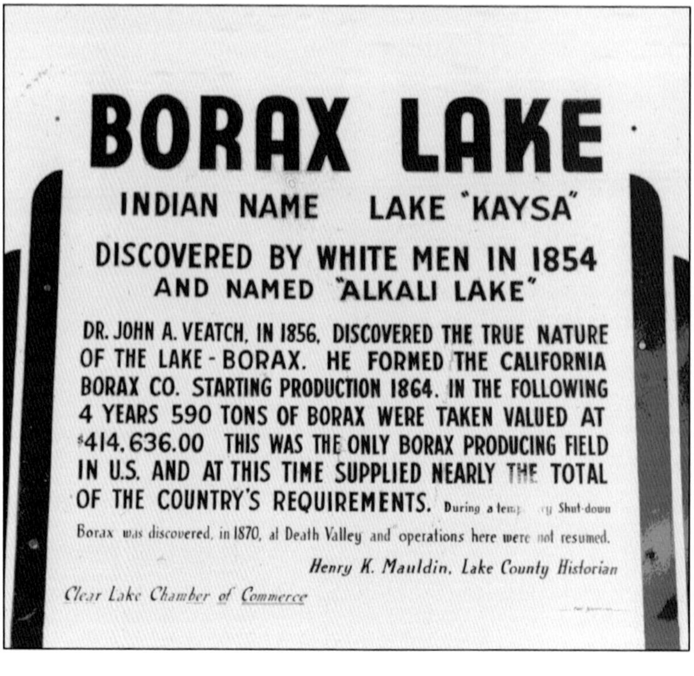


**MINING THE MINERALS.** The California Borax Company opened for business in 1859 according to historical records employing Native Americans to haul tons of borax through Middletown. In 1862, the superintendent drilled too deep through clay and hit fresh water, which dissolved the lake's crystals. The company shifted to Little Borax Lake for a short time, but its real demise came when a source in Death Valley was discovered. (Photograph by Henry Mauldin, courtesy Lake County Historic Courthouse Museum.)

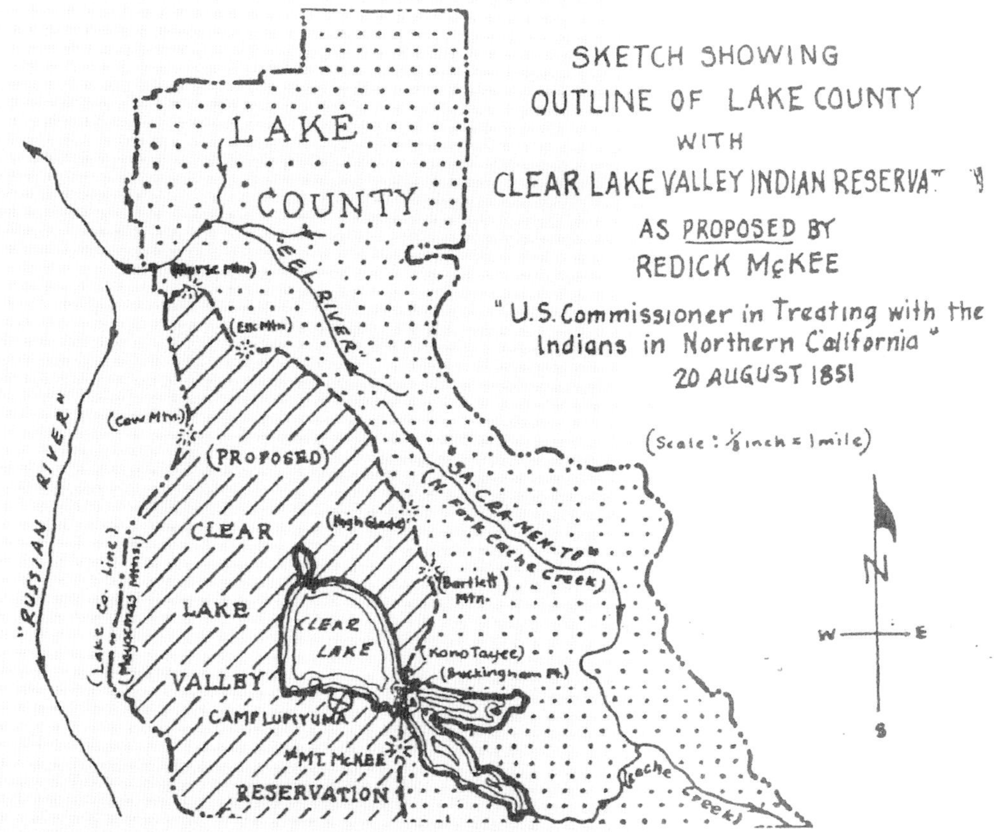


**Losing the Land.** In 1851, Pres. Millard Fillmore sent Redick McKee and his guide/translator, George Gibbs, to negotiate treaties with the California Indians. The tribal representatives agreed that much of the Clear Lake Basin would be reserved for the Native American peoples and that they would relinquish claim to all the rest. The treaties were sent to Congress in Washington, D.C., and the Pomo began to move onto their reserved land, where they might be safe to hunt and gather as before. Californians pressured Washington to deny the agreements. The Senate refused to act on all 18 treaties and placed a 50-year injunction of secrecy on the action. At the same time, Congress passed the Land Claims Act, which required that claims to all lands in California be presented within two years. Since this was not publicized to the Native Americans in any language, they failed to meet the deadline and thus were deprived of all legal titles. (Map used by permission, from *The Distant Bells of St. Turibius.*)

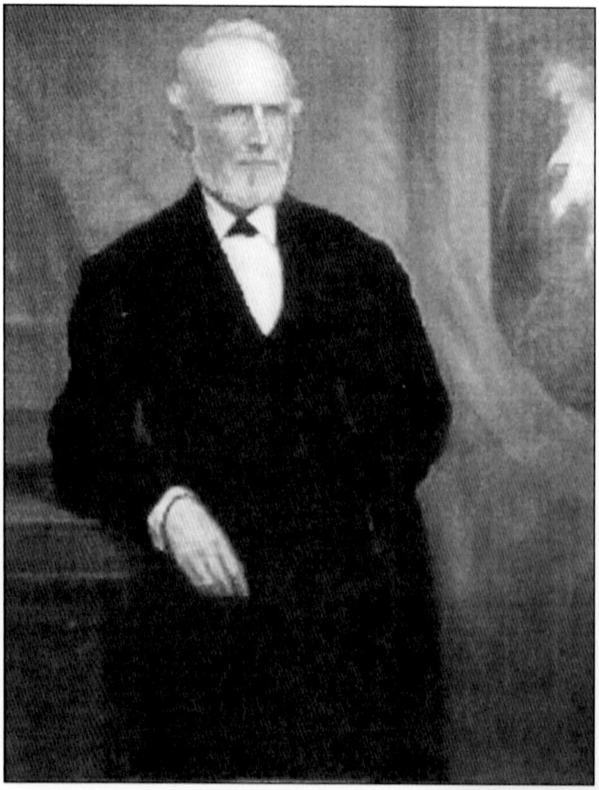

**PUBLIC POLICY.** In Peter Burnett's inaugural address on December 29, 1849, the first governor of California (portrait at left) said, "That a war of extermination will continue to be waged between the two races until the Indian race becomes extinct must be expected." The policy continued with successive state administrations (John McDougall, below) for several decades. In 1850–1851, the California legislature enacted a law "for the protection of the native population." The law effectively stripped Native Americans of all civil rights, justified "apprenticeship" or enslavement of children or "vagrants," and offered a $25–$50 bounty for evidence (scalps) of dead natives. (Courtesy California Governors portraits.)

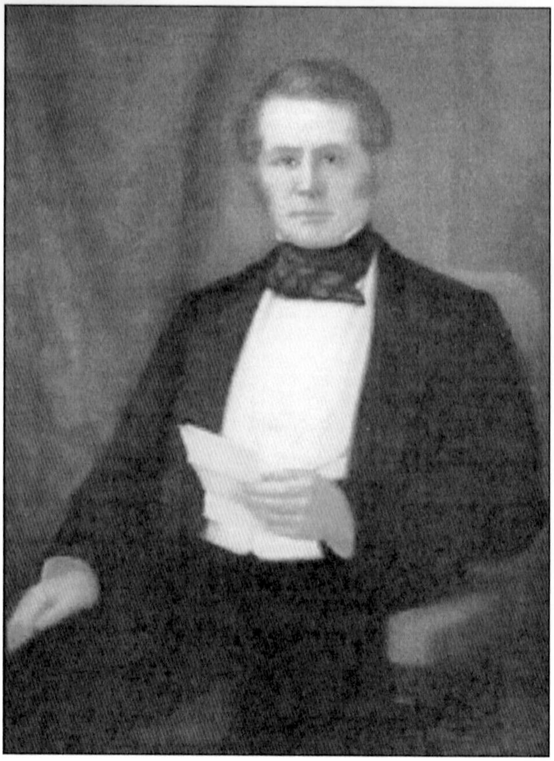

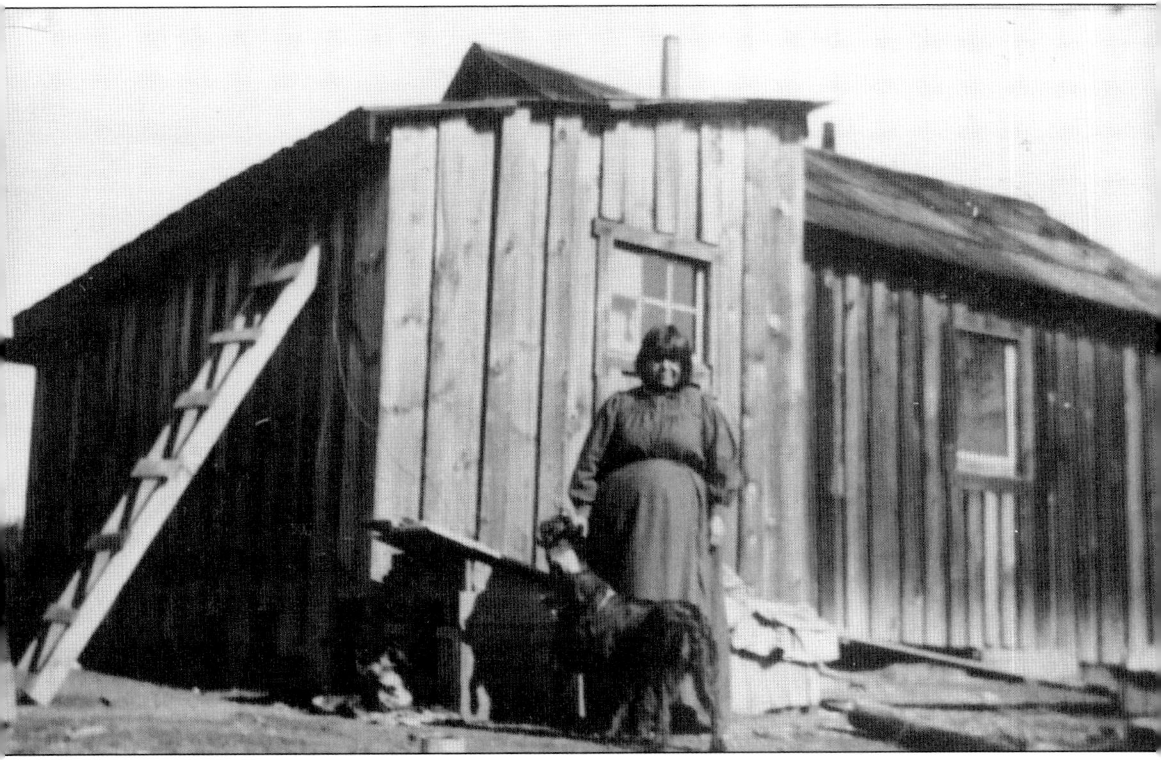

**INDIAN SQUATTERS.** For the first time, Northern California Indians were forced from their homelands and sent to a Mendocino Indian Reserve at Fort Bragg, without resources, along with their traditional enemies. It was so badly mismanaged that within 10 years, even the government abandoned it and natives drifted back to where they had once lived. They found thousands of white settlers in their place. Again, in 1856, nine tribes from Northern California were forced to march to the newly established Nome Cult Indian Farm in Mendocino County, which became the dreaded Round Valley Indian Reservation at Covelo. For various reasons, most Lake County Indians did not go: their lack of resistance to Anglo takeover, the farmers' need for an agricultural labor force, and the already diminished numbers of indigenous people here. They still lived on other peoples' land as in the photograph above. (Courtesy Lake County Historic Courthouse Museum.)

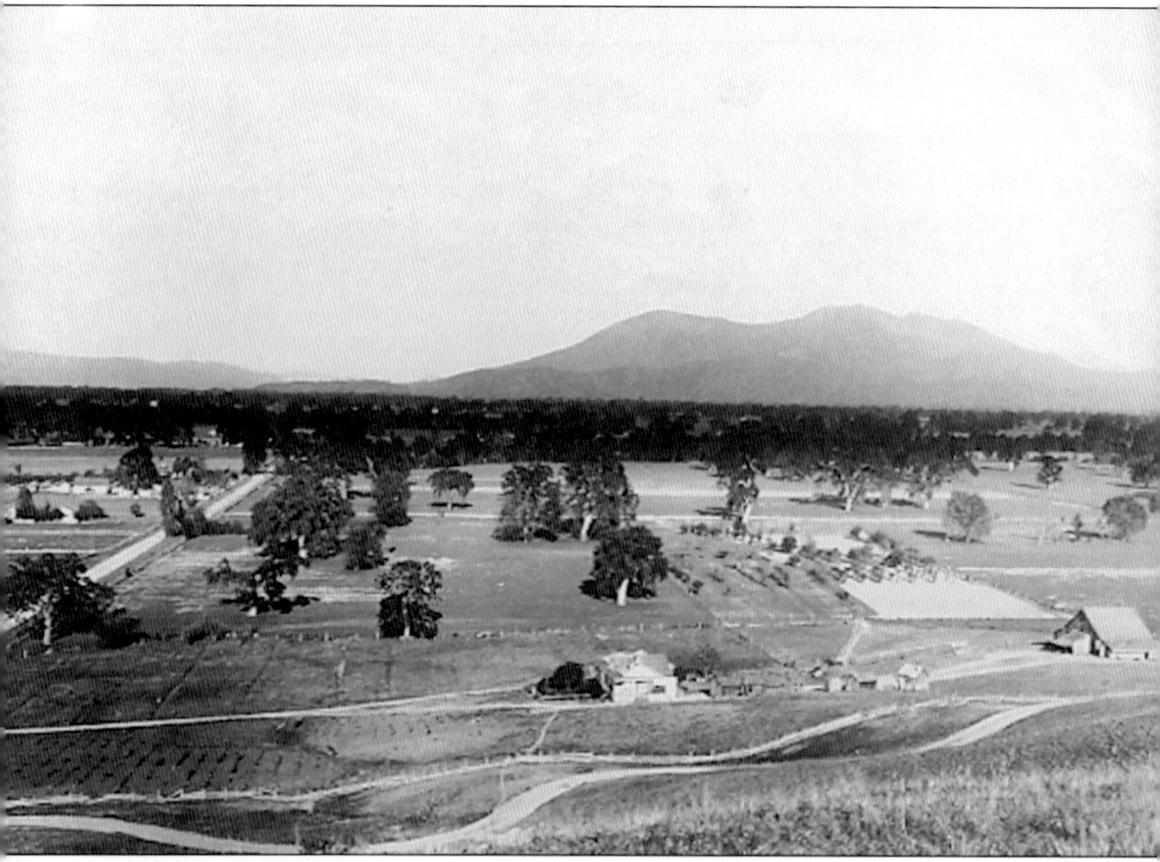

**Learning to Plant.** Not everything had been negative under Spanish and Mexican rule. While neither country acknowledged Indian land ownership, they allowed the Natives to continue to occupy their villages. Although both farming and grazing had a bad effect on habitat, the experience gave Native Americans skills necessary to survive in the coming years. In two short decades, everything had changed in Big Valley (above). The oak groves were cleared and annual grasses planted. Gentle contours had been flattened and made into geometric squares, streams had been rerouted, roads cut into the land, and heaps of unused materials and garbage were near each dwelling. Market hunters had made the elk, bear, wild turkey, and some waterfowl disappear. (Photograph by O. E. Meddaugh [Bishop], courtesy Lake County Historic Courthouse Museum.)

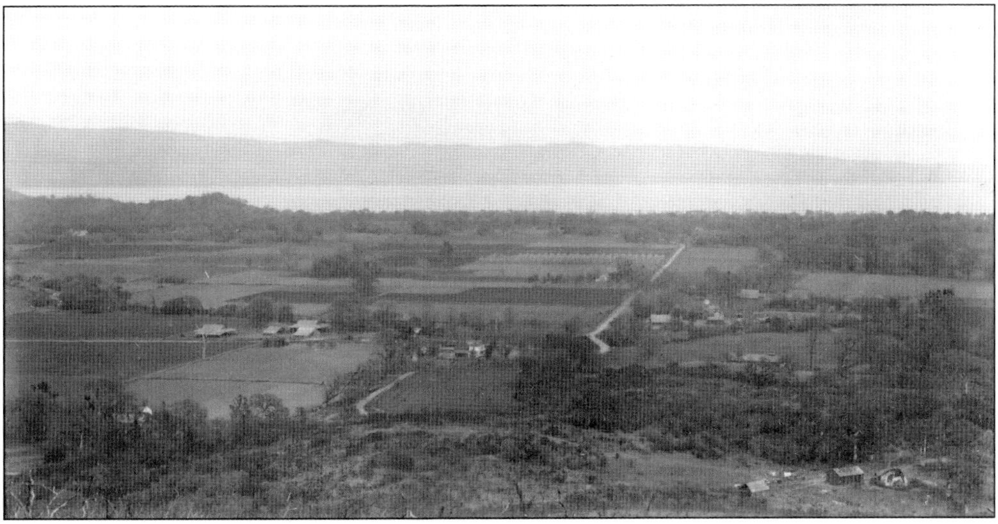

**WHAT WERE THEY THINKING?** The elders wondered this as they looked down at the new Scott's Valley. The newcomers had said it was so perfectly created, so why did they change it all? Why did they tear out the heart of the mountains so mud runs down? Why did they put dirt in the lake and take rock from the streams so fish no longer spawn? Why must they cut down every tree so there is no shade or acorns? Why do they kill animals they do not need to eat? Why did they come to live with us if we are so hateful and imperfect? (Photograph by O. E. Meddaugh [Bishop], courtesy Lake County Historic Courthouse Museum.)

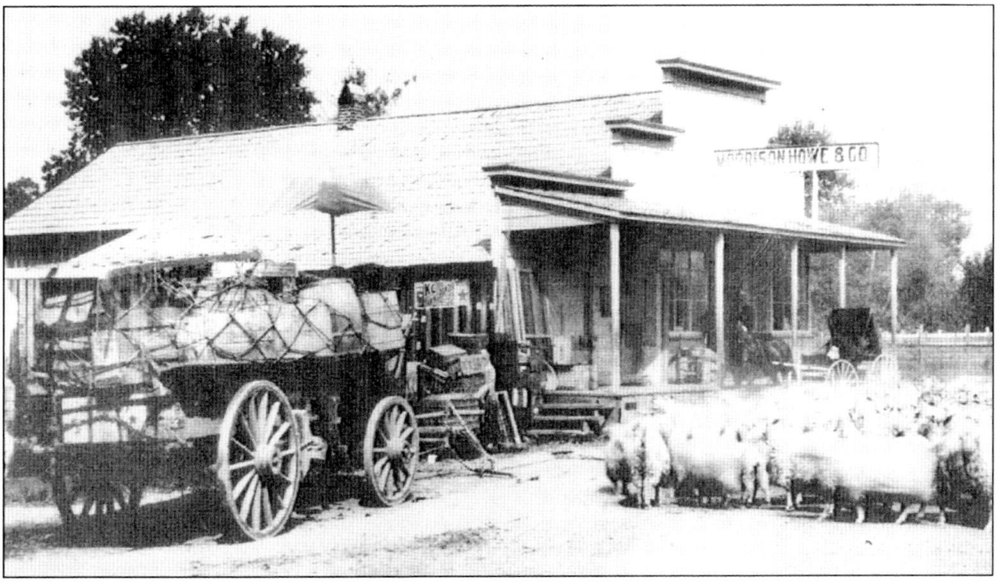


**SELLING FOOD.** "Wild stuff" should not be sold according to the rules of the Pomos—only manufactured articles such as deerskins, rabbit skin blankets, and baskets. Food was given away but not sold. Land was not owned, but gathering or hunting sites and their boundaries were carefully defined. Livestock and its by-products were some of Lake County's first exports. Native Americans knew beef cattle and were good vaqueros, but dairy cattle, sheep, and goats were foreign. Milk, cream, and cheese were new to the native diet, but cheese became one of the county's first marketable products. Workers on ranches learned how to shear sheep and process the wool. (Courtesy Lake County Historic Courthouse Museum.)

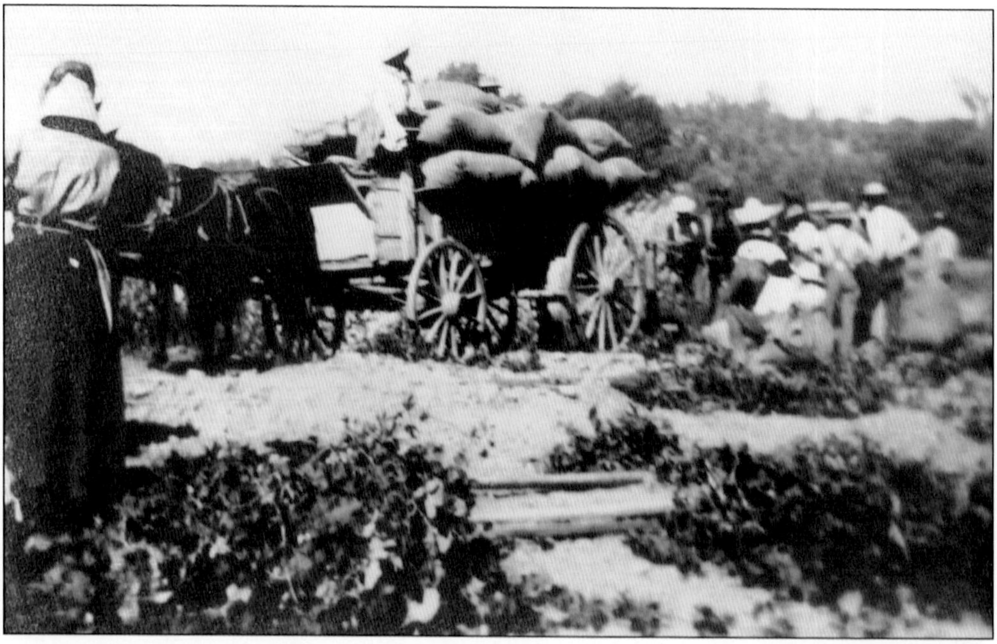

**BEGINNING OF MIGRANT HARVESTING.** Hops were in heavy production from 1858 until the early 1900s. The Riggs ranch (above) was all in hops, and much of Scott's and Big Valley's acreage was as well. Indians trained the vines, then from late August through early September, before the dew was off, they harvested. In the beginning, vines were trained low and handpicked; later they were trained to grow high, most picking was done mechanically, and drying kilns were heated by diesel in place of wood (below). That meant less and less work for Indian families, especially when poor whites started camping in the fields too. (Courtesy Lake County Historic Courthouse Museum.)

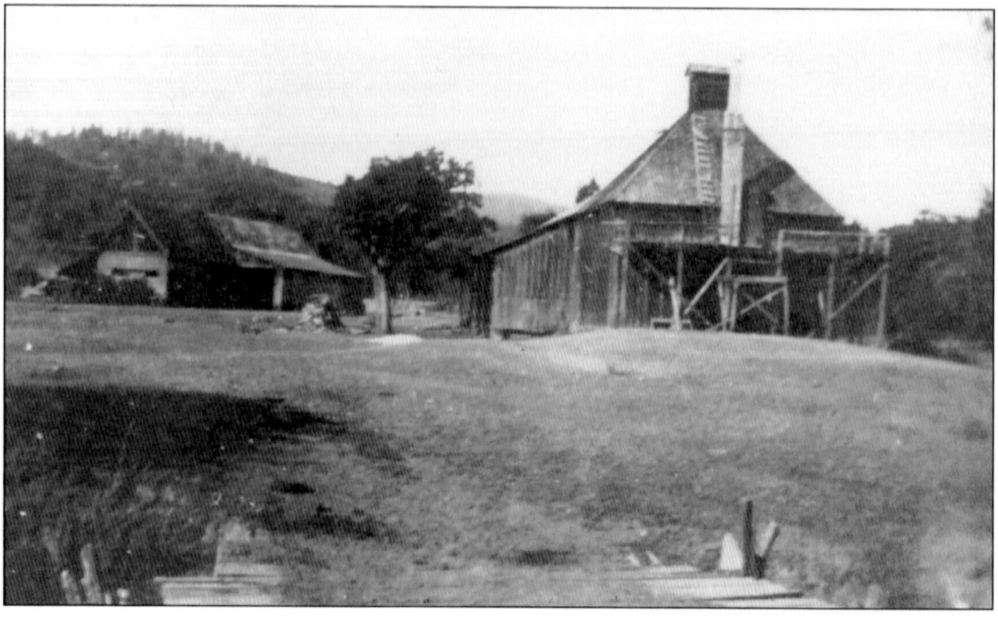

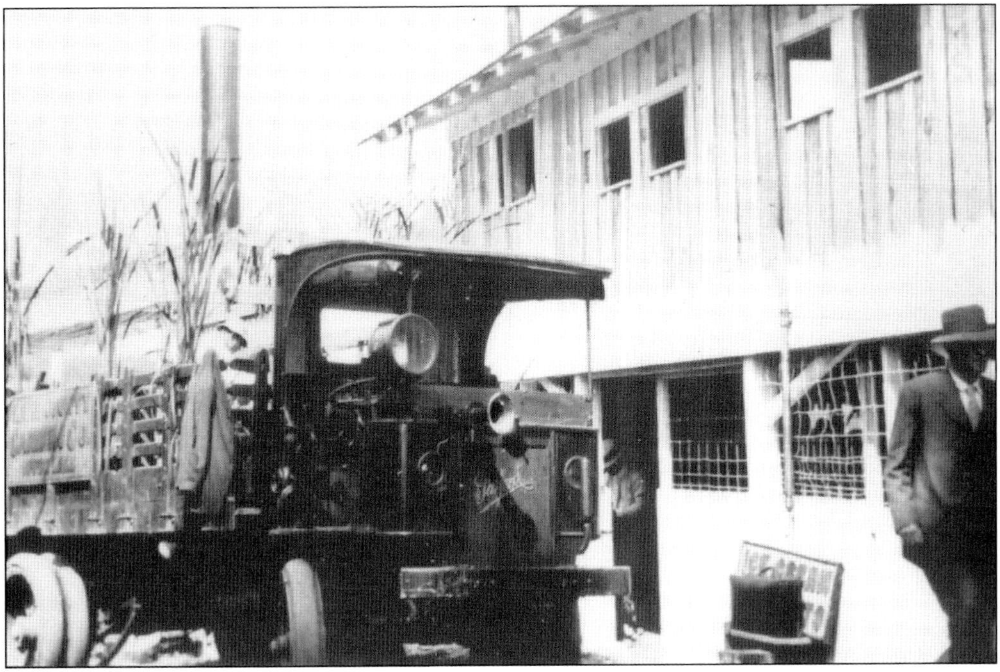

**IN THE FIELDS AND IN THE CANNERIES.** In 1899, Henry Wambold began to grow string beans in the rich alluvial soil near Blue Lakes, and Mrs. Wambold canned them at home. W. B. Mundy, who operated a small fruit cannery in Bachelor Valley, helped Wambold build a bean cannery at Laurel Dell on the lakes. In 1897, A. Mendenhall opened a second bean cannery near Upper Lake, and Lake County Pomo families became bean harvesters too. The seasons fell so that pickers could move from one crop to another. (Courtesy Lake County Historic Courthouse Museum.)

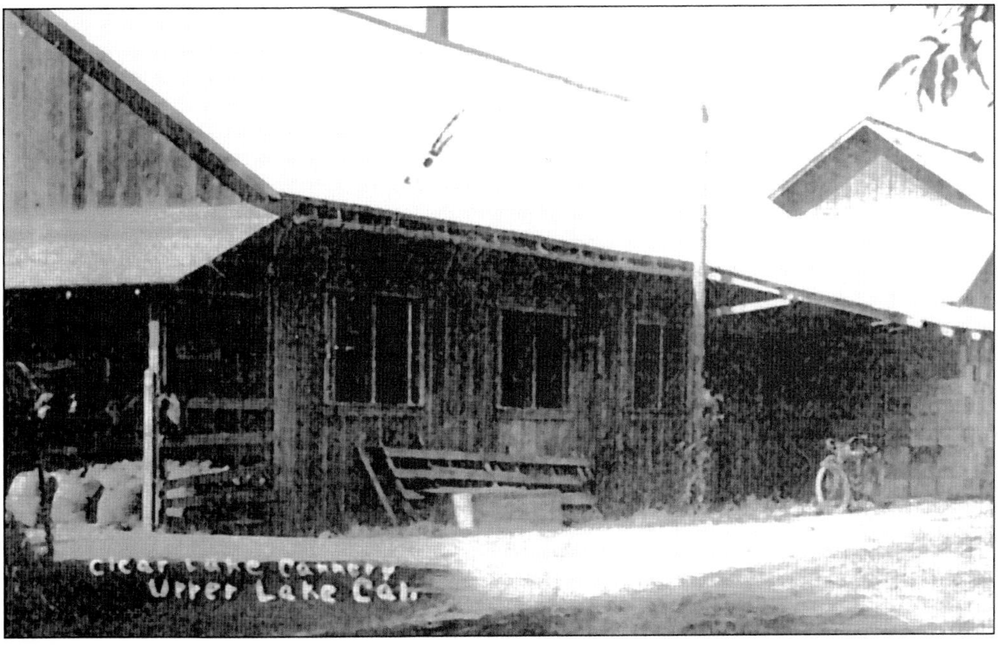

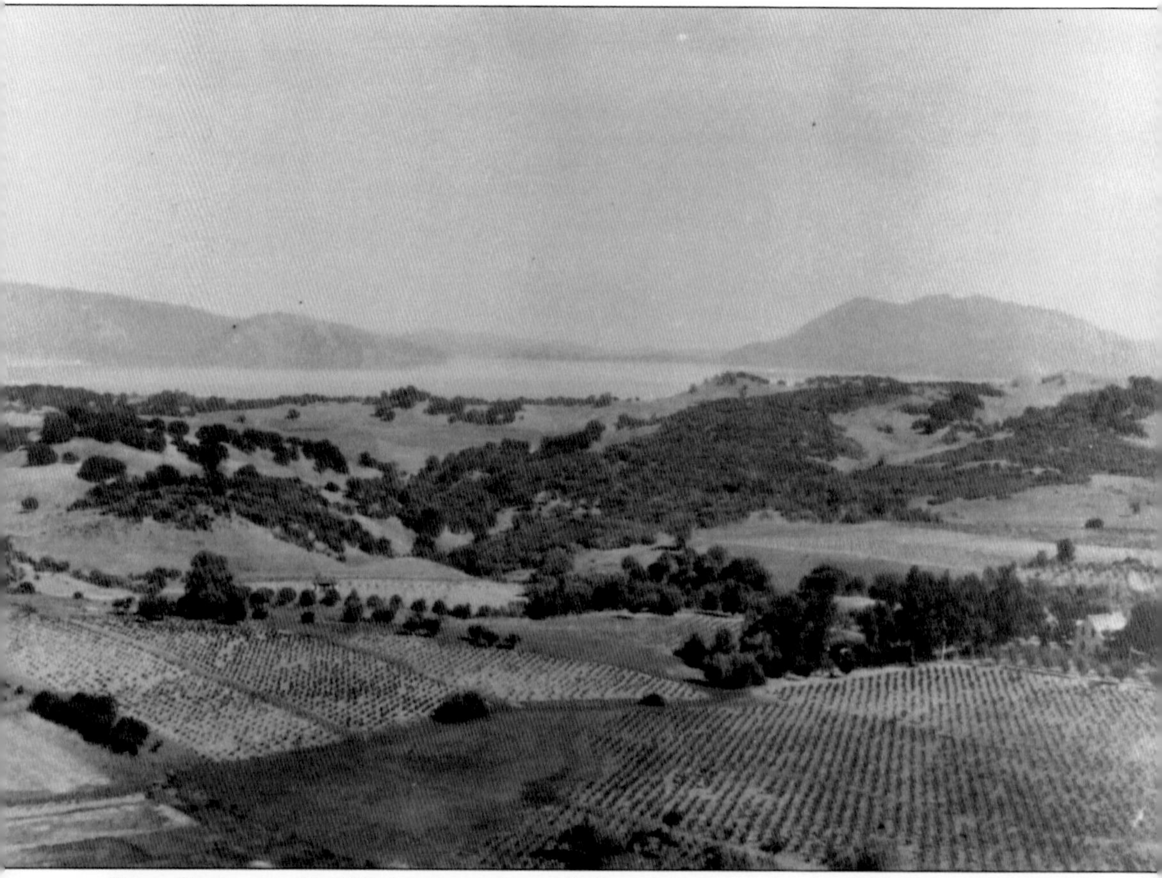

**THEY COME AND GO.** Wine grapes, vineyards (Lyons vineyards in the 1920s is pictured above), and wineries were big business in the first half of the 20th century and provided yet another crop for Native American families to work. The market for wine disappeared during Prohibition in the 1920s and 1930s, but vineyards have been replanted, replacing pear orchards since the 1990s. All harvesting of the delicate grapes was done by hand up to a point, but now machine harvesting is more and more prevalent. Indian children worked or played in the fields with adults and usually missed some school at the beginning of the term. Native American families hoped to make enough harvesting wages to last until spring. (Courtesy Lake County Historic Courthouse Museum.)

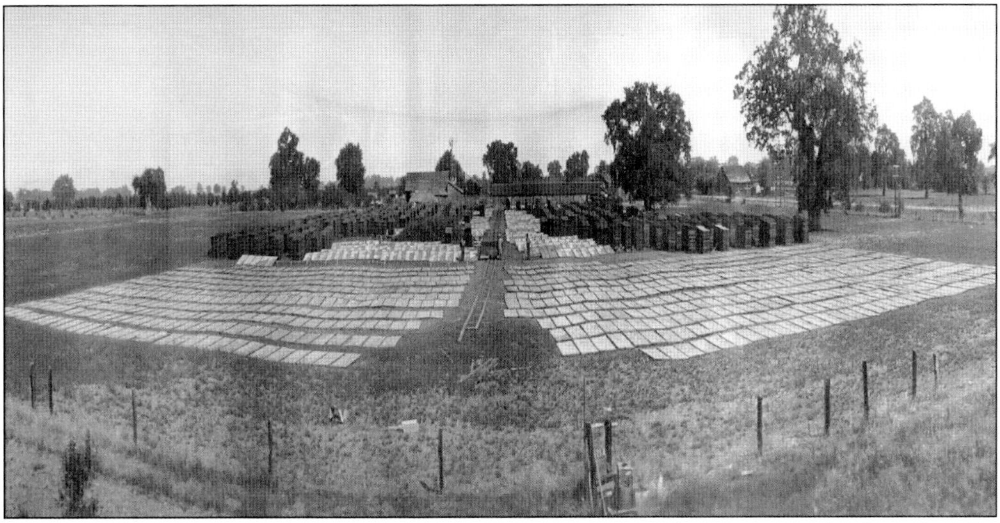

**PEARS AS EARLY AS 1868.** In 1885, a state committee came to Lake County and collected apples and pears to send to the New Orleans Worlds Fair. Growers started planting orchards of Bartletts and other varieties. California Packing Corporation had the largest dry yard for pears in the world in 1922, when practically all the fruit crop was dried (one dry yard in Finley is shown above). Tonnage was so great that farmers looking for other markets built packinghouses and shipped to California and Eastern fresh fruit markets. Mexican migrant workers became competition with Native American workers during World War II because there were so few people available to work in the orchards. (Courtesy Lake County Historic Courthouse Museum.)

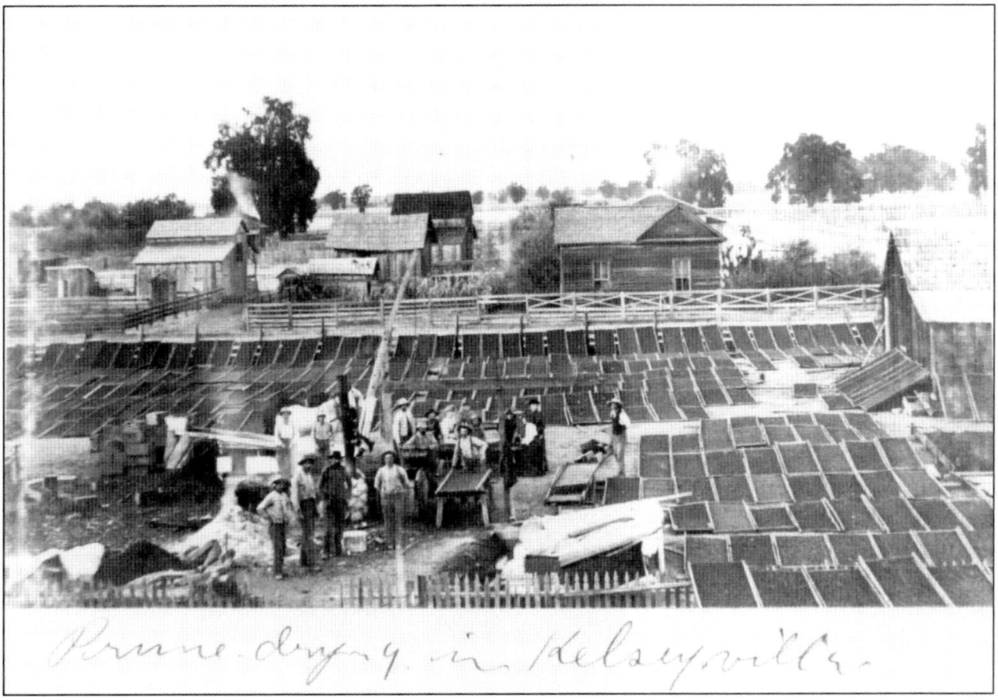


**NOT JUST PEARS.** Prunes and walnuts had to be harvested and dried following pear season. Trays of prunes dry in the sun in Kelseyville (above). (Courtesy Lake County Historic Courthouse Museum.)

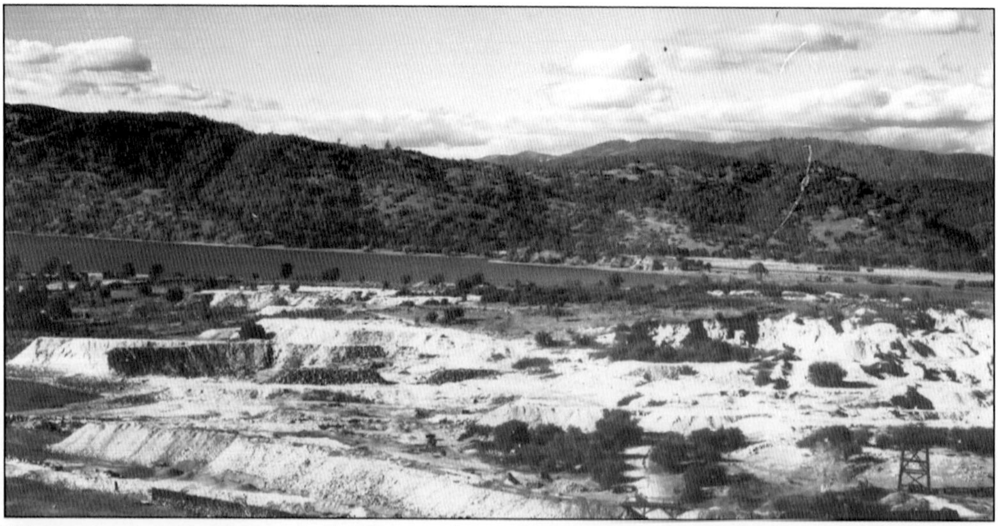

**Working in the Mines.** In 1875, cinnabar and mercury were discovered. Sulphur Banks Quicksilver Mining Company hired hundreds of workers, including 300 Chinese. The mine supplied much of the world's quicksilver from its mine shafts and open pit mining during each war and closed finally in 1957. Great Western in Middletown operated from 1876 to 1900, when it was exhausted. Mirabel and Oat Hill, partly in Napa County, also provided jobs. The work was dangerous and the mercury toxic. (Courtesy Lake County Historic Courthouse Museum.)

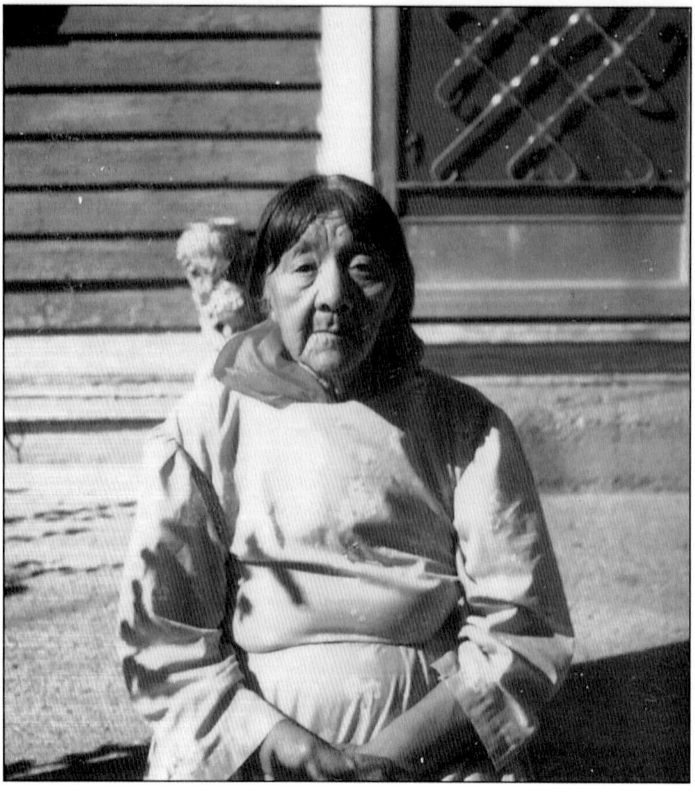

**What Else Is There?** Seasonal farm labor and domestic work were about all that a Lake County Indian could hope for. Around 1912, the Department of Interior bought land for rancherias near some tribes: two in Upper Lake, one in Scott's Valley, one in Middletown, one in Lower Lake, and one in Big Valley. They had just about moved in by 1917 when the United States joined the war. In World War I, 10,000 American Indians served their country, and they saw how others lived and imagined greater possibilities. (Courtesy Lake County Historic Courthouse Museum.)

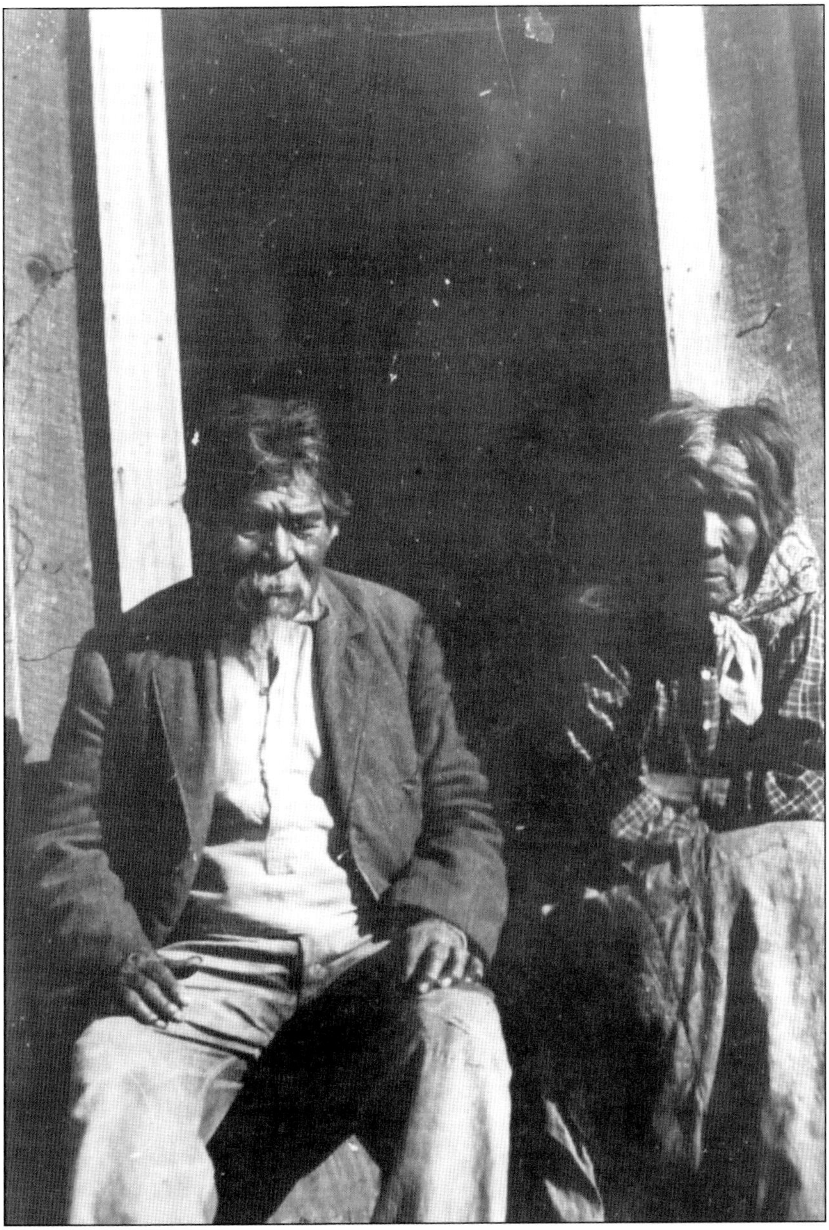

**Bi-polar Policies.** Big Valley Rancheria elder Nelson Hopper says, "They either want to hate us to death or they want to love us to death." From unabashed genocide, to paternalistic caretaking, governmental policies toward Native Americans have switched regularly, often because of lawsuits. After the original unsigned treaties were discovered in the Senate's secret files, public attitude shifted and court cases were launched for restitution for lost native land. The cases were won, but the government charged back the costs they attributed to benefits including the operation of the Bureau of Indian Affairs (BIA) and forced boarding schools, and then withheld part of the money in trust for people they judged still incapable of handling their own affairs. In another land claims case, the reimbursement was based on an 1840s land value of about 47¢ per acre. The anticipated millions of dollars never came. Above, an unidentified couple waits for a home of their own. (Courtesy Lake County Historic Courthouse Museum.)

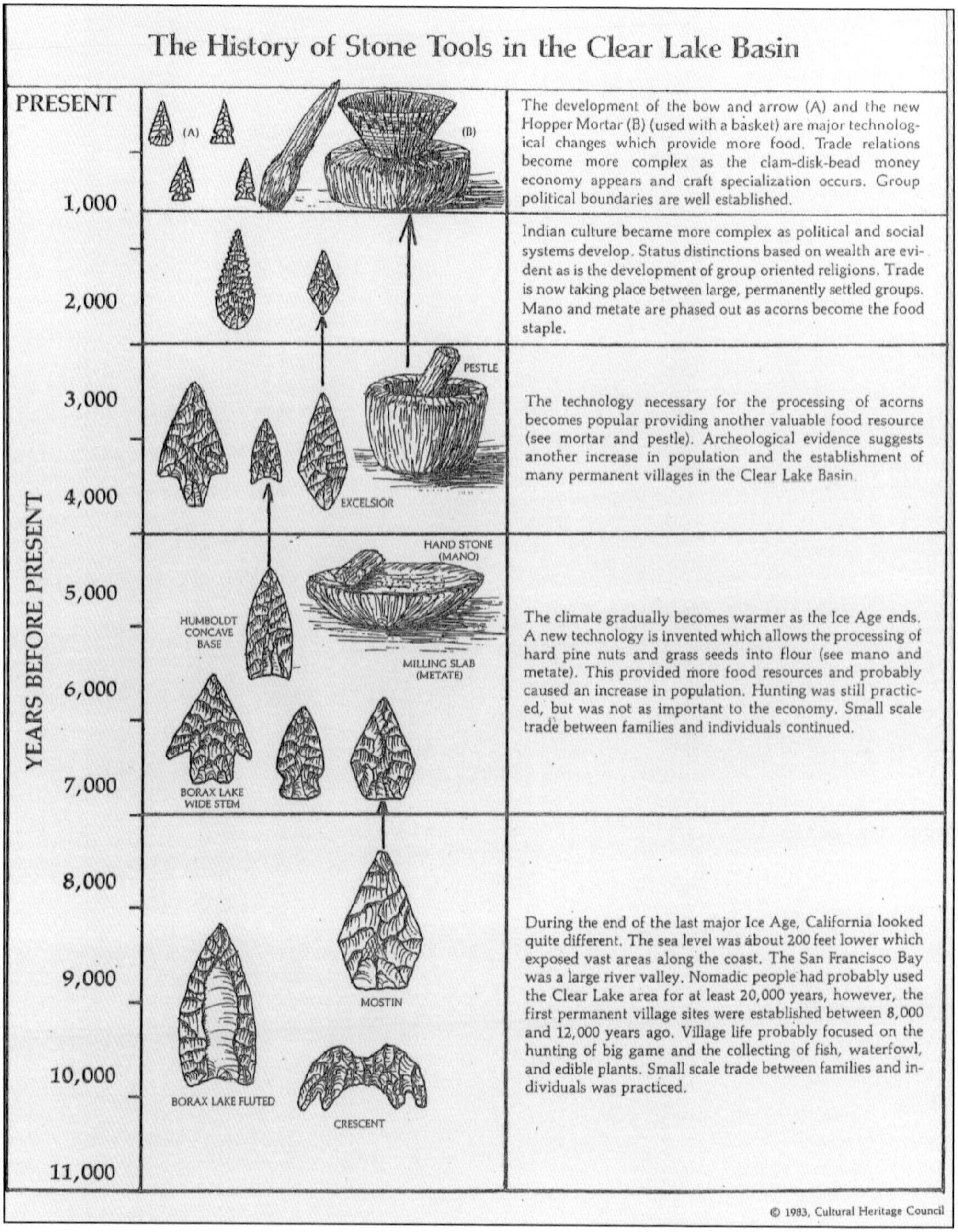


**CHARTING HISTORY.** The above chart shows developments through the ages. (Courtesy Cultural Heritage Council.)

# *Two*

# Looking around and Back

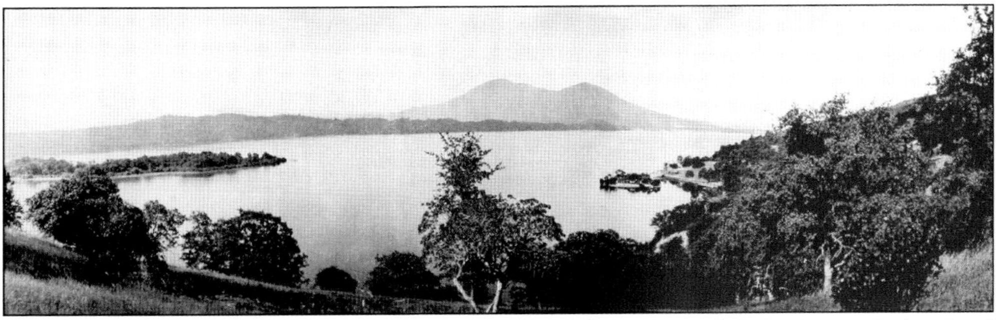

**Examining the Gem.** Around 1900, scientists of all kinds began to study Lake County. Isolated and insular, it had retained, unspoiled and unexplored, a larger view for anthropologists. Geologically and historically unique, it nonetheless was past the point of tule huts and naked gatherers by half a century. Old-style roundhouses, photographed in the 1920s, were no longer seen. Without a written language, people remembered long and well. Before European diseases and homicide were introduced, life spans approached 100 years. Large mechanical devices like earthmovers or hydroelectric dams had not yet come into common use, so geology and archaeology were mostly intact. Lake County was a good case study. The site of several early Pomo villages (above), landfill linked Stubbs Island to the shore creating the town and canals of Clearlake Oaks. (Courtesy Lake County Historic Courthouse Museum.)

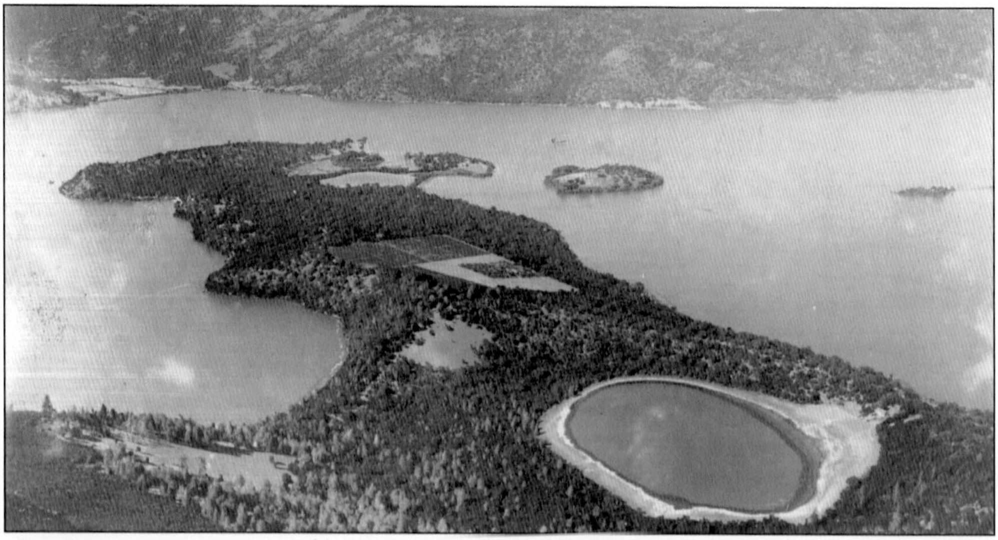

**The Clear Lake.** Traditional home of the Kamdots, Buckingham Peninsula forms the narrows that separate Clear Lake from the Lower and East arms. On the peninsula is Little Borax Lake. Clear Lake is the largest natural lake entirely within California. Its shoreline is 100 miles long, with roadway all around. Reclamation efforts in the 1920s made Upper Lake a series of canals and a wide slough. Clear Lake is shallow and nutrient-rich, with a fault line running through its middle. The lake bottom sinks at precisely the rate sediment feeds into the lake, so its depth remains relatively constant. The lake is at least 2.5 million years old, perhaps the oldest in North America. (Courtesy Lake County Historic Courthouse Museum.)

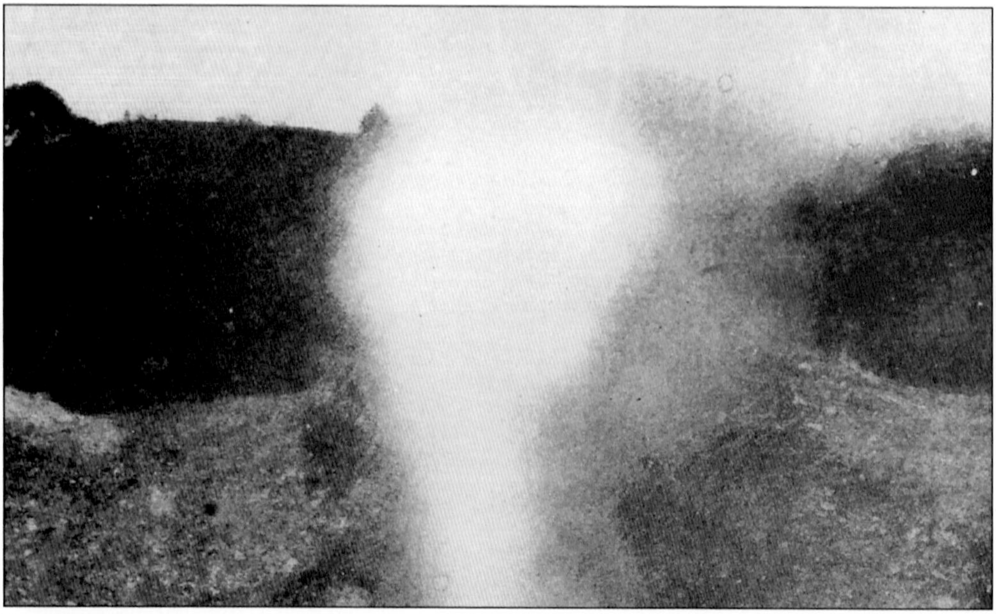

**The Mountains.** The mountains surrounding the lake are layer upon layer of sedimentary rock thrust upward as part of the Coast Range as well as remains of volcanic eruptions. Artesian wells and mineral hot springs that Pomos enjoyed continue to flow, and one of the world's largest geothermal power plants is just south of Middletown near Geyserville. A deep layer of obsidian was a source of widely traded arrowheads and spear points made by skilled Pomo craftsmen. (Courtesy of Lake County Historic Courthouse Museum.)

**DIG DEEP INTO THE PAST.** People have lived in the Clear Lake area for 12,000 years or more. The temperate climate and adequate rainfall were ideal, and people lived simply, so they have never been studied for their drama as, for example, the Egyptian or the Mayan civilizations. They were good fishermen and hunters, and they built houses and boats and manufactured clamshell money to demonstrate honor, wealth, and social values, such as gifting and gambling. The women made all the baskets except fish and hunting traps, and they are thought to make the finest baskets in the world. (Courtesy Lake County Historic Courthouse Museum.)

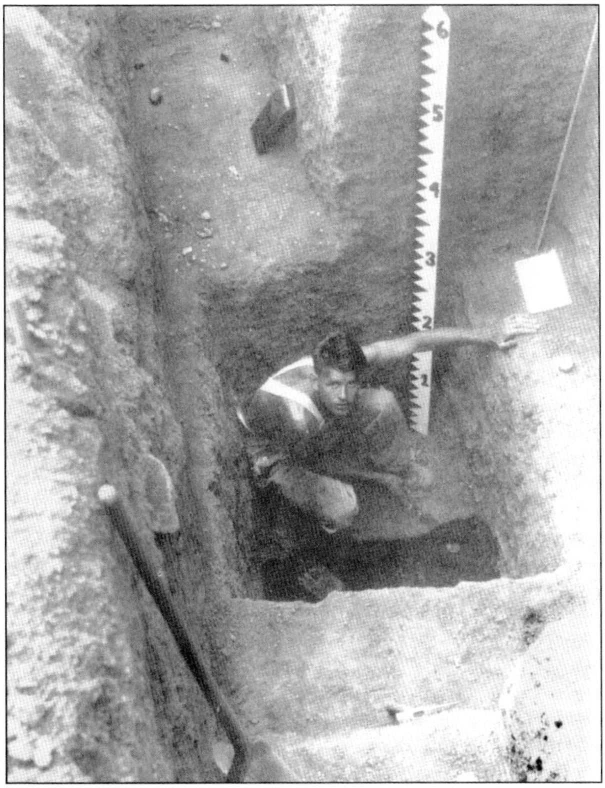

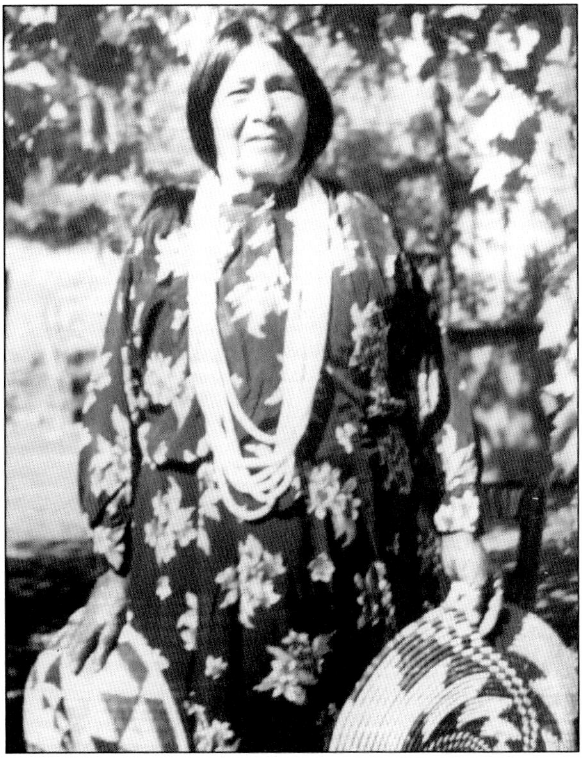

**JOB SPECIALIZATION.** Women gathered acorns, the food staple. Food was cooked in baskets with heated stones. A few skilled workmen made nets for fish or waterfowl. Every man fished, and songs and charms were used to help. The village shared in the catch. Arrow and spear making were the skills of the few who knew where to gather and how to shape obsidian. Bows were bought from the Long Valley Patwins, who obtained them from the people in the northeast. Skilled craftsmen prepared the coin beads like those Coddie Graves wears. (Courtesy Lake County Historic Courthouse Museum.)

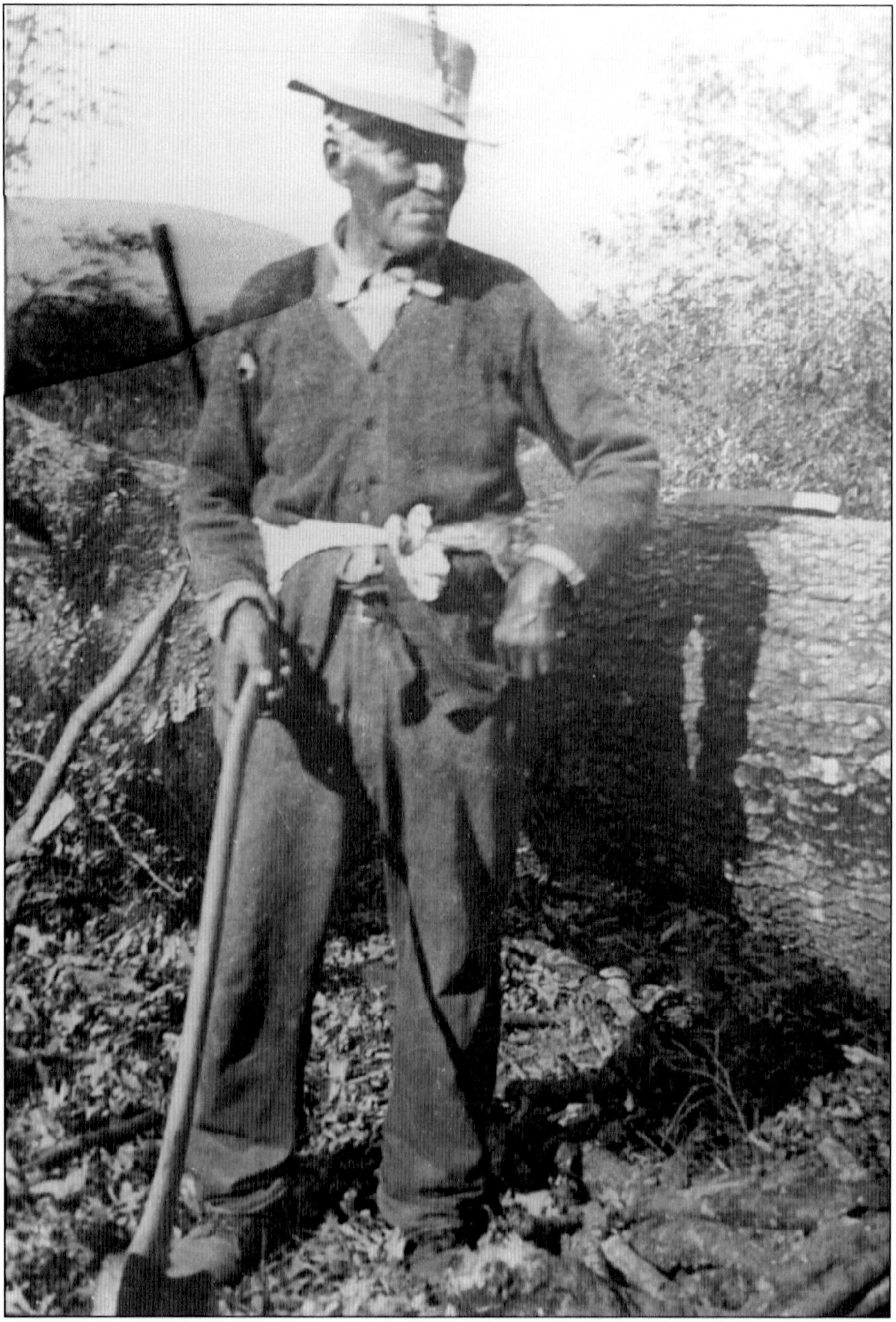

**LEADERSHIP.** Joe Augustine (above) would have been in line for chief if the tradition had continued. Historically, a chieftain was not always chosen to take his or her father's place; a certain quality of "goodness of heart" was required. The tribe rejected one man because he was impatient, could not make speeches, and always wanted to fight someone. Mateo was chief of the Kamdots; he followed his father as chieftain and held the place of ceremonial fire tender. He said to his people, "Work, do not steal, do not fight, and do not become angry." (Courtesy Lake County Historic Courthouse Museum.)

# *Three*

# Family Life

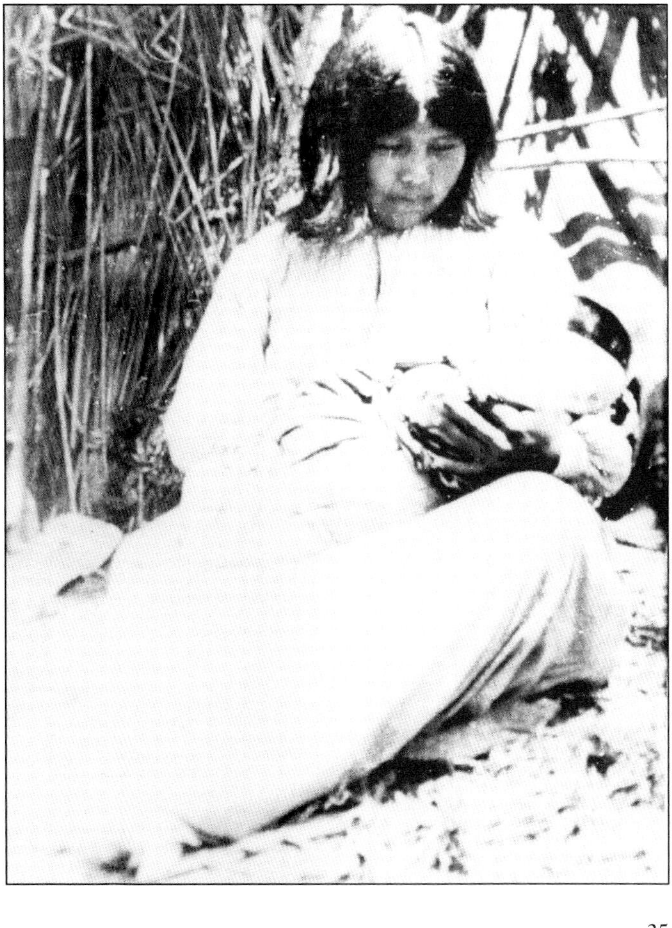

**From the Beginning.** Pomo love their children and elders. Here Minnie Thompson Boone (*c.* 1876–*c.* 1920) admires her baby daughter, Rosalie. Perhaps because infant mortality rates were 50 percent, each person was precious to the community. Early in pregnancy, elaborate gifting rituals began between maternal and paternal families, culminating at birth. Multiple births were rare. Births took place at home, accompanied by a midwife or mother's family, since Native Americans were not treated at hospitals until legislation forced it in the mid-1930s. In the event of a mother's death, her mother or family raised the child lovingly. (Courtesy Lake County Historic Courthouse Museum.)

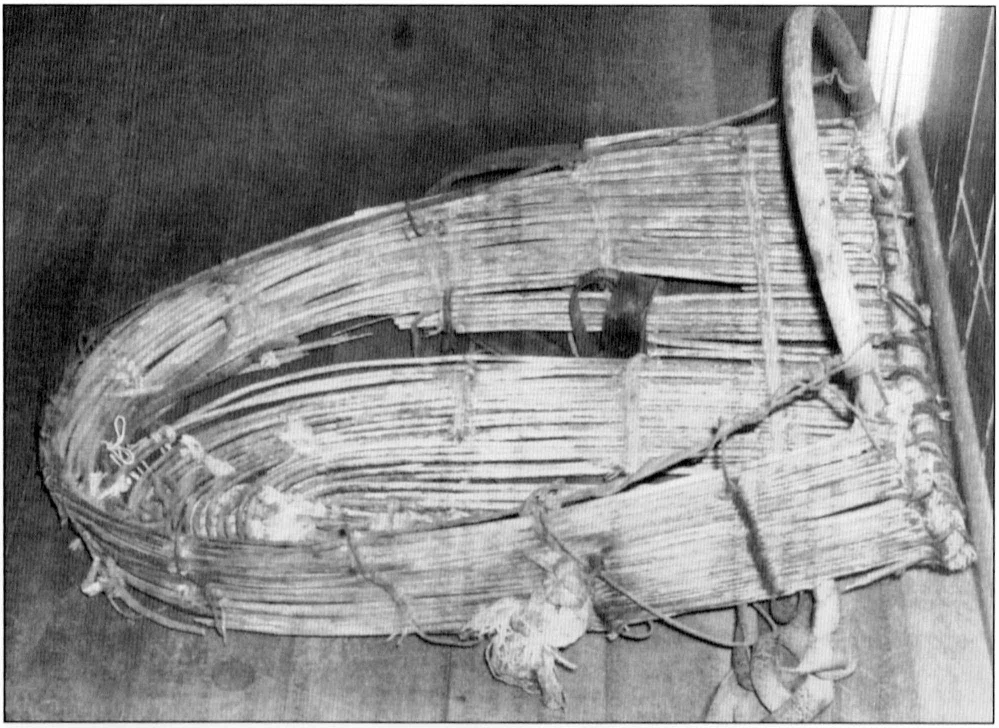

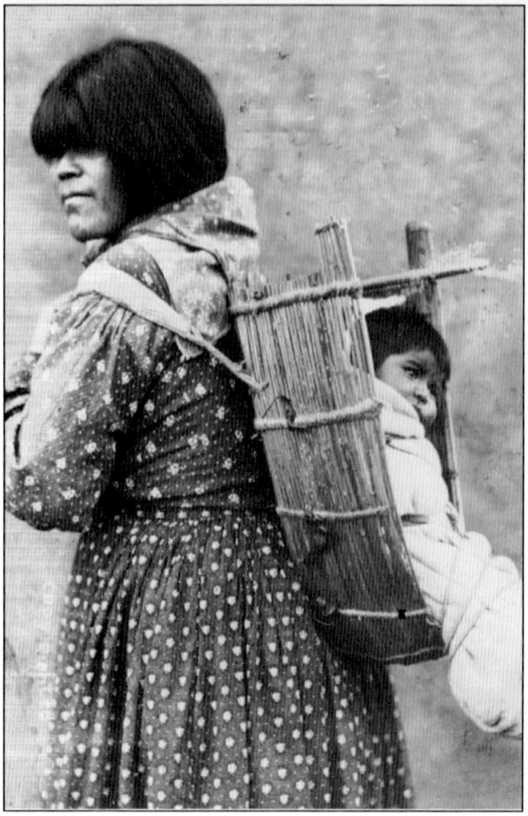

**CARRIED EVERYWHERE.** Traditionally fathers wove the basket that would house the tightly swaddled baby, but in modern times, it is more likely to be the mother or a member of her family. Families with no weaving heritage generally contract a tribal member who can construct a sturdy and elegant carrying cradle known as a *kee-wee*. This basket above was made by the wife of Jake Knight (born 1831 in Middletown) to carry grandchildren. The last to be carried in it was James Knight, who was born in 1916. (Courtesy Lake County Historic Courthouse Museum.)

**GREAT CARE.** Babies were kept very clean. Water was heated to a comfortable temperature with hot stones, and the baby was bathed twice a day. Diapers were made of clean shredded tules. The child was tightly swaddled and returned to the basket. They were carried on the mother's back so she could continue about her work. Later the basket could be set down and the toddler used it as a seat. (Courtesy Lake County Historic Courthouse Museum.)

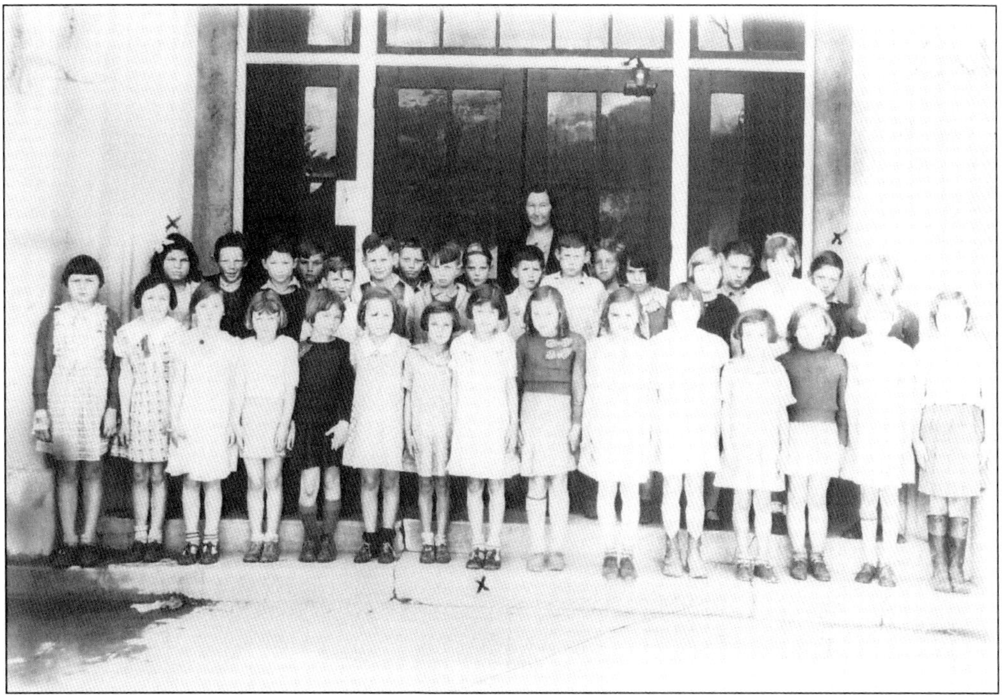

**Mainstreaming.** Not until 1932 did law abolish separatist policies in Lake County so that Indian children could attend public schools together with everyone else. In the class picture at Kelseyville Elementary School's first integrated year is Katherine Martin (later Ray) at left in the back row and non-Indian Chris Mauldin, son of the Lake County historian, second from right in back row. Betty Nitka, a Middletown elder, was in the first class at Lower Lake. (Courtesy personal collection of Chris Mauldin.)

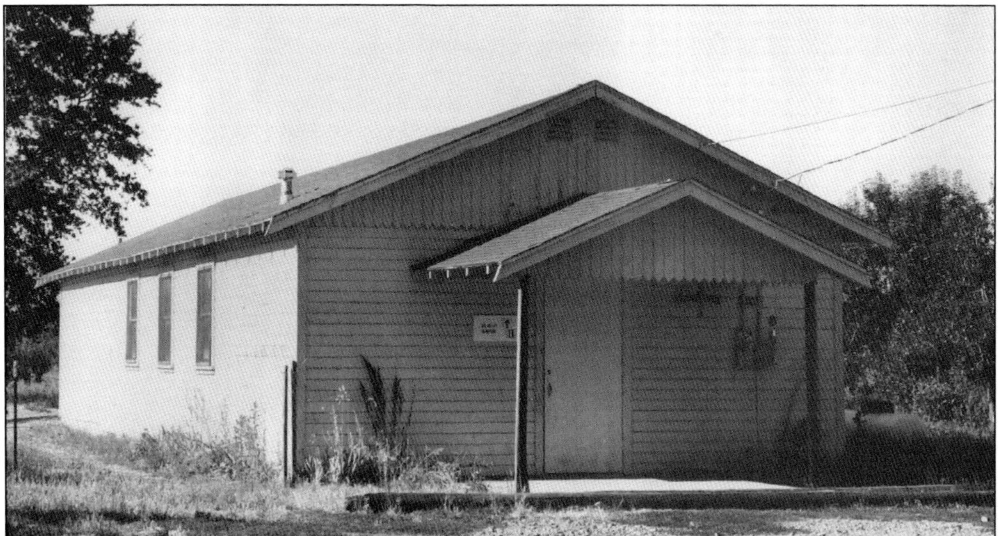

**Headstart at Big Valley.** In the 1960s, preschool children attended head-start programs at Big Valley Rancheria started by Nelson Hopper and his wife, Marina. (Courtesy Lake County Historic Courthouse Museum.)

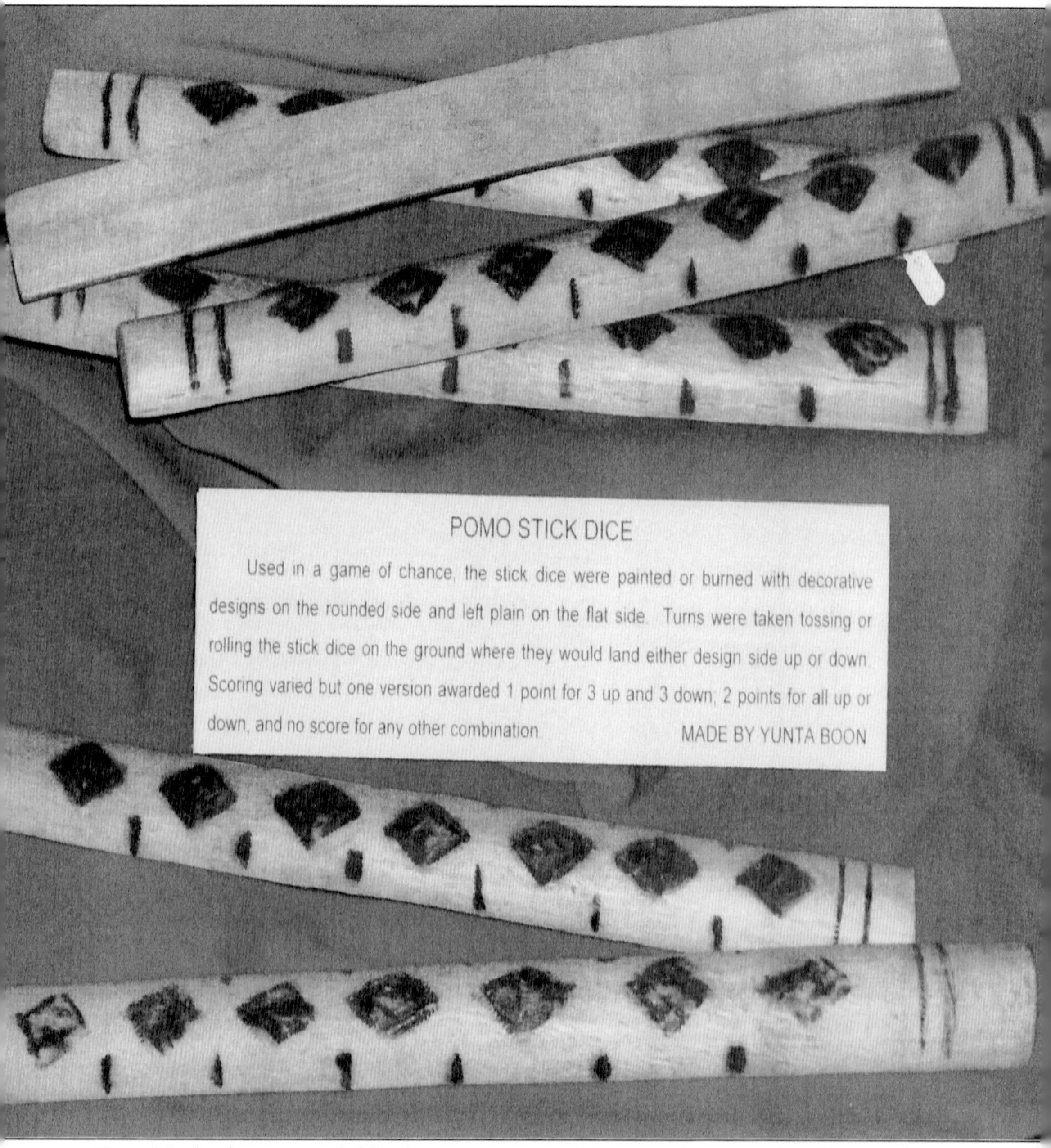


**PLAY.** Much of a growing child's play was experiential learning: how to gather, hunt, and prepare food and running and racing to develop endurance and strong muscles. Girls learned to be women with tule dolls, beginning basket weaving and sewing. Boys learned to hunt and catch skillfully with their families. Beyond races, children and adults loved to play games of skill and luck. Gambling was constant, with women's gaming sticks (above), men's grass game and shinny, and children's dice and acorn tops. Scores were kept with counting sticks, and wagers were made with clamshell money. Indian gaming connects a long heritage of exercising luck. (Courtesy Lake County Historic Courthouse Museum.)

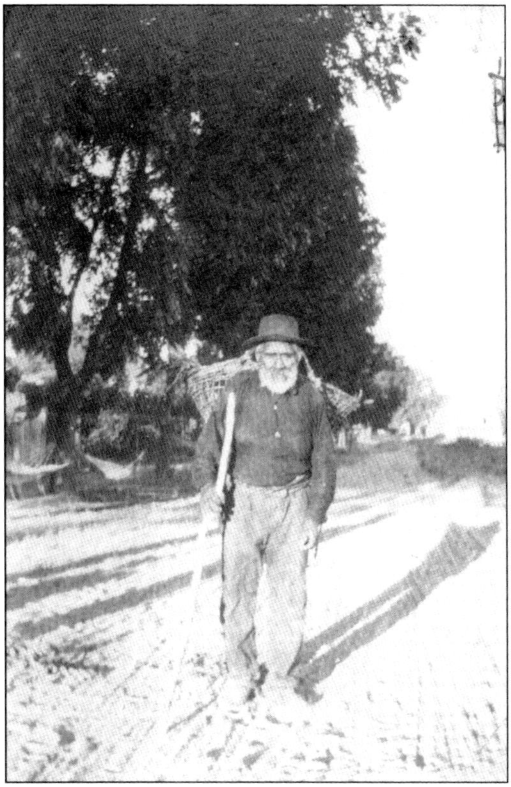

**LIVING SLOWLY.** Native Americans lived long, and there was no hurry to grow up, learn everything, and practice a role in the community. Old Tom, in 1945 said that his father told him he was born the year the stars fell (a meteor shower) in 1860. The Pomo elder lady (below) from Long Valley was said to be between 110 and 120 years old. The Pomo calendar was 12 lunar months, each named for the time, such as the month to harvest acorns. Time was a leader's responsibility. Death came as a part of life and with an understanding of an afterlife. Most tribes had rituals for cremation of the dead until the time the priests came. Since accumulation of wealth or possessions was not part of the culture, favorite possessions and gifts of mourners were burned or buried with the deceased. (Top photograph by Henry Mauldin; courtesy Lake County Historic Courthouse Museum.)

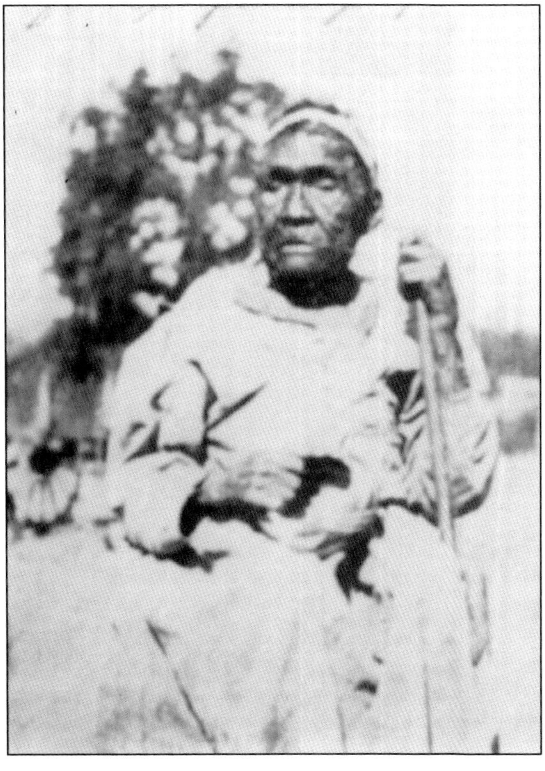

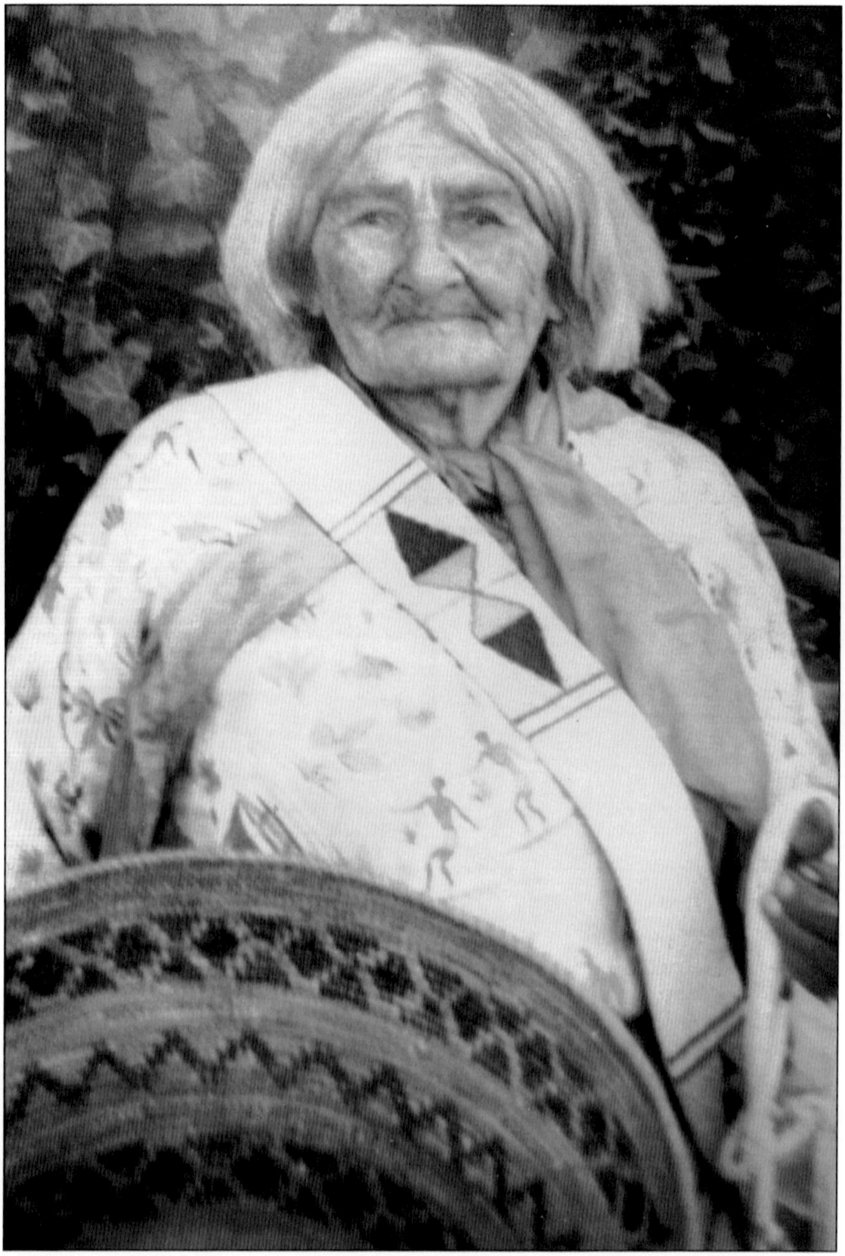

**MAY BE THE LAST SONG.** Two eras of Indian life ended at graveside services for William Graves (88), December 1960, and his sister Lydia Sleeper (108), June 1961, (above). Modern services were held with the favorite belongings buried with each. According to ancient custom, chants or "sings" were held for a full day before burial by Jonathan Moore of Upper Lake, and Clifford Salvador of Cache Creek. Sleeper and Graves were said to be the only Pomos who knew the complete ceremonies and language of the ancients. At the time of his death, Graves was recording them for the University of California. Sleeper was considered one of the most skillful basket makers in the tribe. She escaped death many years ago when she was on Clear Lake in a storm with eight Pomo men, all of whom drowned. She was found, nearly dead, clinging to the boat. (Summarized from obituaries in *Santa Rosa Press Democrat*, June 12, 1961, and December 1960.)

# *Four*

# Koi Nation and Lower Lake Rancheria

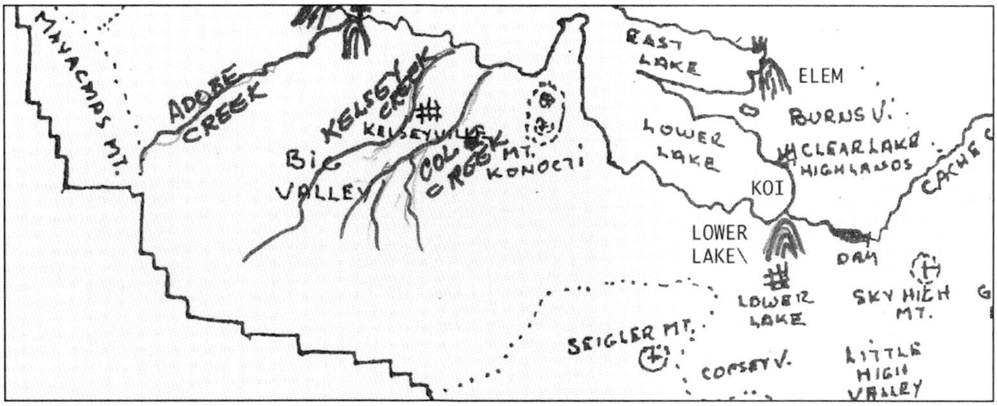


**Where Is Koi?** The Southeastern Pomo village of *xqoyi* (Koi) was located on the eastern shore of Indian Island (Lower Lake Island) at the southern tip of Lower Lake. The island is designated as an archaeological site of great interest, but it is under private ownership. Repeated slave raids and genocidal massacres decimated the native populace. Capt. R. S. Floyd and a partner purchased Indian Island around 1880 as part of a railroad construction project that never materialized. Garner Island and Slater Island, also ancient habitation sites, were similarly considered Koi territory.

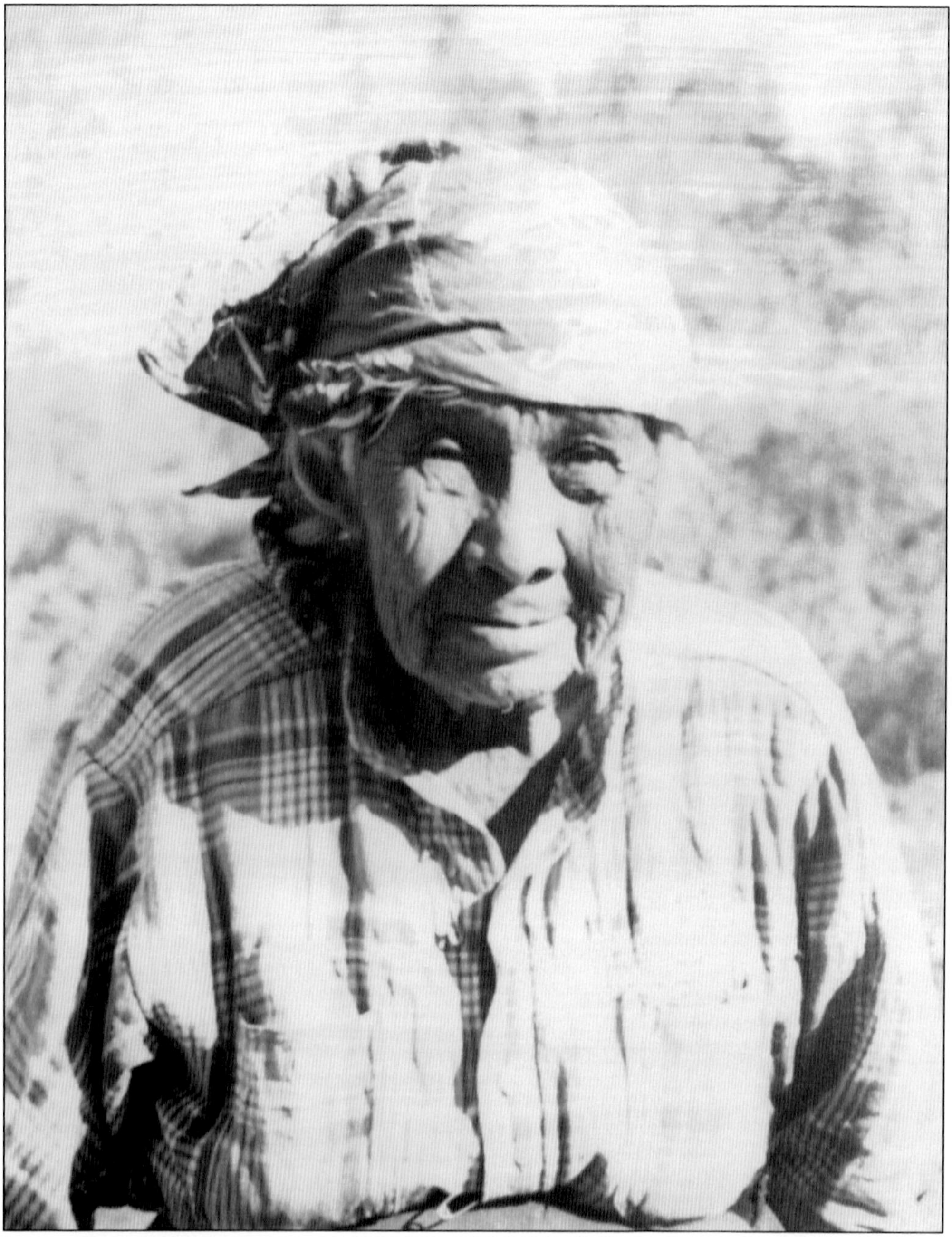

**Koi or not Koi?** An old Indian village lay just below the steel bridge across Cache Creek, but in 1916, the Bureau of Indian Affairs purchased Purvis Flats specifically for "the benefit of the landless Indians residing in the immediate vicinity." The 140-acre rock pile was called Lower Lake Rancheria (sometimes mistakenly called Cache Creek Rancheria) and remained uninhabited for decades. Etta Grant (above) was the grandmother of Pete Smith, a key family there, along with the family of George Patch. Patch is buried in the Pioneer Cemetery and Indian Burial Ground. (Photograph courtesy Lower Lake Historic Schoolhouse Museum.)

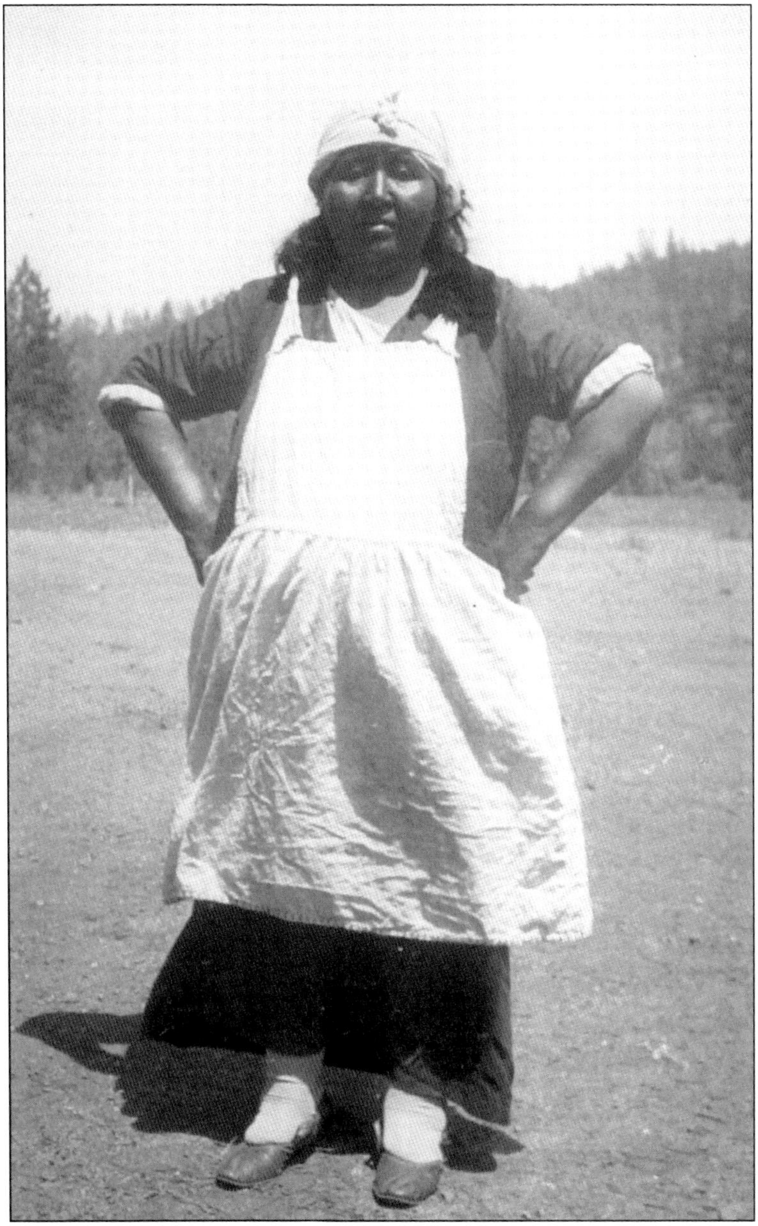

**TERMINATION?** In 1956, the 84th Congress passed Public Law 443, selling Lower Lake Rancheria to Lake County "for the purpose of establishing an airport," except for 40 acres gifted to Harry Johnson and his wife, who were said to be the only two Indians living there in 1953. Brothers Harry and Ned Johnson were said to be from Long Valley, and Ned and his wife, Maggie (above), lived at Middletown in the 1930s. When the airport was discontinued, the land was sold to the city of Clearlake, but the tribe itself was forgotten but not terminated. BIA director Kevin Gover placed the Koi back on the Federal Register on his last day with the government, December 29, 2000. Alan Ginsburg, a Florida real estate mogul and entrepreneur, is banking the re-organized Koi tribe's planned gambling casino on land near the Oakland airport. The 53-member tribe, chaired by Daniel Beltram, has a mailing address in Santa Rosa, California. (Photograph courtesy of Merriam files, Calisphere.)

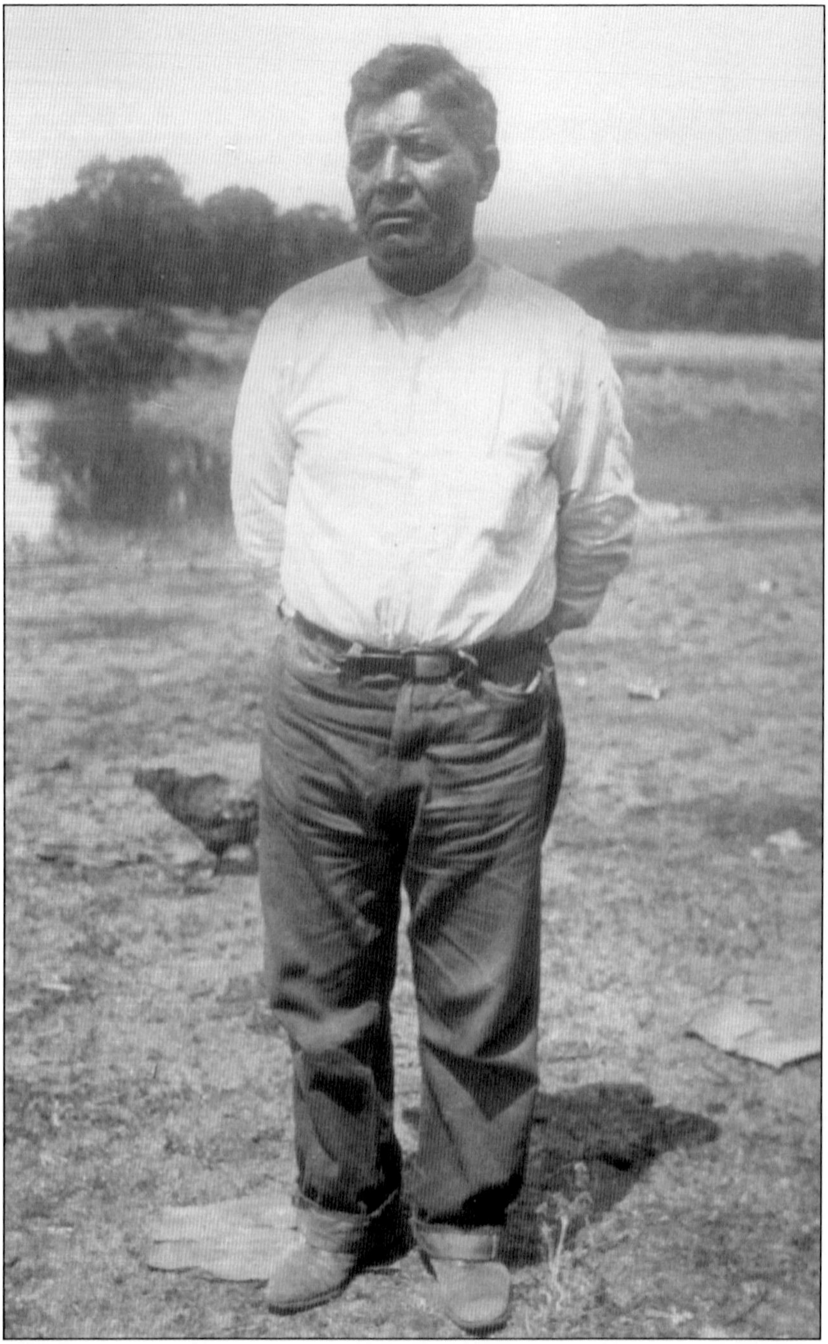

**TAKEN CAPTIVE.** Around 1836, the Spanish made a raid into Koi territory to take Indians back to Sonoma as forced labor. Many were killed, and those remaining were marched over the mountains to be enslaved. The ancestors of Clifford Salvador (above in the 1930s) narrowly escaped capture at their home on Koi (Indian Island). Subsequently the soldiers caught the Indians on Yo (Slater Island). One captive was a nine-year-old boy who took the name of his master, Salvador Vallejo. After 10 years, Salvador returned to his old home at Indian Island, where he married a local Indian girl and started a family. (Photograph courtesy of Merriam files, Calisphere.)

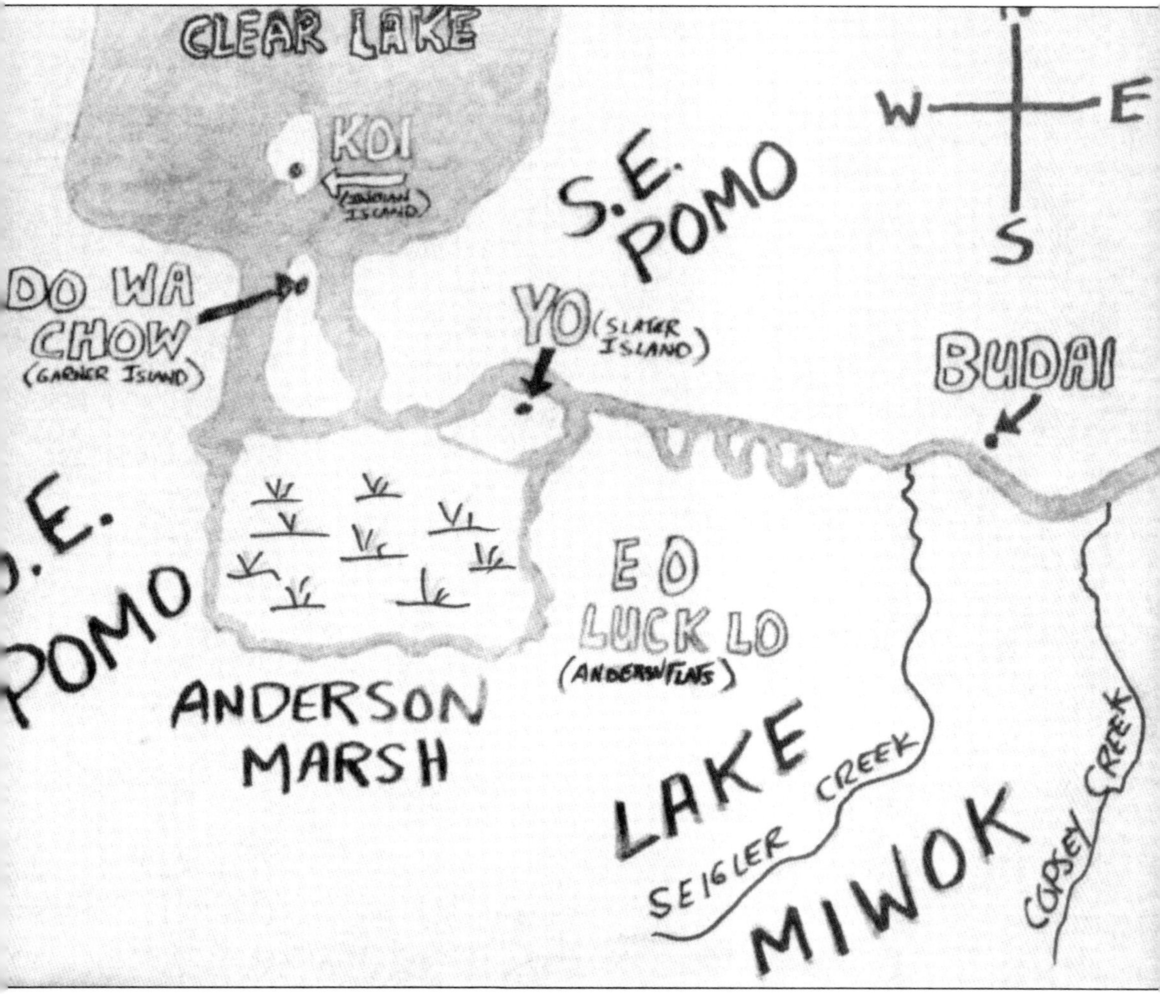


**FIGHTING INTERNMENT.** In 1856, the order came to remove all Lake County Indians to Round Valley Reservation. The Indians and local white farmers who needed the natives as laborers protested. Salvador, it is said, went to his old master Salvador Vallejo but to no avail. Desperate, he went to Sacramento, and this time the order was rescinded. Salvador told his son that he had been given a paper that granted him the right to live on Indian Island. As time went on, the homes on the island burned and the paper was destroyed. The Salvador family moved to Ba-di-chow-claul (Creek Home) on the north bank of Cache Creek just below the old steel bridge. Refugees from other tribelets moved there too. (Map courtesy of former state park ranger Tom Nixon.)

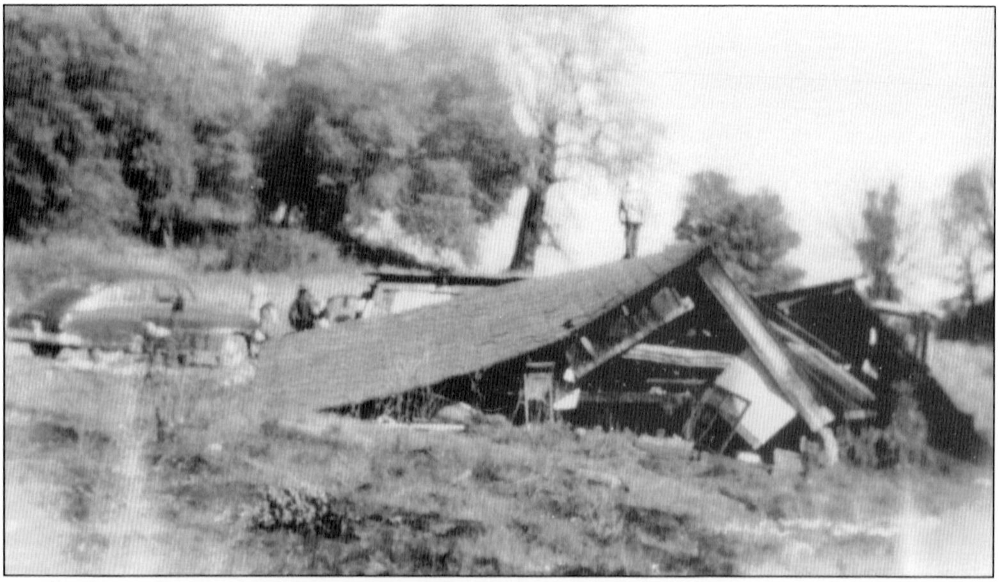

**No Right.** Clifford Salvador, a son of Salvador and his wife, was born and raised at Ba-di-chow-claul (1870–1965). In 1959, resort developer Paul Lewis bulldozed the house and belongings of Clifford and the other resident families (Pete Smith's house is at right). It was a classic example of culture clash, as an ensuing court case demonstrated. Lewis maintained that the land belonged to him; Salvador maintained he belonged with the land. (Courtesy Lower Lake Historic Schoolhouse Museum.)

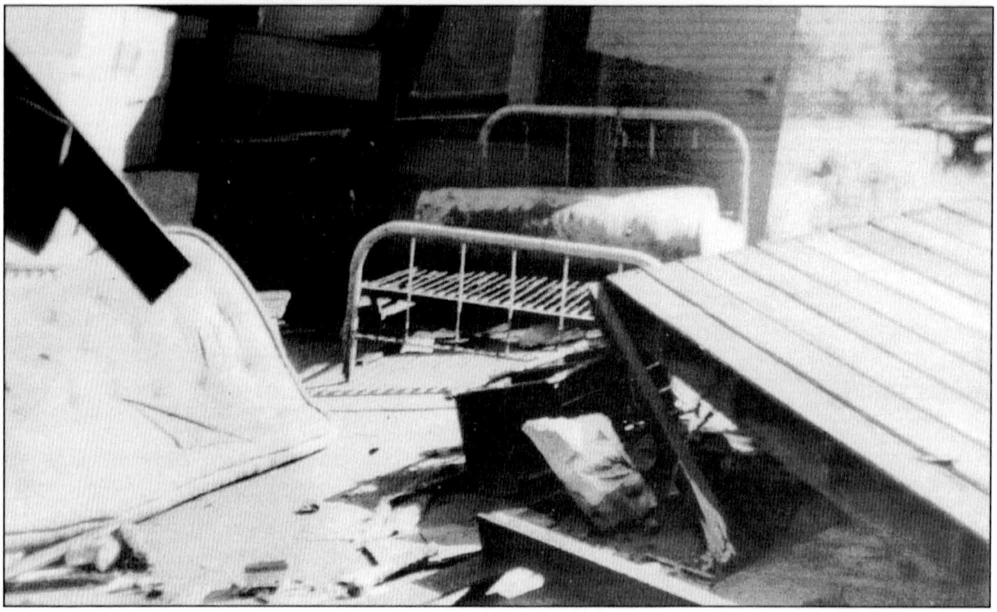

**Losing the Land Again.** The Indian Bureau told Lewis that the tribe had no claim to the land, and so he acquired it to develop a mobile-home community. Prosecutors questioned the aged Salvador about mundane items. Salvador didn't understand. He knew only that this had always been Indian land, that it was wrong to have been pushed off it, that he had lived there all his life, and that he wanted to die there. Salvador died at Robinson Rancheria and is presumed buried at the Pioneer Cemetery and Indian Burial Ground at Creek Home. An extensive mobile home community now lies along Cache Creek. (Courtesy Lower Lake Historic Schoolhouse Museum.)

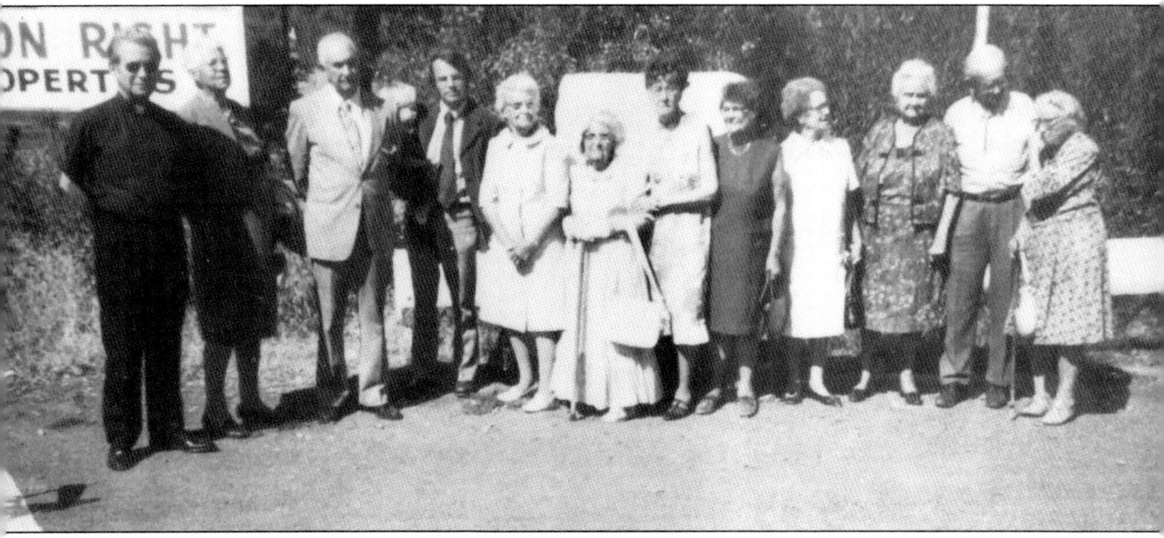

**MEMORIALIZED.** On October 1, 1972, a plaque was dedicated to Clifford Salvador for his struggle as a resident of Lower Lake and his help in telling the history of the area and his ancestors. It was due largely to the writings of Ruth Tennyson in local papers and the efforts of the Women's Civic Improvement Club. The marker now stands in the yard of the Historic Schoolhouse Museum. From left to right at the ceremony are Father Mahole, unidentified, Henry Mauldin, unidentified, Cora ?, Ruth Tennyson, Marika West, Phoebe Peasley, Maude Peasley, Louise Melson, George Miller, and Mrs. George Miller. (Courtesy Lower Lake Historic Schoolhouse Museum.)

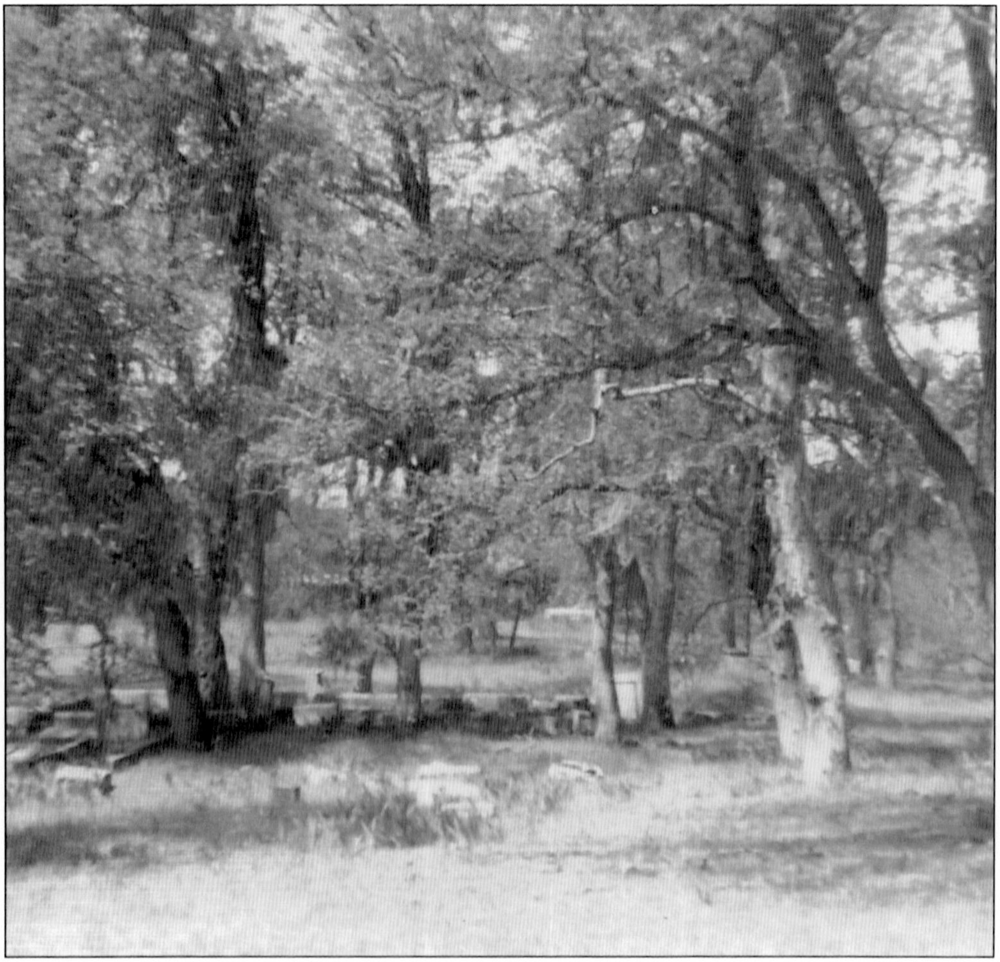

**NO REST.** A developer's bulldozer that threatened Lower Lake's Pioneer Cemetery and Indian Burial Ground was stopped in 2006 by community activists led by Kevin Engle with the support of the Lake County Historical Society. (Courtesy Lower Lake Historic Schoolhouse Museum.)

# *Five*

# THE ROMANTIC ERA

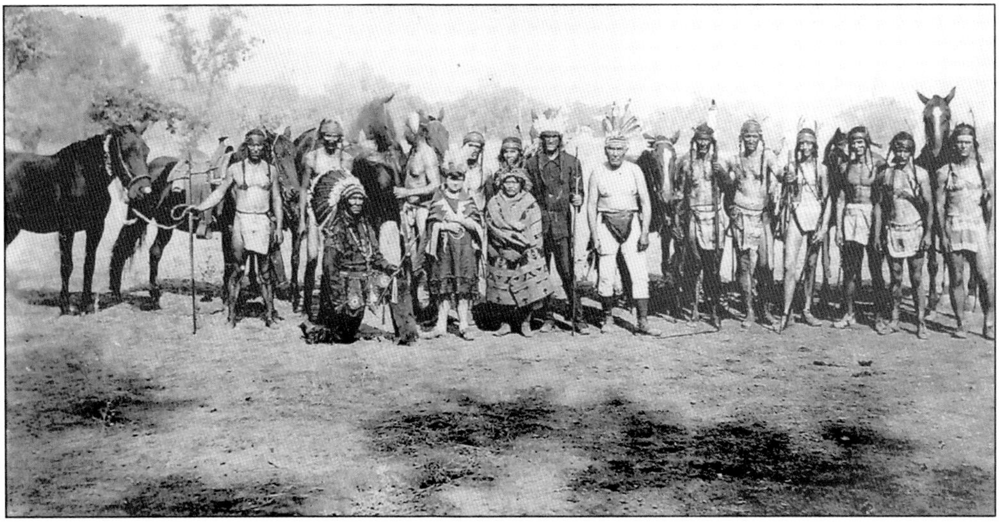

**CASTING CALL.** Helen Hunt Jackson's books *A Century of Dishonor* (1881) and *Ramona* (1884) changed the way Americans thought about Native Americans. Both were widely read, movies and songs were written, and a groundswell of public opinion followed. Suddenly the noble savage was in vogue, especially those set against a backdrop of brilliant sunsets, as this costumed Lower Lake group seems to be. (Courtesy Lower Lake Historic Schoolhouse Museum.)

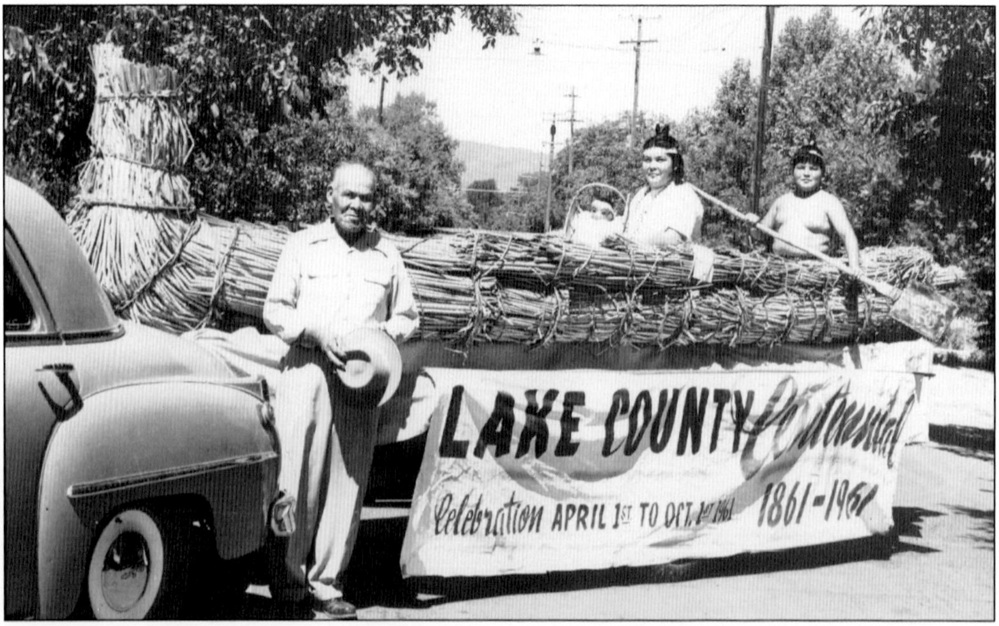


**DRESSING THE PART.** Lake County Pomo were in trouble; they didn't look like the stereotype. In Lake County's temperate climate, men and women originally went without wardrobe once they left the cradle. Then calico and kerchiefs accompanied the vaquero look, followed by California castoffs. Now people had to dress up to look like Indians. Beaded chamois "buckskins" and eagle-feather war bonnets topped mass-produced moccasins. Lincoln Dennison pulls a balsa (tule boat) with Katherine (Martin) Ray's children dressed as "Indians." (Courtesy Lake County Historic Courthouse Museum.)

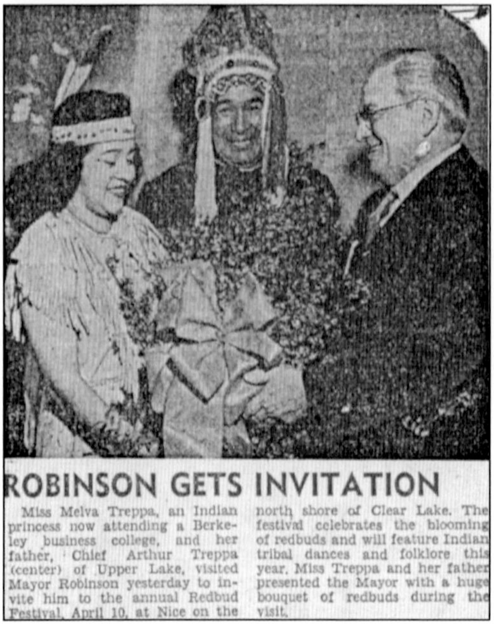

ROBINSON GETS INVITATION

Miss Melva Treppa, an Indian princess now attending a Berkeley business college, and her father, Chief Arthur Treppa (center) of Upper Lake, visited Mayor Robinson yesterday to invite him to the annual Redbud Festival, April 10, at Nice on the north shore of Clear Lake. The festival celebrates the blooming of redbuds and will feature Indian tribal dances and folklore this year. Miss Treppa and her father presented the Mayor with a huge bouquet of redbuds during the visit.

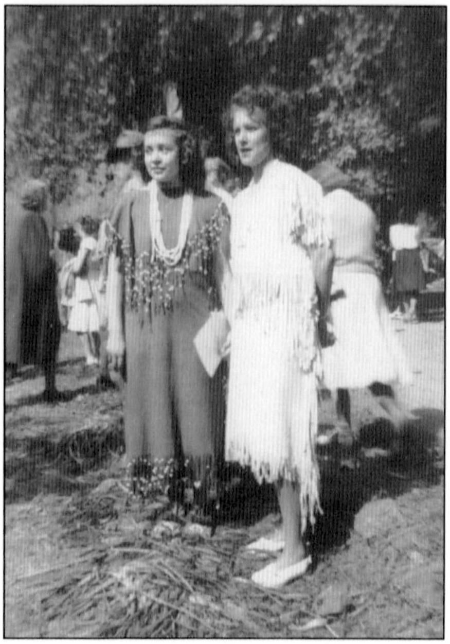

**FOR THE MEDIA.** "Chief" Arthur Treppa dressed the part, and his "princess" daughters showed off their buckskins in the 1950s to promote the annual Redbud Festival in Nice. (Courtesy *San Francisco Examiner*; Treppa family archives.)

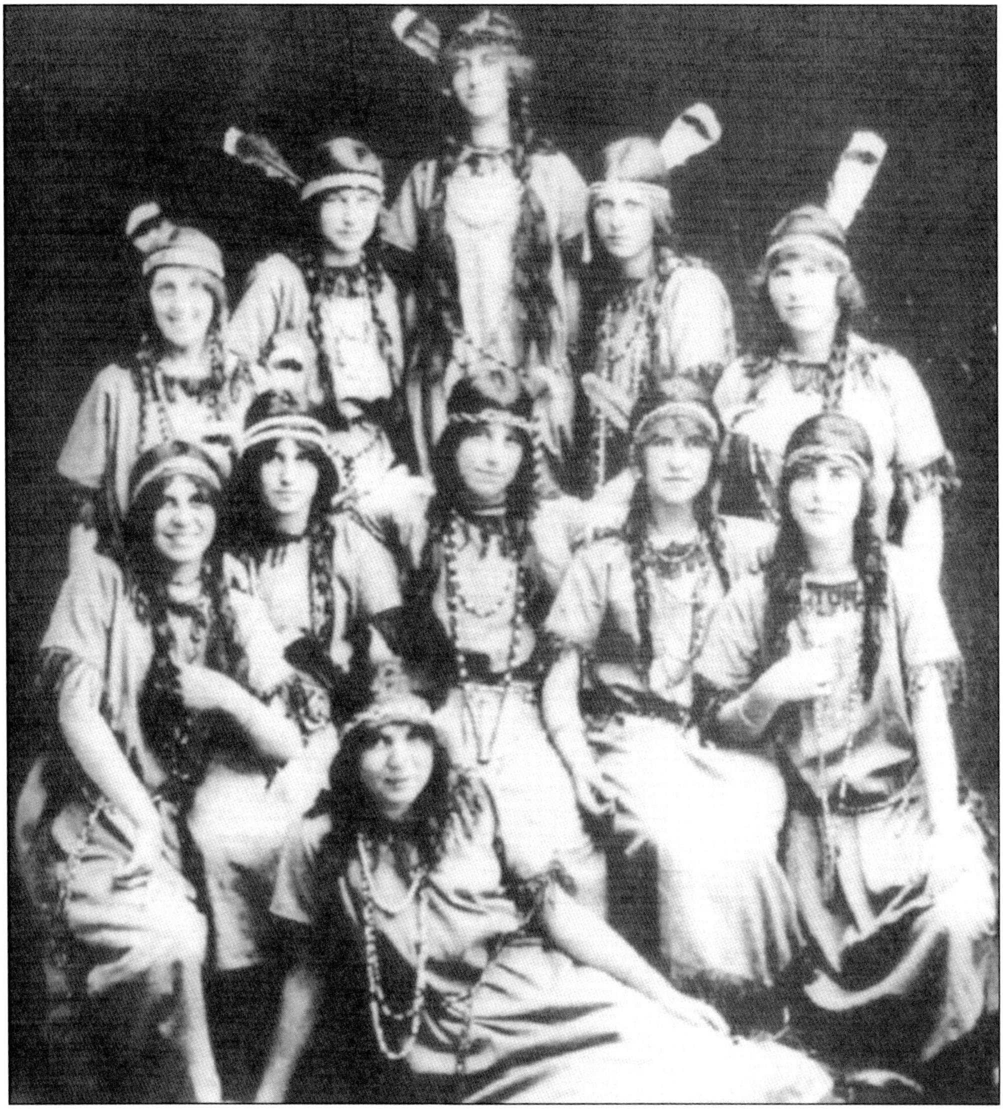

**EVERYWHERE YOU LOOK.** The Pocahontus [*sic*] Club (*c.* 1920s) still did not allow Indians in high school when a local play, *Kabatim*, advertised that the cast included seven real Indians and genuine mortars and pestles. In 2006, Pomo activists persuaded Kelseyville High School to replace its team logo with something less offensive to the county's 12,000-year native tradition of unwarlike culture. In the past, local activists asked that Him Konocti, a whimsical figure with a giant nose, be removed as the Lake County Fair emblem. Images aren't everything, but they do carry unintended messages. (Courtesy *Lake County Record-Bee*; private collection.)

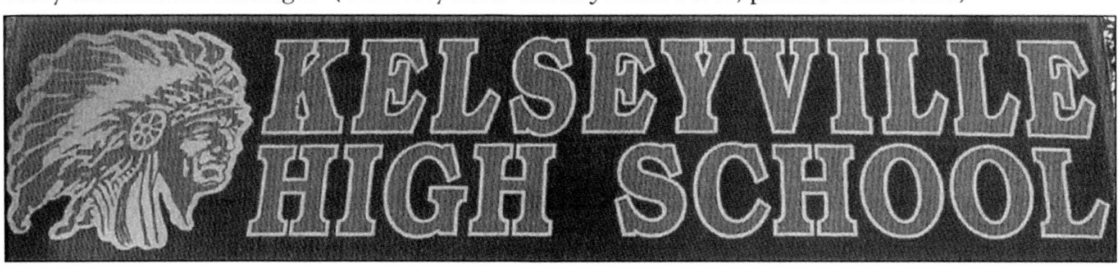

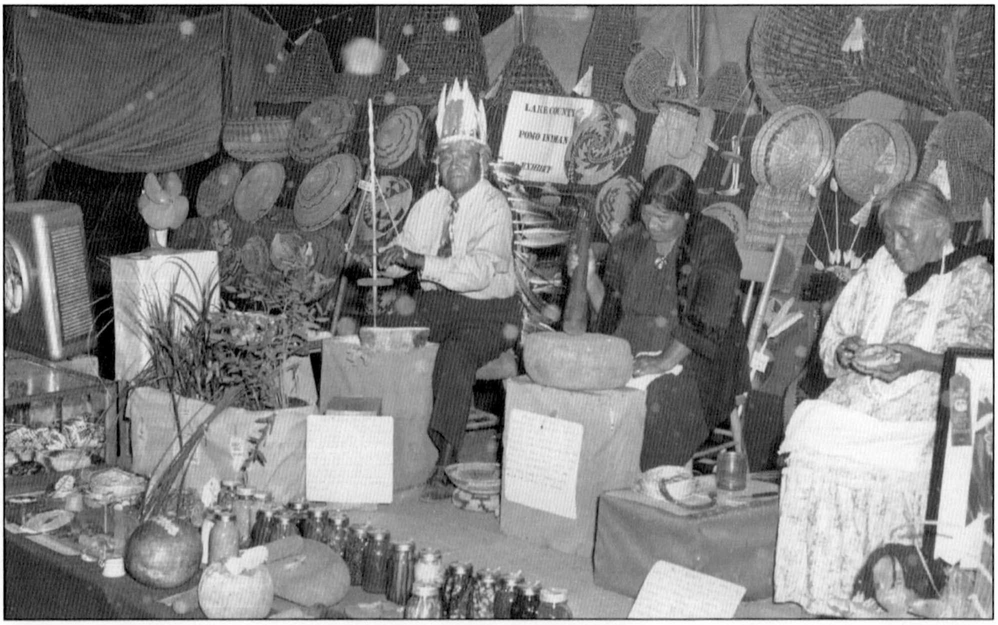


**REAL POMO SKILLS DISPLAYED.** A 1948 exhibit of Pomo crafts and arts won ribbons at the 1948 Lake County Fair, and it consisted of real Native American craftsmen and artifacts from the Lake County Museum's Pomo displays. The booth was designed and entered by Lake County historian Henry Mauldin and Belle Davidson, founder of the Lake County Museum. It shows Frank and Mary Norton with weaver "Goldtooth" May John. (Courtesy Lake County Historic Courthouse Museum.)

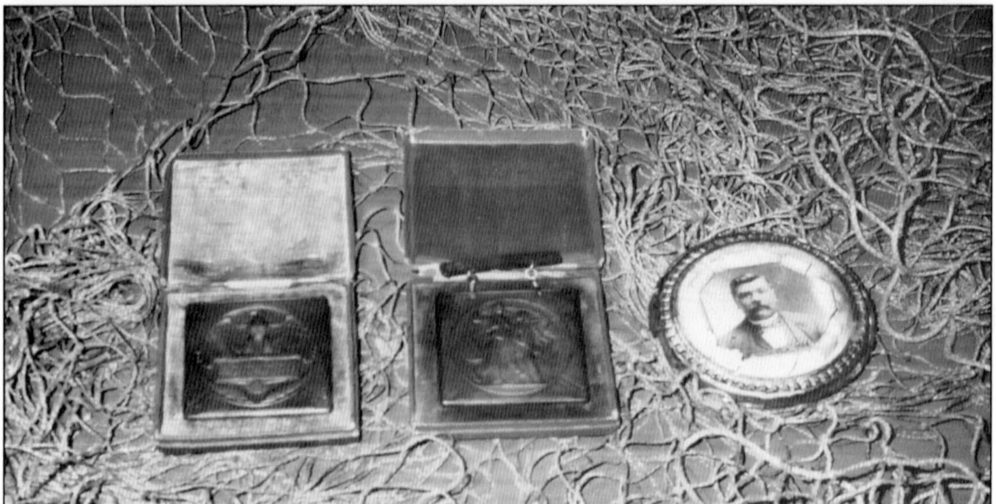

**PRIZE-WINNING ARTIST.** William Raganal Benson was the son of a white father and an Eastern Pomo mother. He was born on the Benson ranch in Kelseyville but married a Yokaya Pomo and lived there. An artist, Benson and his wife, Mary Knight Benson, a well-known basket weaver, went with Dr. John Hudson to the St. Louis World's Fair in 1904 (their medals are exhibited at Lake County Courthouse Museum) and were honored for their Pomo artifacts. Benson made many objects now in museum collections and was a valuable informant to ethnologists. (Photograph by Donna Howard, courtesy Lake County Historic Courthouse Museum.)

# *Six*

# RANCHERIAS

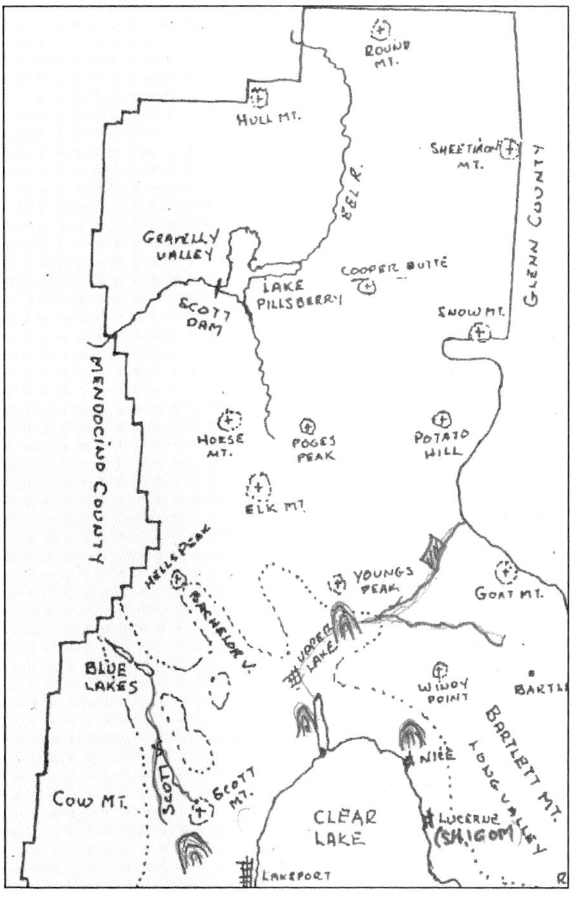


**AFTER YOU.** Scott's Valley was named for early pioneer William Scott, who built a cabin in 1848, stayed in it briefly, and then moved on. Scott's Creek, the drainage channel named for the same individual, regularly changed course and left rich sedimentary deposits across the valley until flood control measures were implemented in modern times. The valley was generally brush-covered and swampy and a good place to hide. The Indian trail from Clear Lake to Blue Lakes, past Tule Lake, through the mountains, and on to the Pacific coast led right through Scott's Valley. There were essentially four tribelets resident there around 1850: some ancient and some relatively new arrivals.

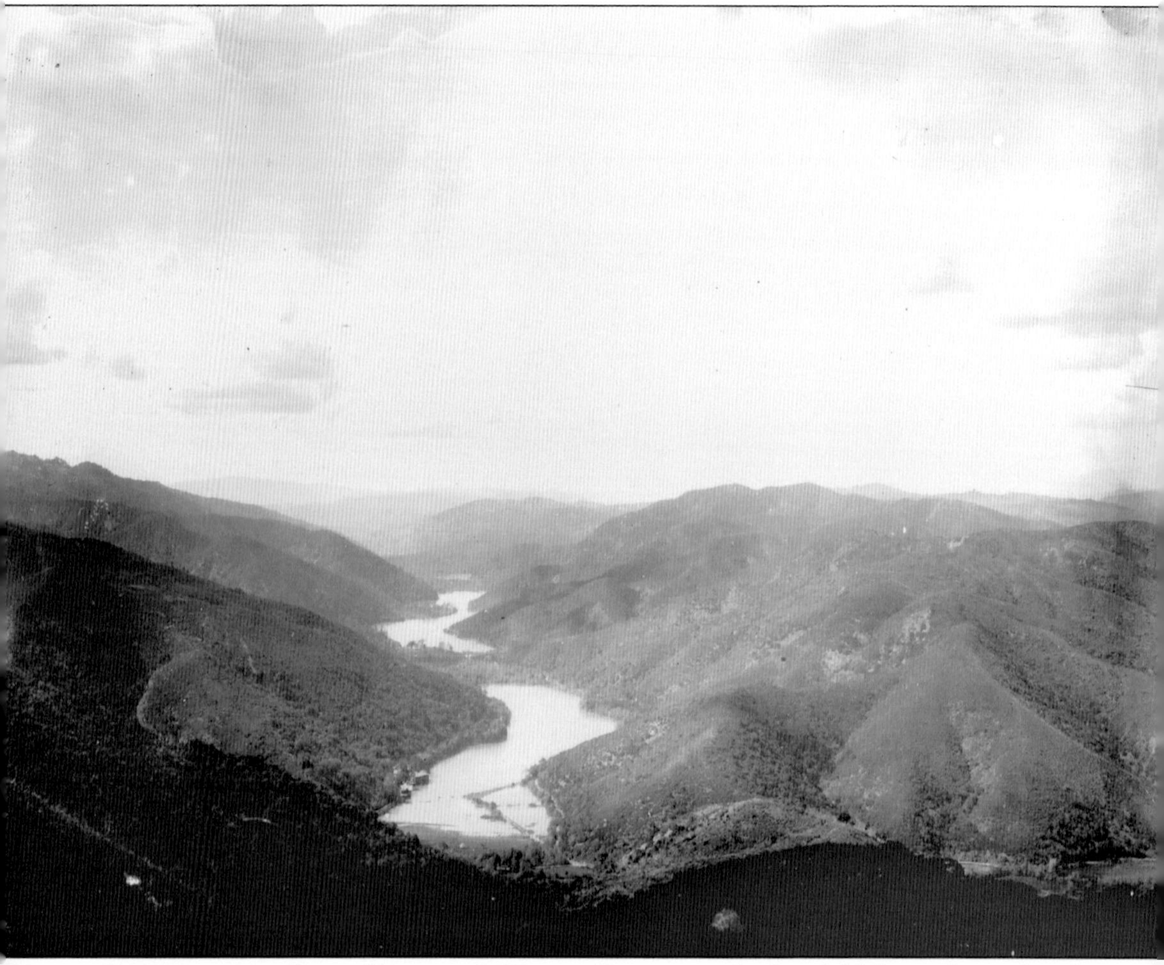

**PLAYERS IN THE BAND.** *Yima* was the Eastern Pomo name for Scott's Valley and *yima-bax* the name for the people. Exactly where their village was located is uncertain, but somewhere just east of Blue Lakes (above). *Kha-yaw* is Eastern Pomo and *Sinal* is Northern Pomo for "head of the valley." Its location at the northwest end of Tule Lake in Bachelor Valley was considered part of what became a Scott's Valley Band territory. *Bowalk-eya* is Northern Pomo and means "ones from the west side." A captain from this tribelet attended the McKee summit in 1851 and was a signatory to the treaties. The *Komli*—Northern Pomo—had apparently been forced out of their territory near Ukiah by a Central Pomo expansion and had moved to Eight Mile Valley and became part of the Scotts Valley Band. Both the Komli and the Bowalk-eya people intermarried with the Kulanapho and Xabenapho (people of Lakeport and Kelsey Creek areas) and vanished as independent "tribes." (Photograph by O. E. Meddaugh [Bishop], courtesy Lake County Historic Courthouse Museum.)

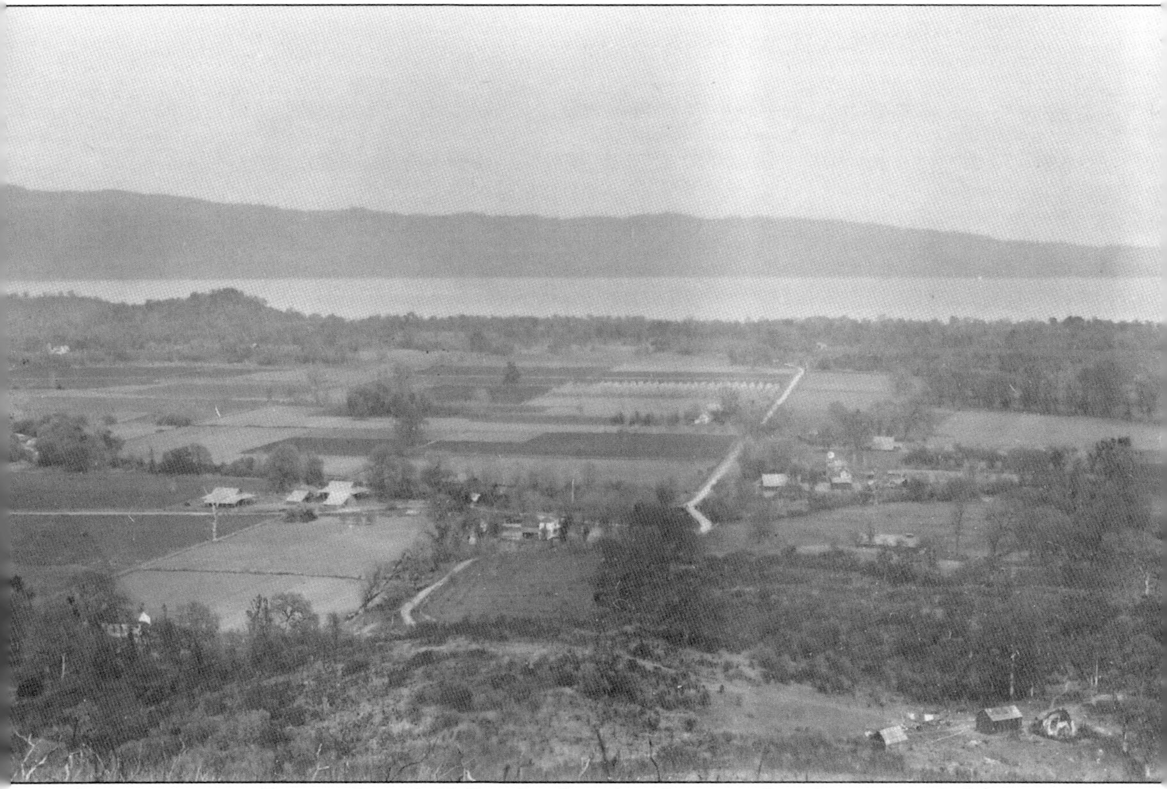

**COMING OF THE ROADS.** Scott's Valley developed within two decades as a settled farming community; small Indian settlements remained on white squatters' land only through their goodwill. (See the Faught Rancheria at lower right above.) In 1873, the government surveyed so residents could homestead and file legal claims to their land. California Indians could not file claims. Local lore says that a member of a Russian Orthodox Church wrote to Indian Affairs pleading for a reserve where the Indians of the Scott's Valley area could be safe and well cared for. It was a bitter irony that the name on the report that authorized reservations was Kelsey. (Photograph by O. E. Meddaugh [Bishop]; courtesy of Lake County Historic Courthouse Museum.)

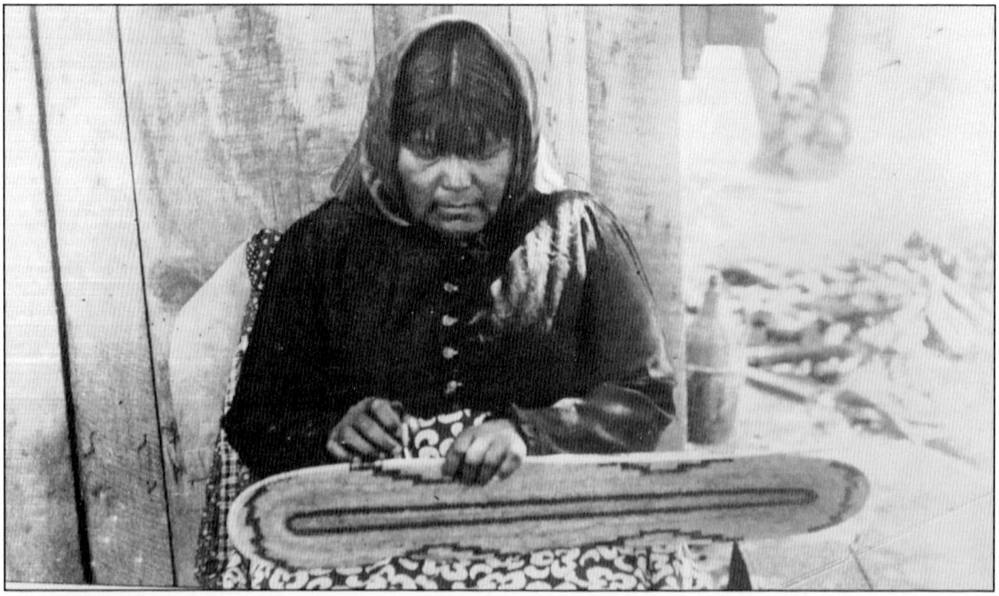

**Living on the Land.** Scott's Valley Rancheria was established on 56 acres in 1911. Nicknamed Sugarbowl, the land sits in a depression with a high water table and relatively steep hillsides surrounding it. Enoch Jones (below) probably moved there when his mother, Ellen Jones, married Peter Boggs. Enoch's wife Lucy was a proficient quilter and basket maker, though her work in collections goes largely unidentified. Lucy died in 1937, but she is remembered as Indian Lucy in *Stories and Legends of Lake County* (1936), where she tells that her mother and baby sister were killed by soldiers in the punishment. She is puzzled by the word Pomo, saying that Chief Augustine always called them *Yima*, for "over the hill." (Robert Lee Collection [Nevin], courtesy Lake County Historic Courthouse Museum.)

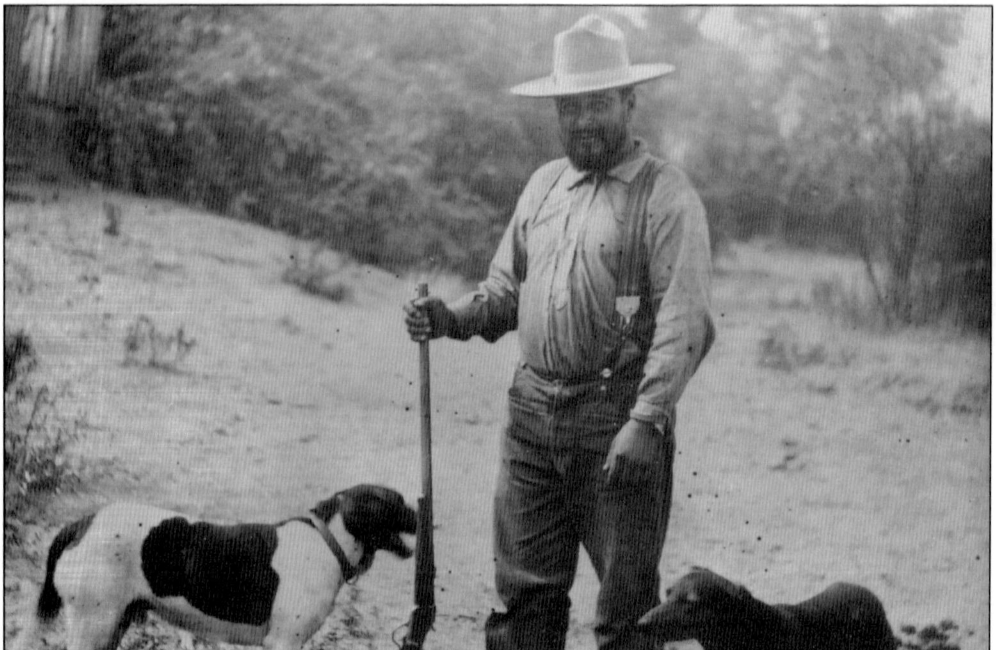

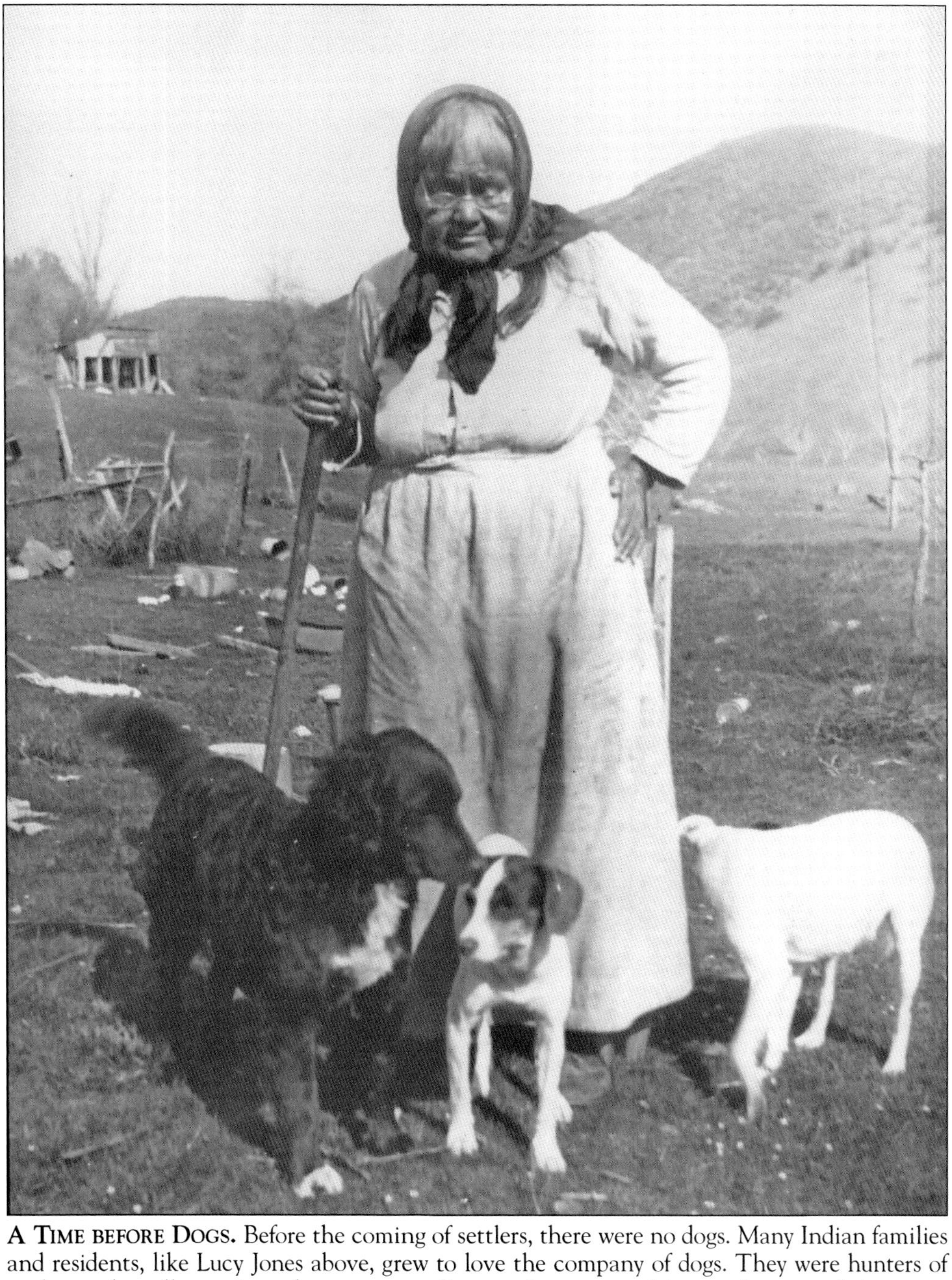

**A Time before Dogs.** Before the coming of settlers, there were no dogs. Many Indian families and residents, like Lucy Jones above, grew to love the company of dogs. They were hunters of snakes and small varmints, they were guardians against approaching predators, and they were entertaining, affectionate, and non-judgmental. Today there aren't many reservation homes without a dog. (Robert Lee Collection [Nevin], courtesy Lake County Historic Courthouse Museum.)

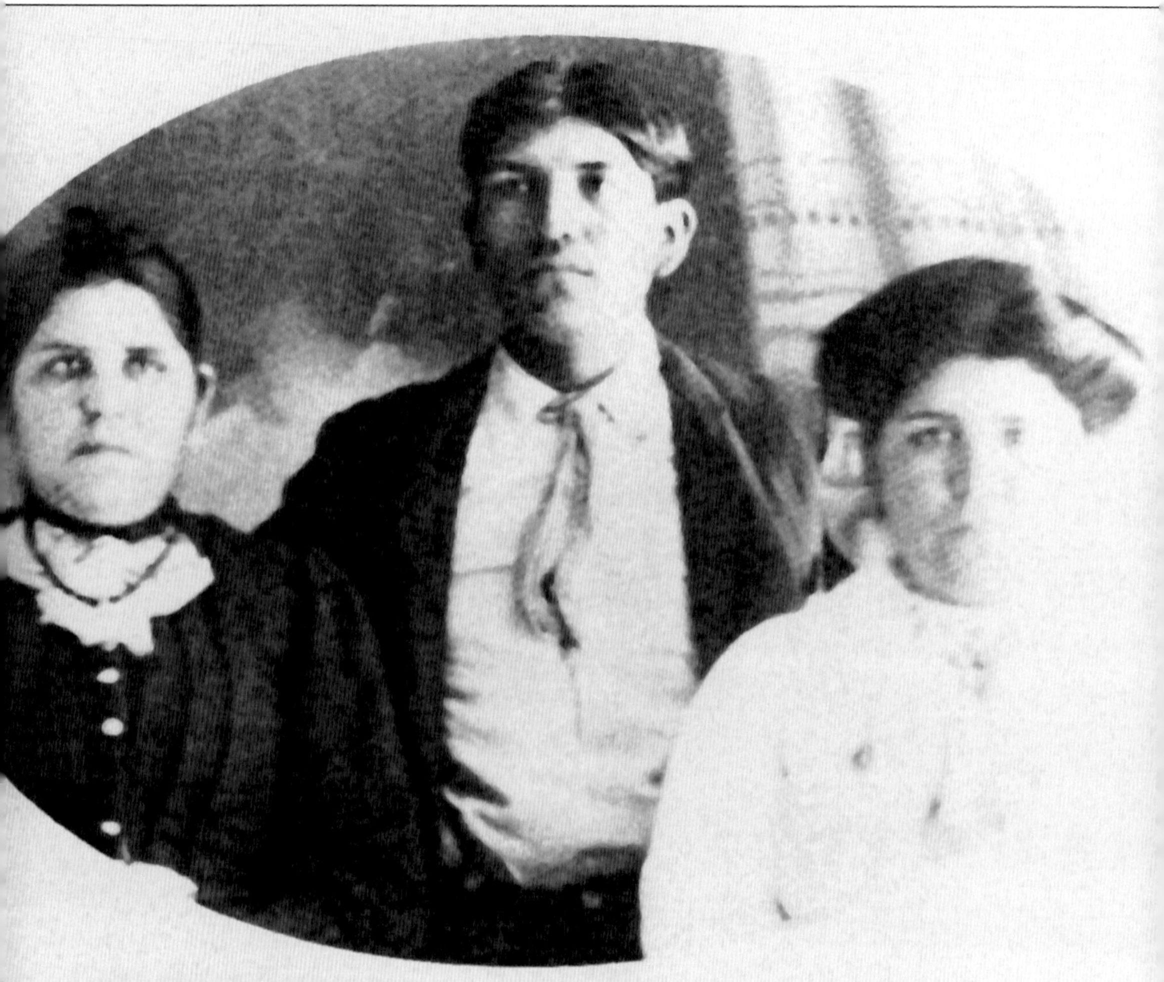

**The Name Resonates.** Augustine is a name taken from a Spanish ranchero owner perhaps or from lessons about St. Augustine learned at the mission. Chief Augustine went down in history as the majordomo at the Stone and Kelsey ranch at the time of the killing and as a reliable informant to historians of the time. Known as a fair and moral man, the name Augustine is part of Pomo history but a little too early for many photographs. The photograph above shows Victoria Juarez Augustine (left), Luis Augustine, and Bessie (Augustine) Ray. (Courtesy *Lake County Record-Bee.*)

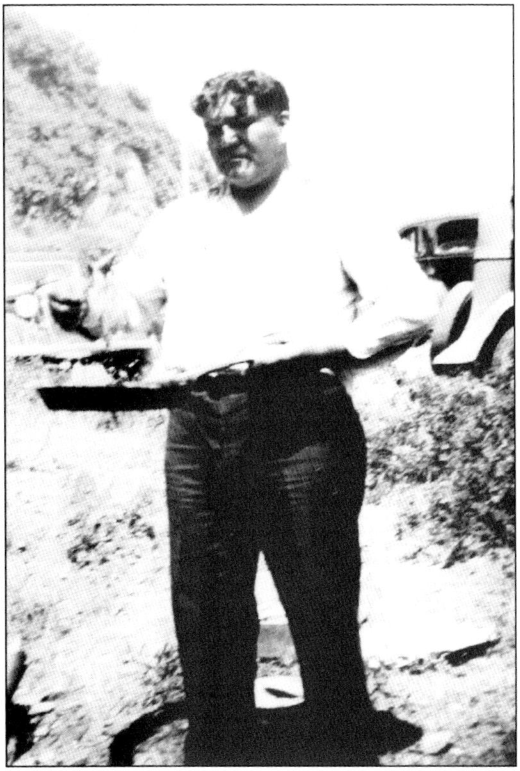

**BUILDERS AND SHAKERS.** When Gene Ray, a Cahto (Kato) from Laytonville (right), married Bessie Augustine (below with daughter Sharon), a Pomo from Upper Lake, they founded the Ray dynasty at Scott's Valley Rancheria. Three generations lived there before termination and distribution of all assets in 1965. Lakeport's high school now sits adjacent to the two remaining parcels of land: Elliott land, which is in trust, and Boggs land, which is not. Les Miller, son of Rose (Ray) Miller and owner of a respected Lakeport business, remembers that no government built their houses. His grandfather had a yard full of tools and he built a house for each of his eight children. They shared one spring for water, which they boiled, but had no other water or septic systems. When the BIA installed toilets in their kitchens, they revolted. Miller served four terms representing 52 of the 104 tribes on the Central California Policy Committee recommending changes to BIA. (Photographs courtesy Miller family archives.)

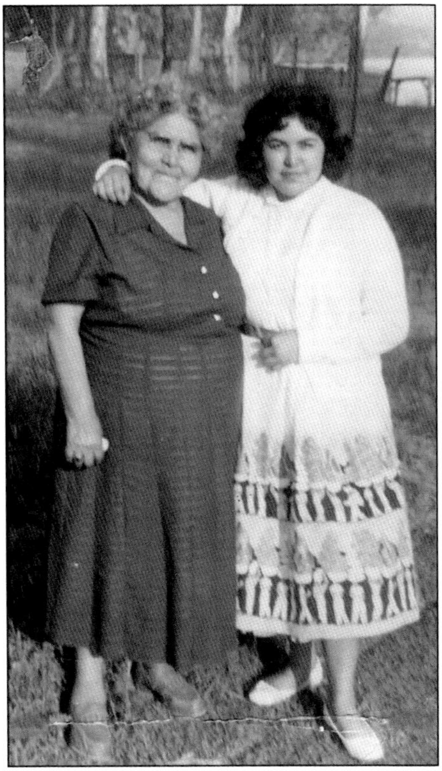

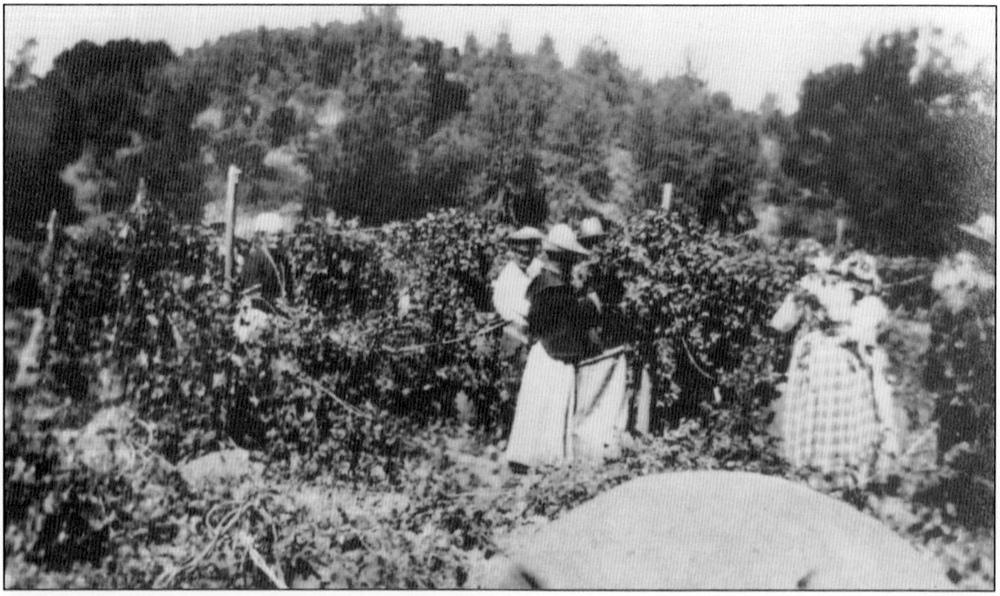

**Don't Look Up.** That's what reservation Indians were taught by everyone but their families. "Just do the work," like picking hops (seen here in E. C. Riggs's ranch) or beans. Indians would miss the first two weeks of school because they would be picking fruit and pickin' walnuts. (Courtesy Lake County Historic Courthouse Museum.)

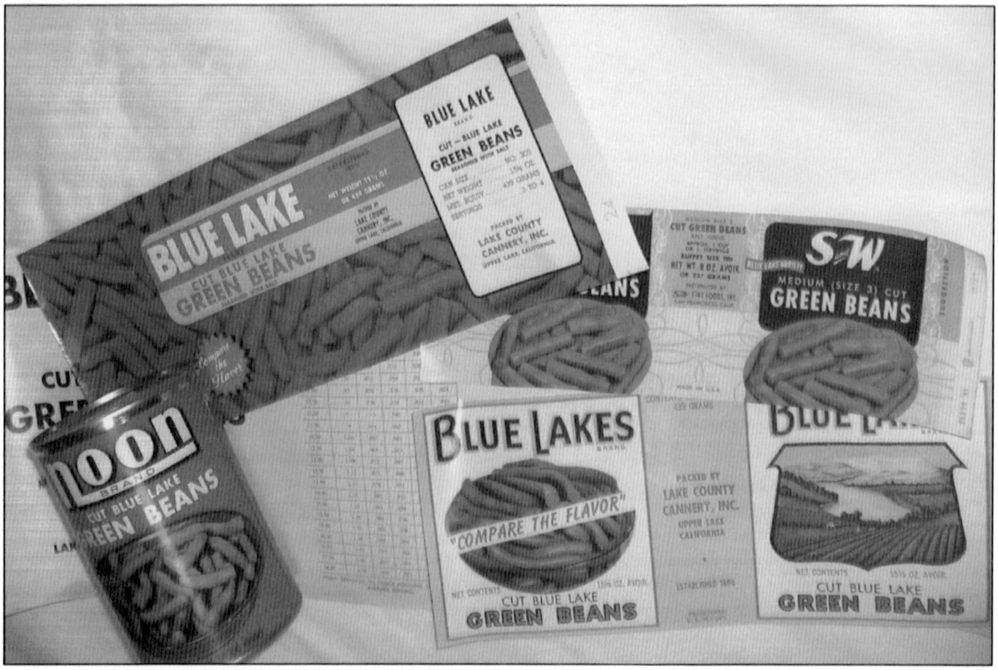


**Just as Good.** "Work hard and do a good job. Always be ready for Monday. You're as good as anyone else, and if you're true to yourself—better." Those were the messages of parents and grandparents as their children worked with them as day laborers or in canneries near Blue Lakes. (Courtesy private collection.)

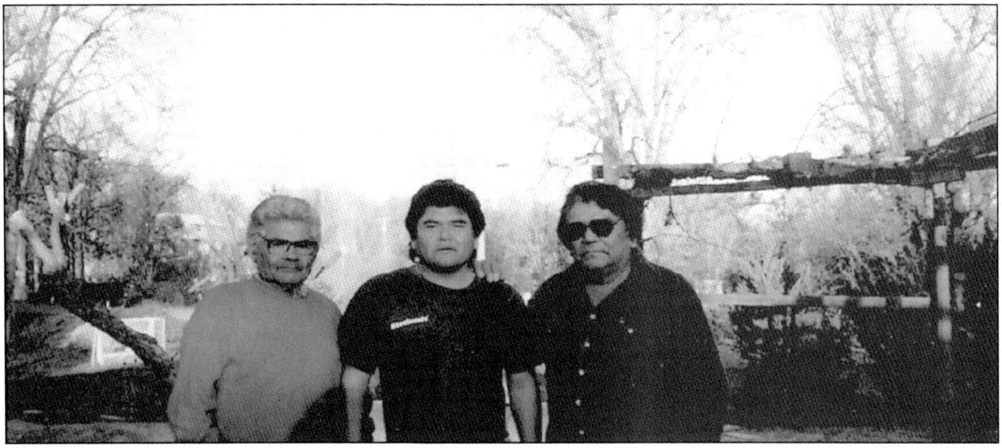

**DOING BATTLE.** Iggy (Steve) Elliott missed the draft but learned to be combative when he helped file suit against the government challenging the legality of its termination policy in the 1960s. The suit was won, but most of the reservation land was lost to other buyers. Here Bennett Elliott, his son Iggy Elliott, and ? Ray stand united. (Courtesy Lake County Historic Courthouse Museum.)

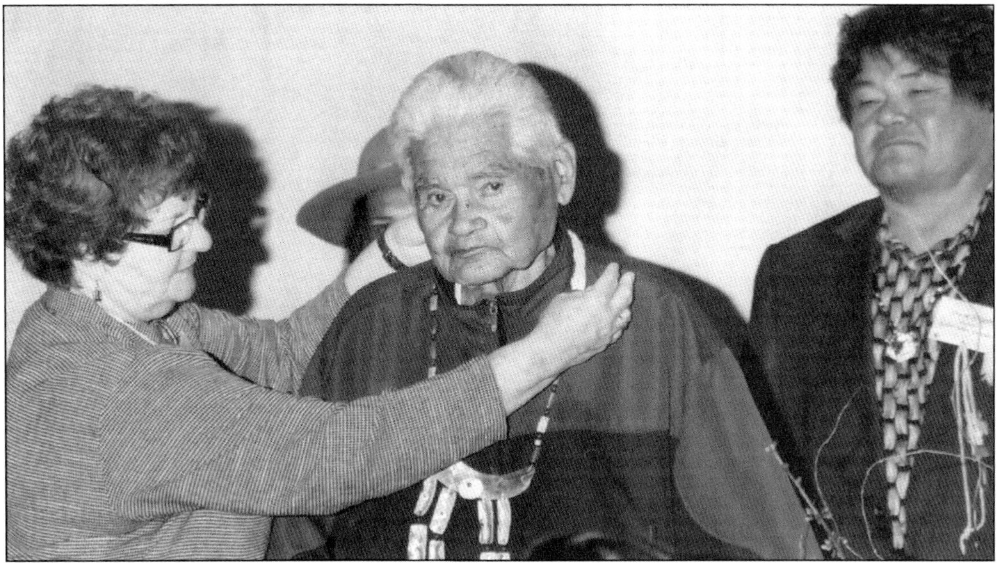

**IT'S A STORY.** Ninety-six-year-old Bennett Elliott is an honored elder at a 2007 Cultural Storytelling of Pomo Basketry conference together with his storyteller son, Ignatius (Steve) Elliott. Elliott's tales evoke the smell of angelica in spring; the flurry of owl wings; the cry of a dog; stories told by his mother, Beulah (Ray) Elliott; and the coarse hands and hard muscles of his father, Bennett Elliott. "I had a hard-working dad who would never thought of leaving us and a mother who loved me. What more could anyone want?" Iggy asks. (Photograph by Trett Bishop, courtesy Friends of the Museum.)

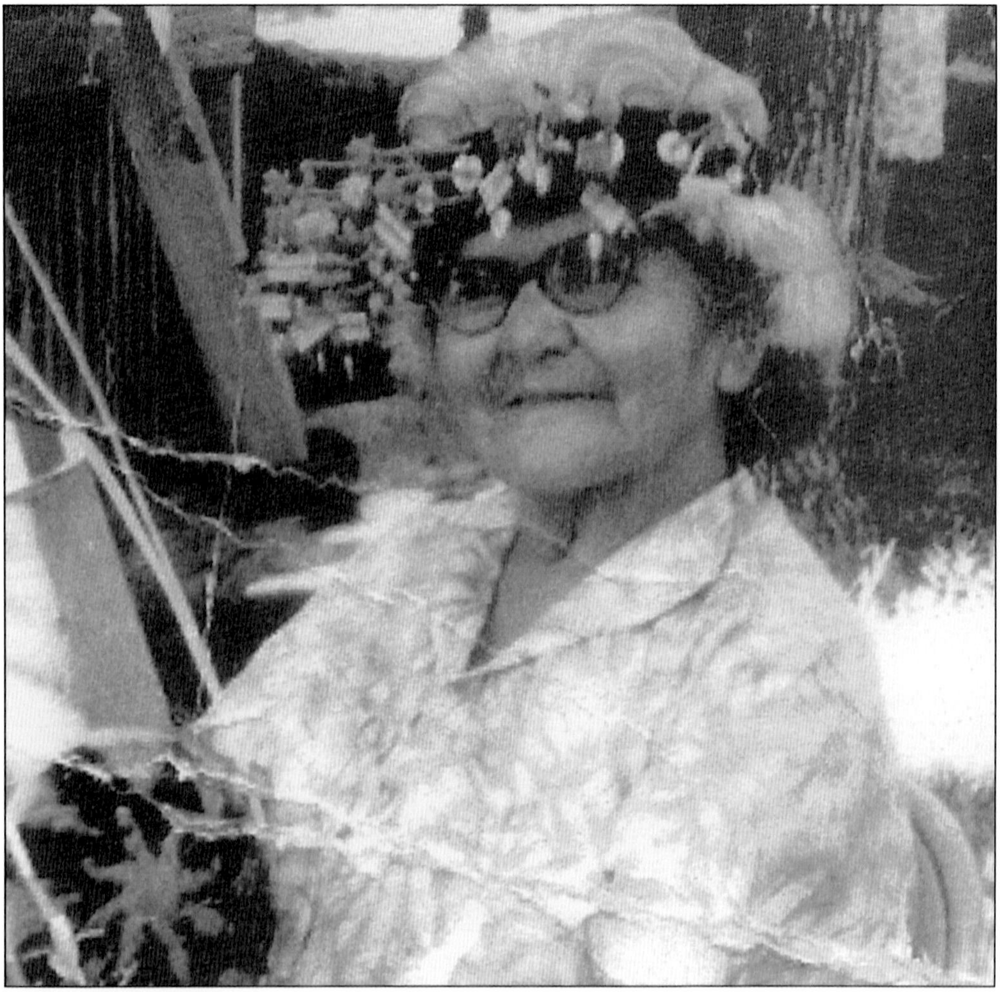

**MOVIN' ON UP.** The current Scott's Valley Band of Pomo Indians wants much more. A picture of Bessie (Augustine) Ray in traditional headgear and holding a Pomo basket now graces the cover of a slick binder of briefing materials from a Richmond, California, address. Since the advent of Indian gaming, investment groups may form partnerships with landless tribes for the purpose of acquiring property in locations advantageous for resort-casino operations. Since the band was formally restored in 1992, a main focus has been to find land on which to build a casino. Scott's Valley maintains a Lakeport administrative office to retain a Lake County presence and address local issues, but the bulk of its members still are reported to live in the greater East Bay area for educational and economic opportunities. Landless doesn't necessarily mean homeless, so the tribal office continues to serve registered members on issues of housing and other administrative concerns. (Courtesy Elliott family archives.)

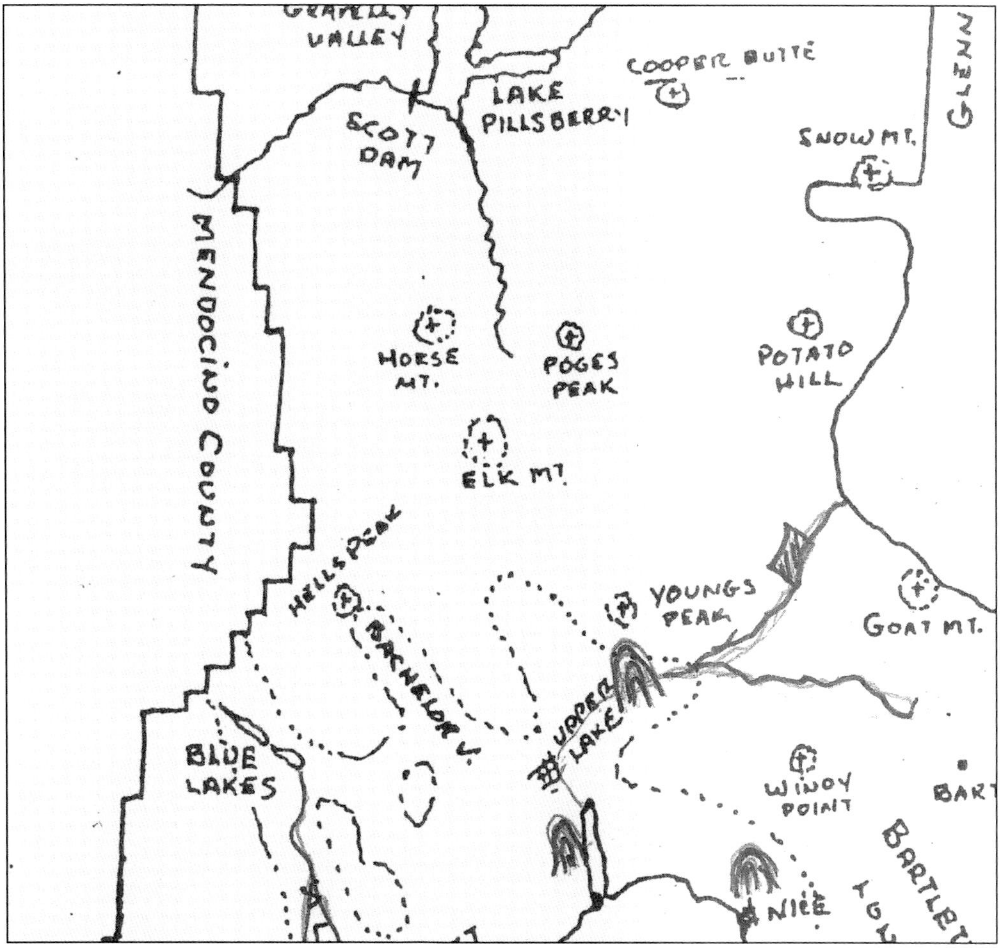


**FOUNDING HABEMATOLEL.** In 1879, a group from the former villages of Shigom, Xowalek, Da-no-xa, and Kayaw/Sinal saved their earnings from summer farm work and together purchased 90 acres north of the town of Upper Lake, thus forming the Upper Lake Indian Community. The 28 new landowners are said to have spoken a combination of Northern and Eastern Pomoan languages (probably Spanish and English as well by this time)

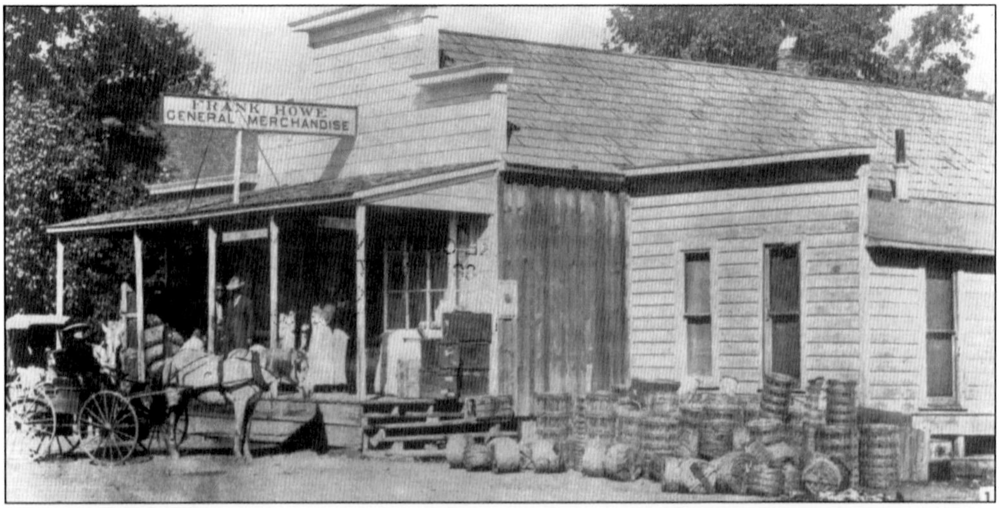


**PULLING TOGETHER.** There were some differences on farming methods between what had been the Hardesty acreage and the Dewell acreage, but they put it together, and the government added 80 acres of hill land for a woodlot. The community functioned very well, with 27 wood-frame houses and several barns, horses, wagons, and plows, harvesting crops as well as hunting and gathering in a more traditional way. Shopping and trading was done at Frank Howe's General Store. (Courtesy Lake County Historic Courthouse Museum.)

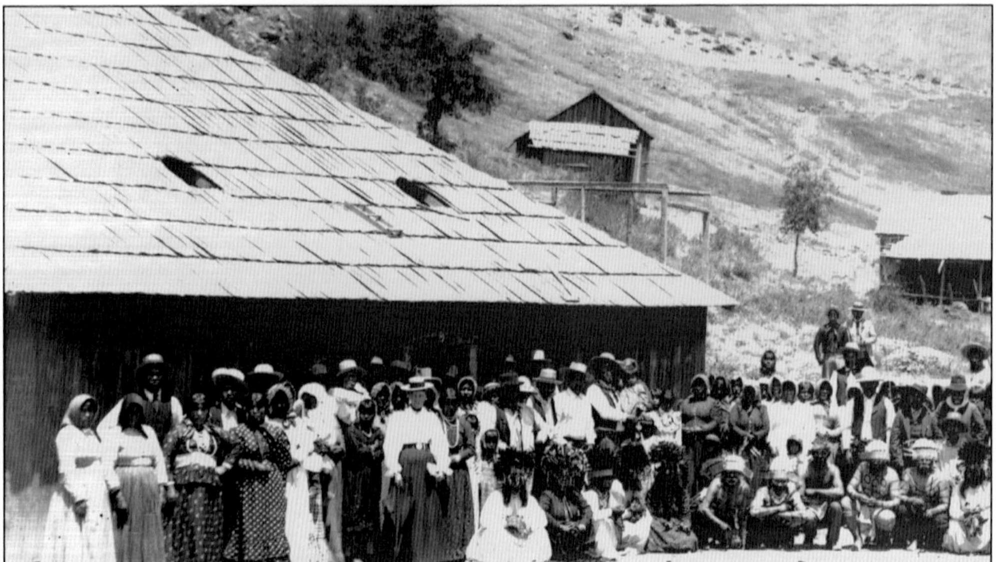

**THE UPPER LAKE DANCE HOUSE.** It burned to the ground around 1906. Great ceremonies had been held there for three decades, drawing dancers from as far west as the coast and as far east as the Sacramento delta. The entire village, including the local storekeeper, ceremonial dancers, and fire-eaters, posed for a picture of history. (Photo by O. E. Meddaugh [Bishop], courtesy Lake County Historic Courthouse Museum.)

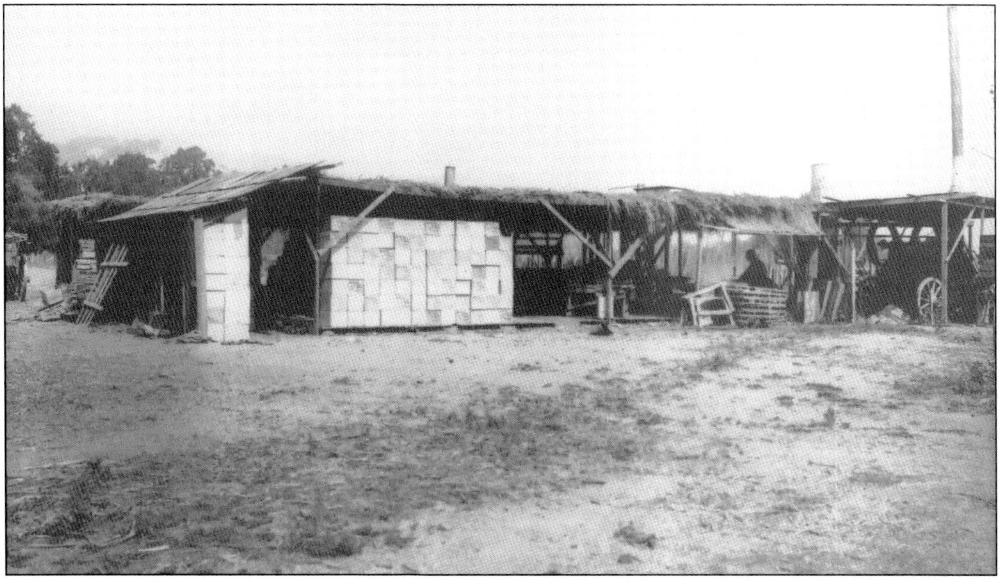

**THERE'S WORK IN THE CANNERY.** Commercial farming had begun on the drained Tule Lake, and green bean canneries were developing (above). From 1907 to 1912, Indian Affairs purchased 483 acres for the Upper Lake Rancheria and also bought more than 500 acres for Robinson Rancheria nearby. After a fire burned several homes and the dance house while families were a few miles away picking beans, some residents preferred to move to new houses on the reservations rather than rebuild at their Indian community. (Courtesy Lake County Historic Courthouse Museum.)

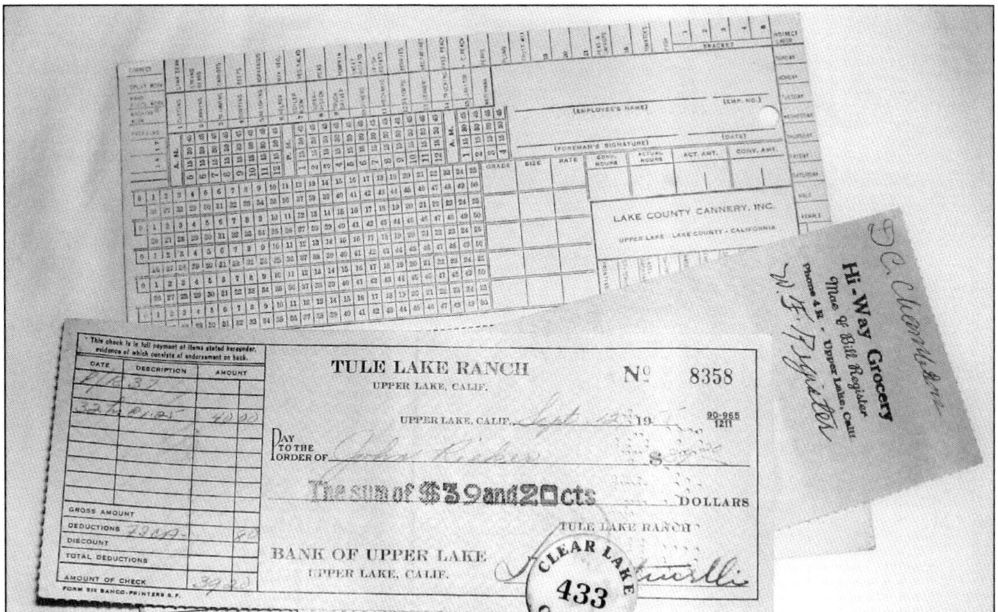


**NOT CLAMSHELLS.** Rich alluvial soil made good green bean land, and canneries were developed to preserve and market the canned product. Native Americans, as hourly or piece-meal workers, had to learn to use timecards and the new banking system's checks that stood for money. (From private collection.)

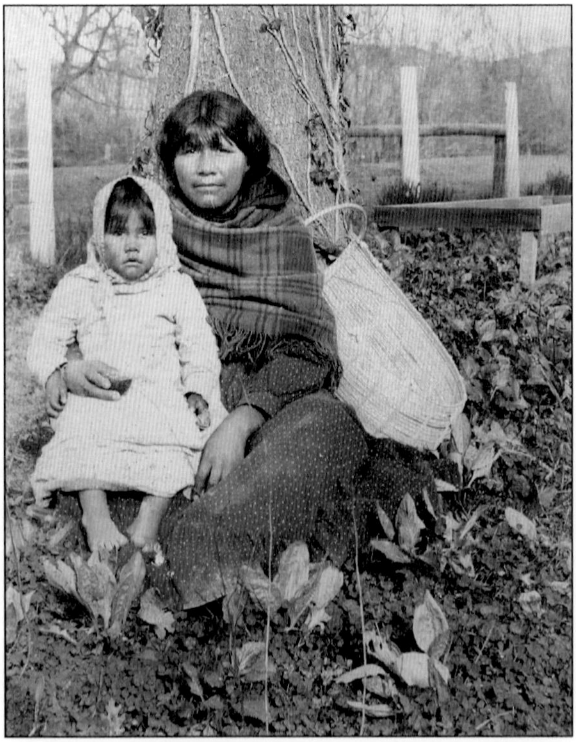

**ARTHUR'S MOTHER.** This appealing photograph of Mary Francisco and her daughter Eva taken on the Banks ranch was made into a postcard to promote the busy town of Upper Lake. Collectors of Pomo baskets and ethnic artifacts traded here because of its convenience and accessibility. (Photograph said to be by Charles Samborn, c. 1915; courtesy Lake County Historic Courthouse Museum.)

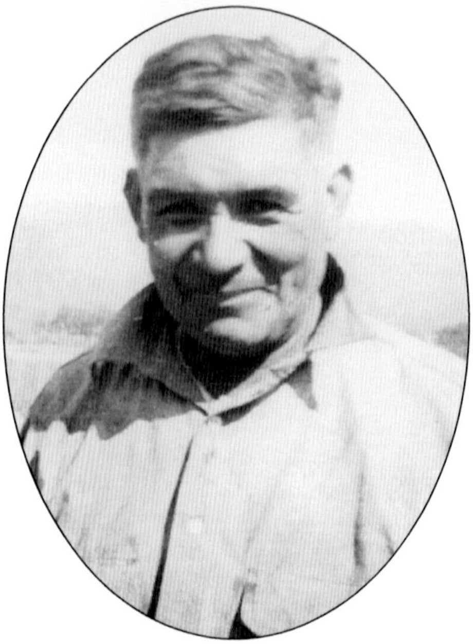

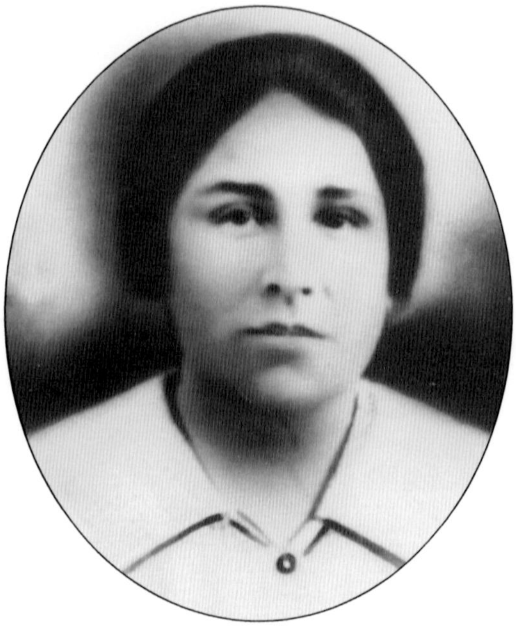

**ARTHUR AND WIFE.** Arthur Treppa was a leading figure in forming Habematolel, and he had a knack for farming that others lacked; he hired crews to harvest carrot and beet seeds. His skills helped mold the Upper Lake Community. Teresa Treppa (right) was often sick, so her daughter, Verna, missed a lot of school to care for her. Teresa died of kidney failure; her great-granddaughter Teresa (Munoz) Meeks is named for her. (Courtesy Treppa family archives.)

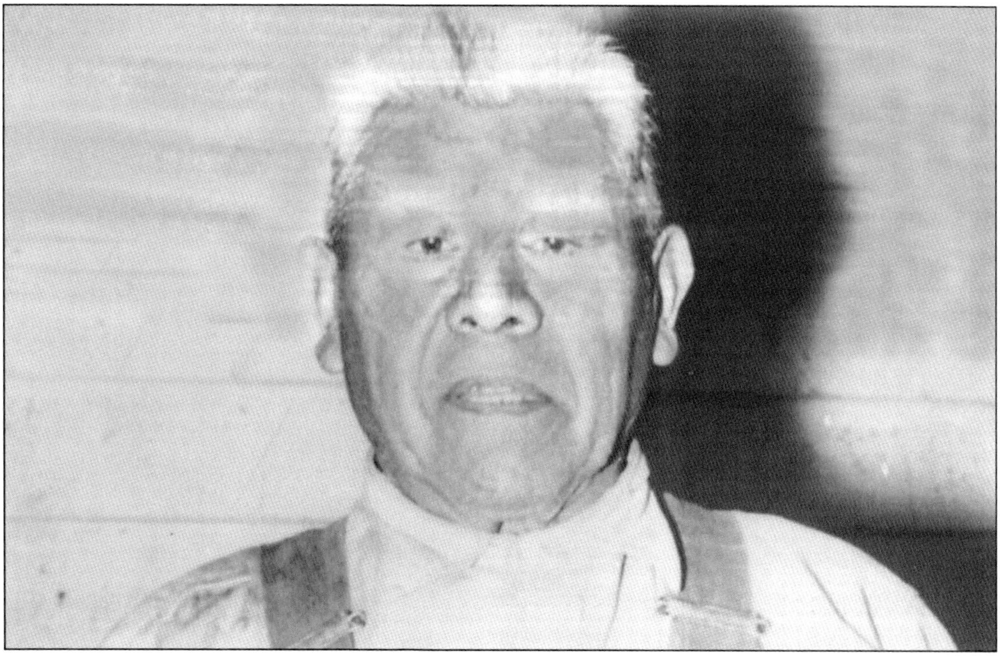

**PART OF THE CREW.** Treppa's children remember playing on the hay baler and harvester. Mike Gomez, of a Big Valley family, worked with Treppa at Upper Lake. Gomez had been to Carlisle Indian School in Pennsylvania, and he was reported to be the best blacksmith in California. (Courtesy National Archives, Sacramento Region BIA.)

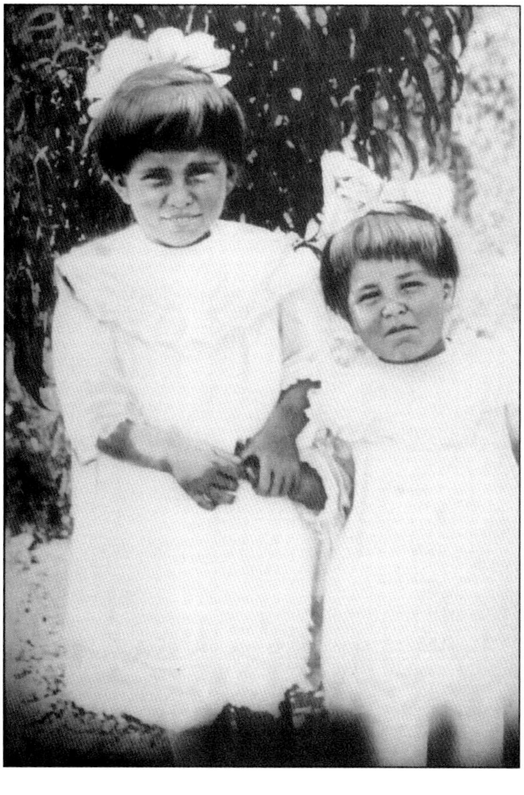

**WHAT FOR THE CHILDREN?** Toys for children were scarce, and Verna (left) hid her favorite doll in the oven to keep her from others. The toy was roasted, unfortunately. The children of the Treppa family attended a local Protestent-run elementary school, but when it came time for high school, they had to go to Indian School in Riverside, California. (Courtesy Treppa family archives.)

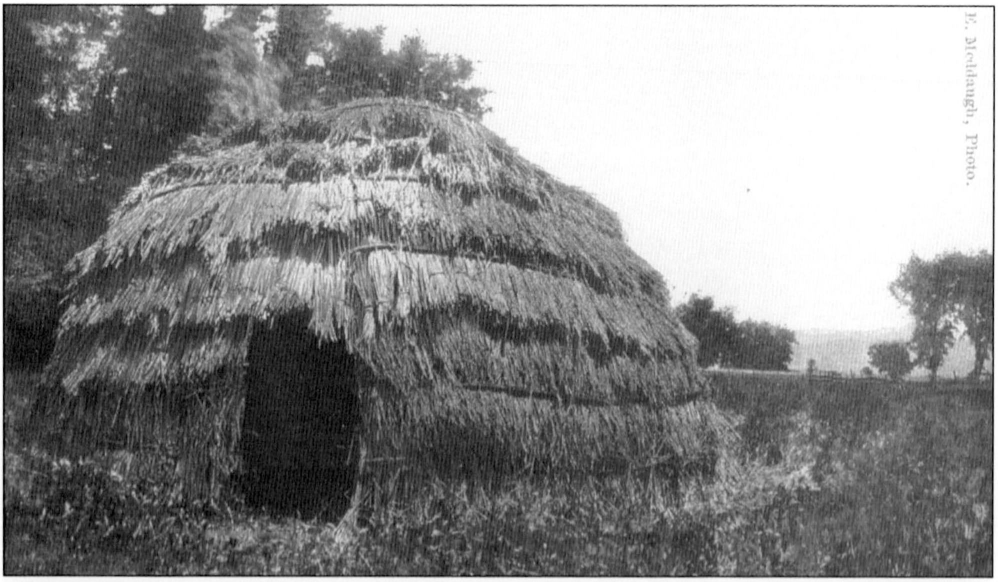


**IN ONLY 50 YEARS.** Most Pomos were forced to enter a wage economy during the 1930s Depression. Many women moved to the Oakland/San Francisco Bay Area or Los Angeles and worked as domestics, while Pomo men found employment as migrant field workers and ranch laborers along with poor whites from the Dust Bowl. It is estimated that the last traditional building was built in 1901, Anglo clothing was worn, and metal and wooden materials were in common use. (Courtesy Grace Hudson Museum.)

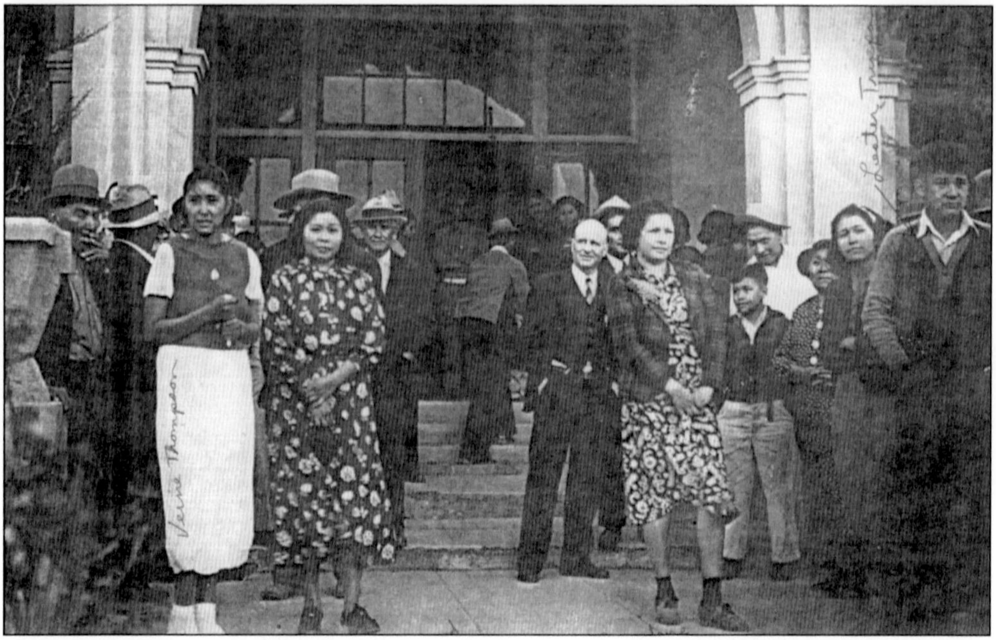


**NO MORE SEPARATE BUT EQUAL.** Lake and Mendocino County political pressure forced an end to segregated schools and facilities around 1932, and Indian children were allowed to attend public schools. Included from left to right above are Vernie Thompson, Vodella Anderson McCloud, Ermadene Treppa, and Lester Treppa in front of Upper Lake High School. (Courtesy Lake County Historic Courthouse Museum.)

Ipper Lake High School Graduating
ass of 1947. Included in the Class of
947 are: Luke Ayers, Ruetta Barney,
Jana Belle Beecher, Jim Beecher,
Harley Beeler, Harold Beeler, Gaye
Burnett, Barbara Davis, Stanley
Pufford, Robert Gordon, Jean Hayes,
Bill Henderson, Robert Jackson,
Kenneth Lightford, Ramona Lyon,
George Madison, Lorraine Manning,
Darlene Rees, Ernest Ridley, Dean
Sleeper, Marvel Sullivan, Frances
Summers, Melva Treppa, William
Wood and Wilma Ward. *Photo courtesy of Sharon Leuzinger.*

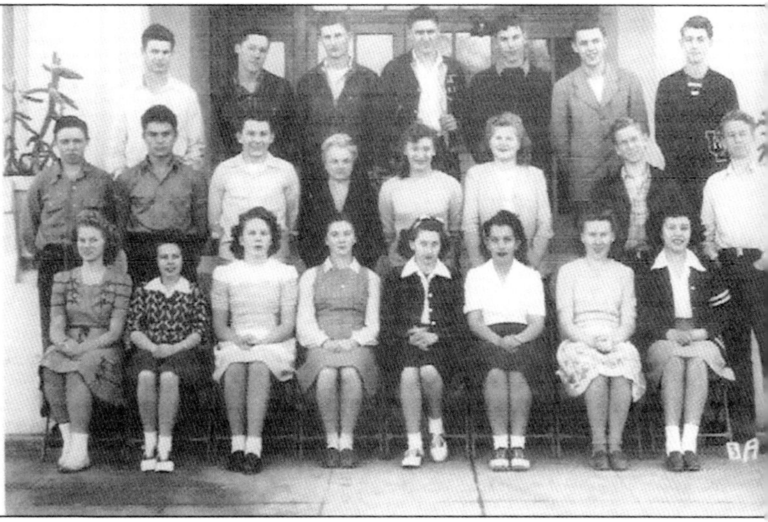

**A Diploma Makes a Difference.** With an Upper Lake High School diploma, Melva Treppa (front right) went on to business college in Oakland. "We were made to feel not as good as everyone else," explained her niece, Charlene (Treppa/Icay) Munoz, who is a member of the 2007 Tribal Council. "My mother felt the old ways weren't going to help us so she didn't give us much of the culture. 'You have to be better, you have to do better,' she said." Respected Lake County Pomo leaders Arthur Treppa and Ethan Anderson went to Sacramento to demand payback for land taken from Native Americans. Standing together in this cause helped form Federated Indians of California (FIC), a pan-tribal consolidation, and initiated the term "California Indian." Gov. (and later Supreme Court Justice) Earl Warren stood with the Indians before the press. The suits were won in federal court. (Courtesy *Lake County Record-Bee.*)

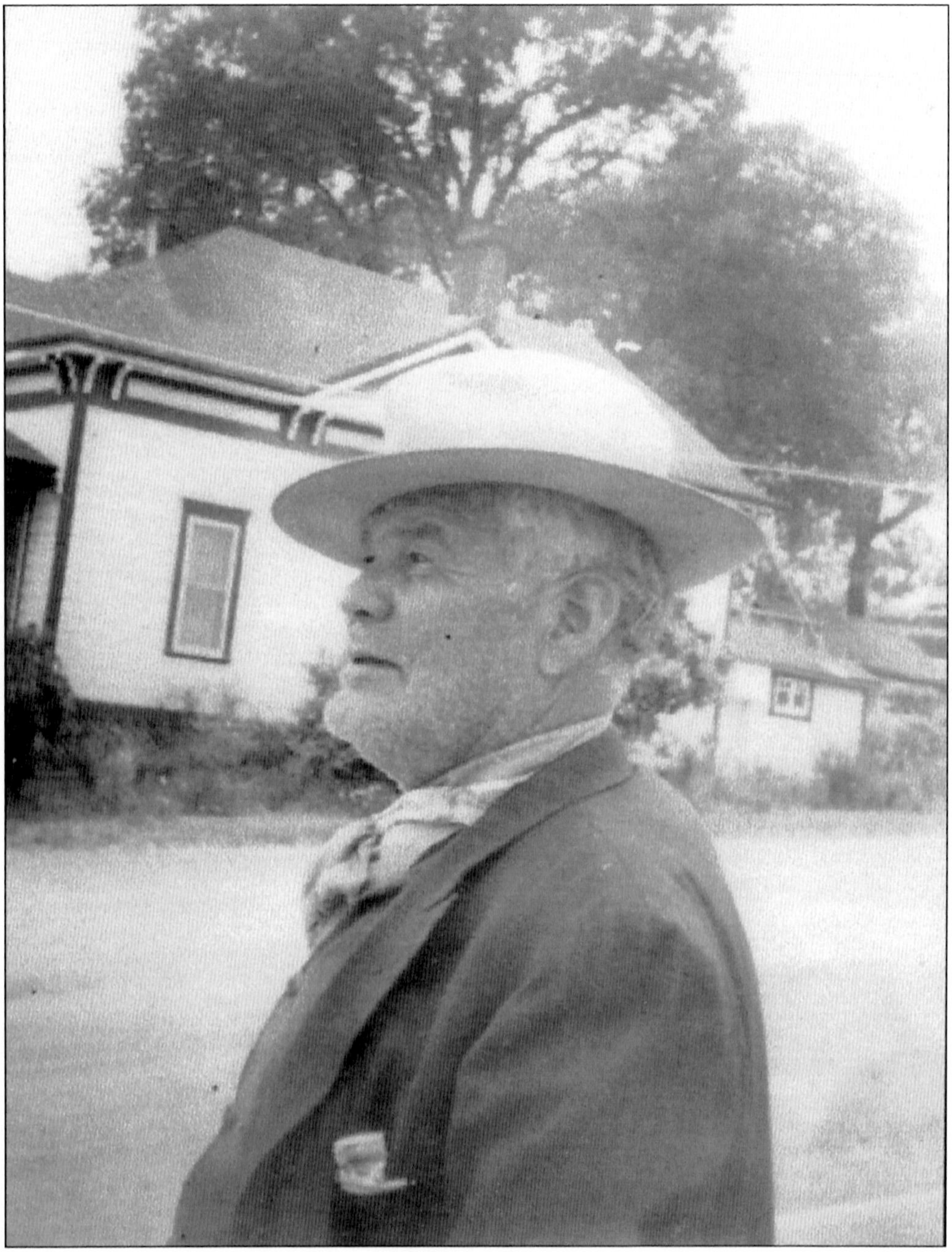

**NEXT IN LINE.** After Arthur Treppa, Bill Graves followed as chief. Although he originated at Guidiville, Graves married and lived at Upper Lake and took his role as chief seriously. He was active in the traditional and contemporary communities. "We felt bad about not getting the history, but Mom was always there," admits Charlene Munoz. "That was her contribution, always part of the community. Now I think it's our time to give back something, to help kids. We, the tribe, give scholarships and tutoring. I think children are where it starts. A good education is the only way out, so they have choices. My husband is from Mexico City and he says, 'If you're born poor in Mexico, you die poor. There's no way to rise above.' " (Courtesy Treppa family archives.)

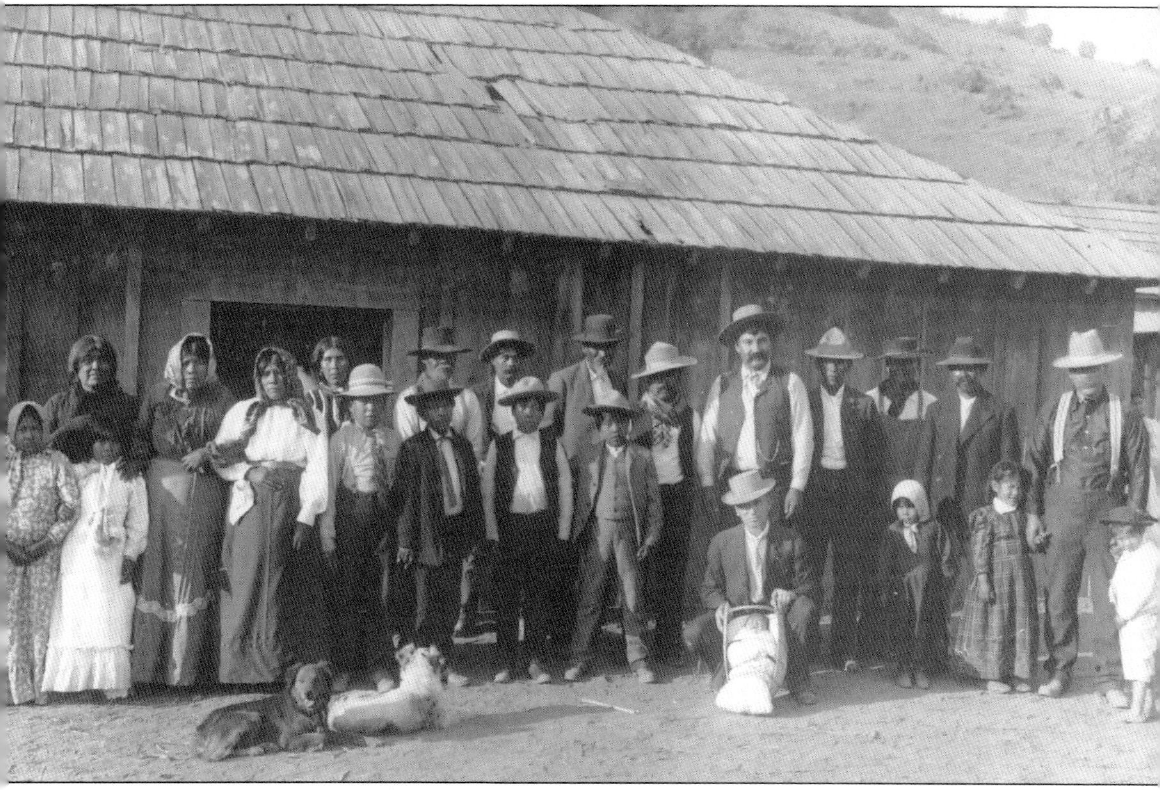

**NO LONGER INDIAN.** In 1959, the Department of Interior terminated its trust relationship with 41 Indian tribes in the state, including those in Lake County, in the California Rancheria Act. The rancherias' assets were distributed by 1961, including the common buildings like dance houses and barns. Only the old parcels communally purchased and still privately held were saved. Treppa's relatives were some of the original 28, but that number dwindled. Property could be sold now, lost for unpaid taxes, or foreclosed on debts, (Photograph by O. E. Meddaugh [Bishop], courtesy Lake County Historic Courthouse Museum.)

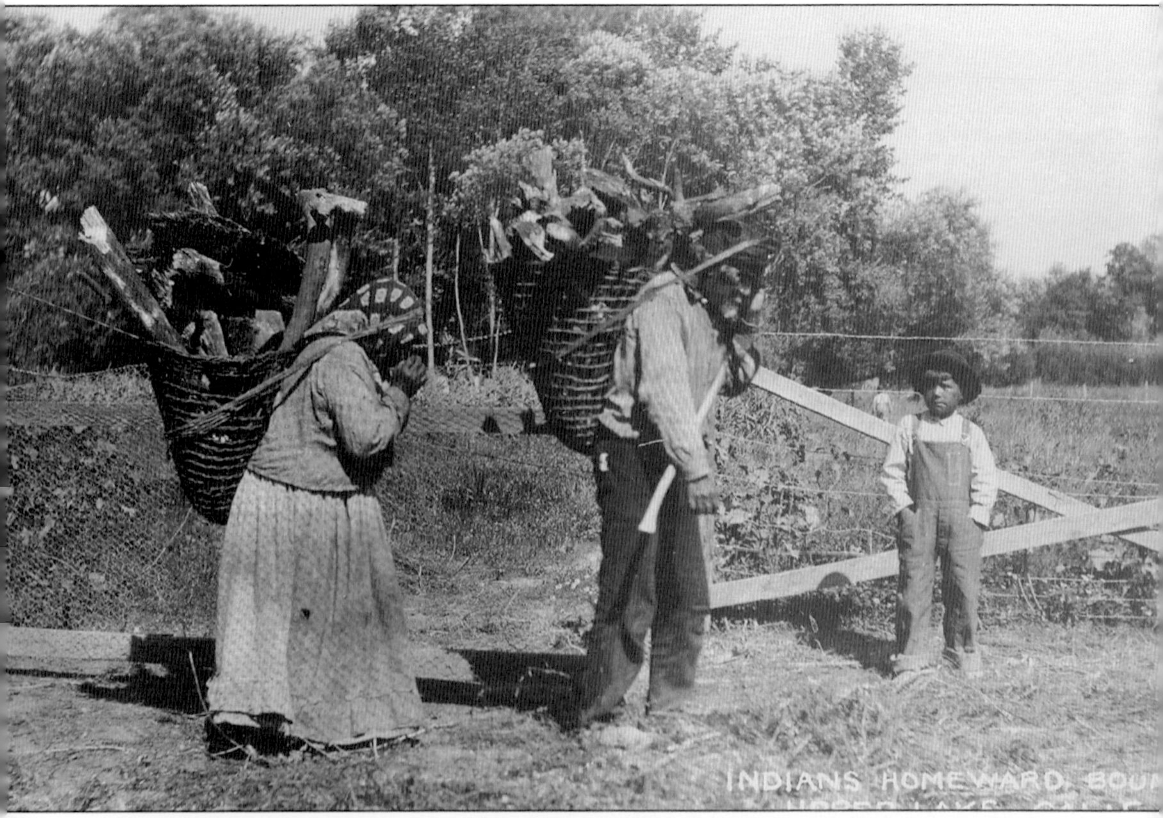


**INDIANS HOMEWARD BOUND AT UPPER LAKE.** The title of this compelling image of Sally and Jim Bateman in 1910 reaffirms the hope for Habematolel. In 1983, the tribe won a lawsuit against the United States for illegal termination (*Upper Lake Pomo Association v. James Watt*) but in the eight-year interim, its reservation lands were already sold. They were once again landless. Federal law now permits such tribes to find a suitable site for restoration of tribal activities and business operations near aboriginal lands. Today's reorganized tribe has 181 members, all of whom are lineal descendants of the 28 who were on the plan of distribution and were plaintiffs in the 1983 court case that led to restoration of the tribe's federal status. (Courtesy Lake County Historic Courthouse Museum.)

*Seven*

# What Part of Me Isn't Indian Enough?

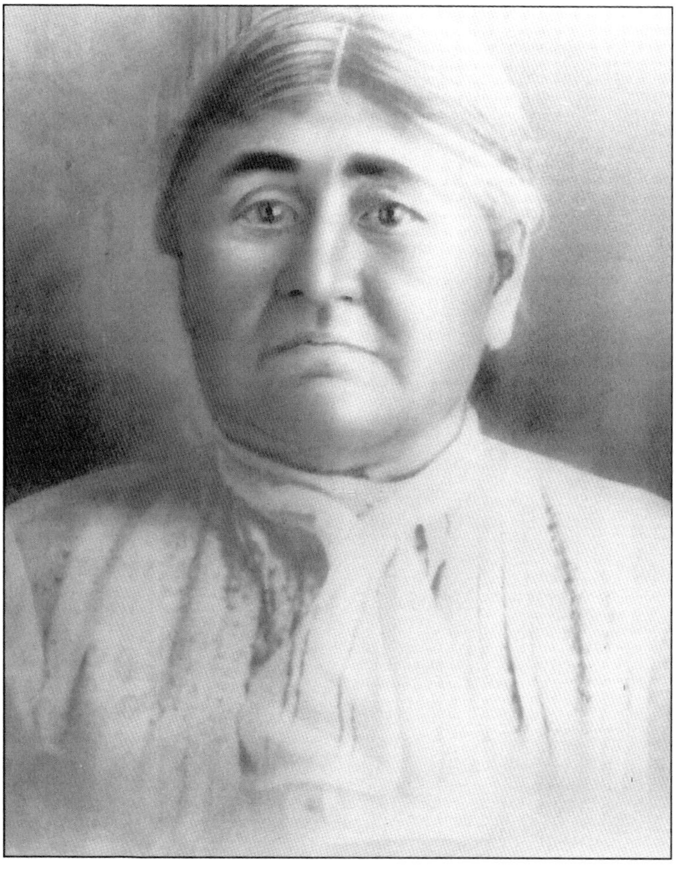

**Belonging?** Donna Herren White grew up off-reservation with all the racial prejudices of a small Anglo community applied to her. Still she often isn't Indian enough. Her story resonates with many others in a time of blended cultures. Great-grandmother Ellen Helena was bought/brought from outside Lake County in the mid-1800s to the Cobb Mountain area. Her tribal affiliation was listed as Berryes. She married a French-Canadian Indian named William Jones. A kindly doctor once emphasized the French-Canadian listing and wrote "white" after it, thereby saving the family from being sent with other Indians to reservations. (Courtesy Herren family archives.)

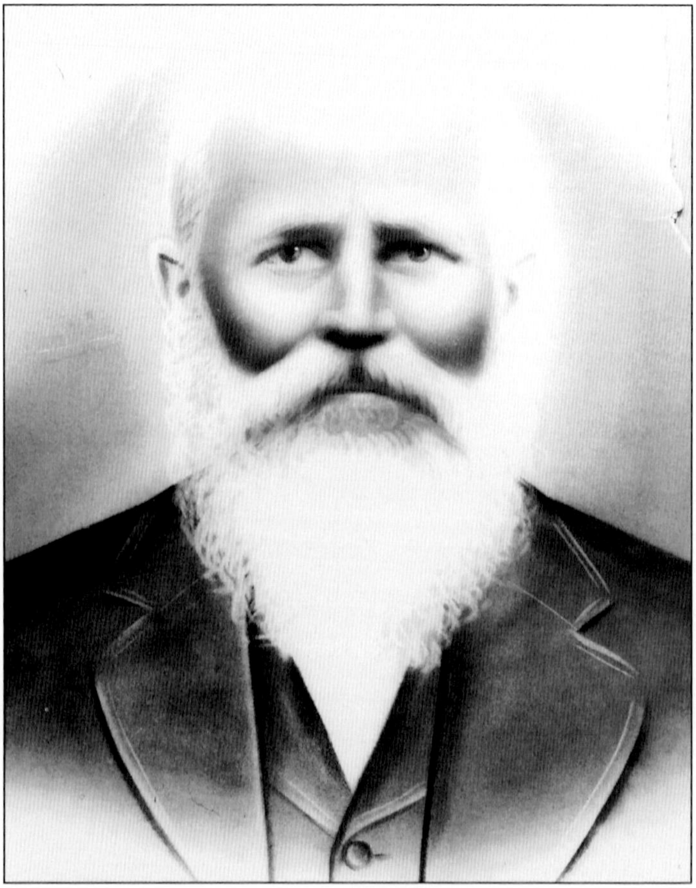

**HERITAGE.** At age 64, William Jones was convicted of murder and hanged outside the county courthouse in Lakeport. Family history says that he had warned an abusive son-in-law that he would shoot him if he beat his daughter again, and Jones was a man of his word. Ellen Jones was pregnant when her husband was hanged, and subsequent Catholic baptismal records show that Ellen Helena Jones (Indian) was born at the Mission Rancheria and Indian Farm on January 16, 1883. The first courthouse burned in 1867; the mission church/monastery survives today on private property. (Courtesy Herren family archives; Lake County Historic Courthouse Museum.)

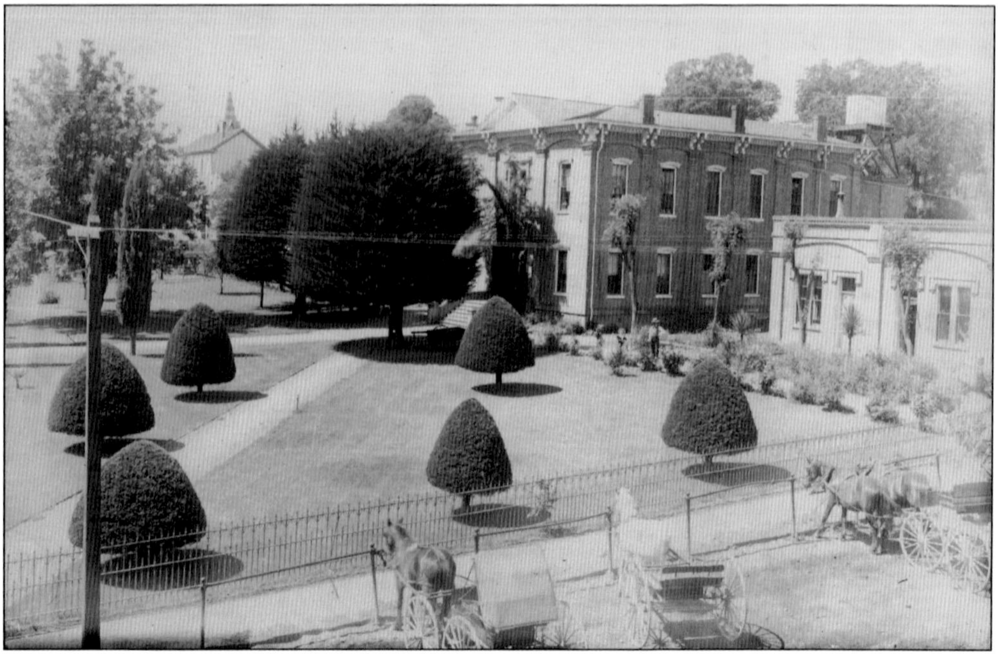

**100 PERCENT INDIAN.** Though the friar's records were in Latin, he translates that Ellen's Eastern Pomo name was Yellow Chicken and verifies that she was born at the mission. She was listed as half Berryessa and half French-Canadian Indian. (Courtesy Herren family archives.)

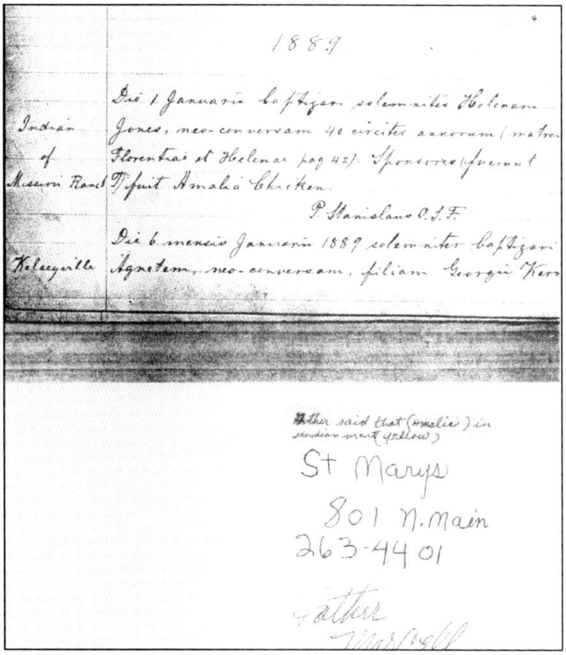

1889

Indian of Mission Ranch — Die 1 Januarii baptizavi solemniter Helenam Jones, neo-conversam 40 circiter annorum (matrem Florentiae et Helenae pag 42). Sponsores fuerunt D fuit Amalia Chicken.

P. Stanislaus O.S.F.

Kelseyville — Die 6 mensis Januarii 1889 solemniter baptizavi Agnetem, neo-conversam, filiam Georgii Kerr

Father said that (Amalia) in Indian meant yellow)

St Marys
801 N. Main
263-4401

Father Marshall

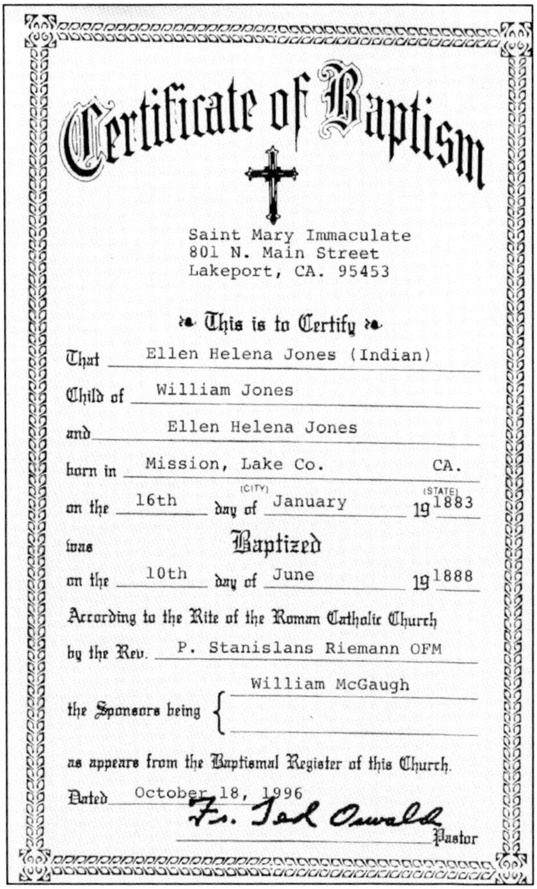

# Certificate of Baptism

Saint Mary Immaculate
801 N. Main Street
Lakeport, CA. 95453

This is to Certify

That Ellen Helena Jones (Indian)

Child of William Jones

and Ellen Helena Jones

born in Mission, Lake Co. (CITY) CA. (STATE)

on the 16th day of January 19 1883

was

Baptized

on the 10th day of June 19 1888

According to the Rite of the Roman Catholic Church

by the Rev. P. Stanislans Riemann OFM

the Sponsors being { William McGaugh

as appears from the Baptismal Register of this Church.

Dated October 18, 1996

Fr. Ted Oswald
Pastor

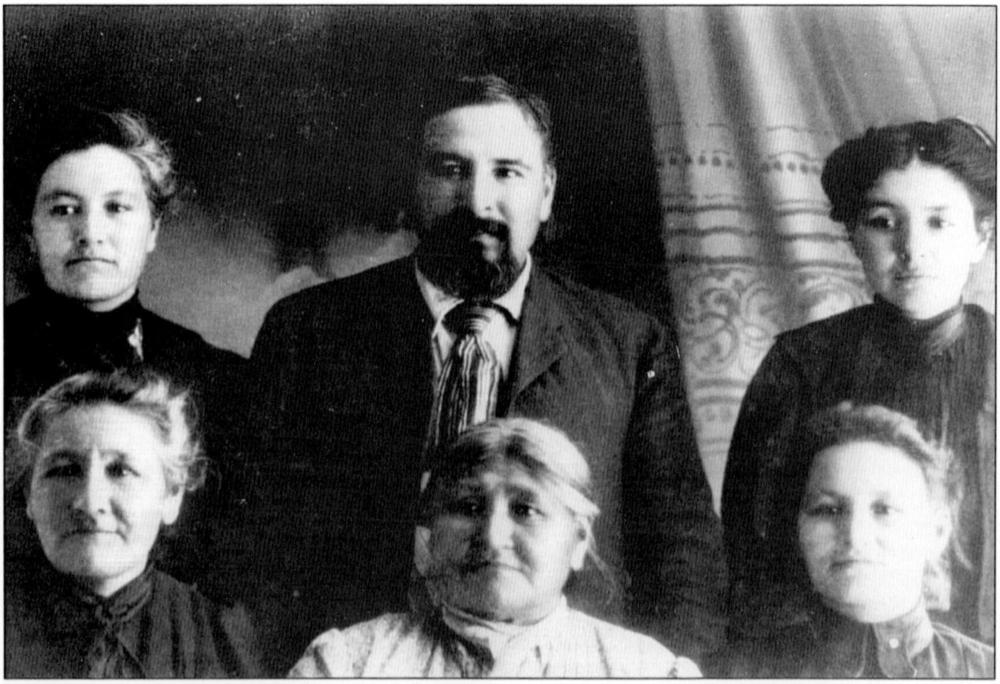

**FAMILY EXPANDING.** Ellen (Jones) took the surname Truely after an employer. Her children were not all quite grown when she married Peter Boggs and moved to Scott's Valley. They are, from left to right, (first row) Rachel Jones, mother Ellen (Jones) Boggs, and May Jones; (second row) Florence Jones, Enoch Jones, and Ellen Jones. Part of the family moved to Scott's Valley and part to the Lakeport Reservation after the mission closed. (Courtesy Herren family archives.)

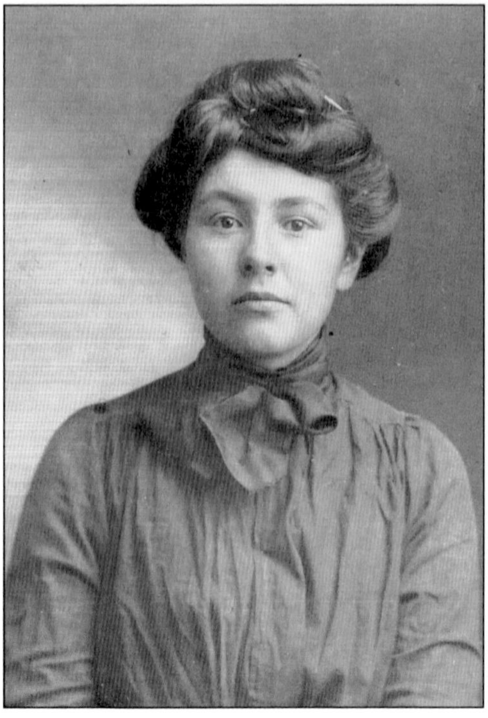

**ROMANCE.** Ellen Jones (left) was working at Adams Springs Hotel and Resort when she met Charles Andrew Herren, an Englishman with seven children whose wife was deceased. In a riding accident, Herren's horse had fallen, and the man's leg was broken. Ellen cared for him during his recovery. They were later married. (Courtesy Herren family archives.)

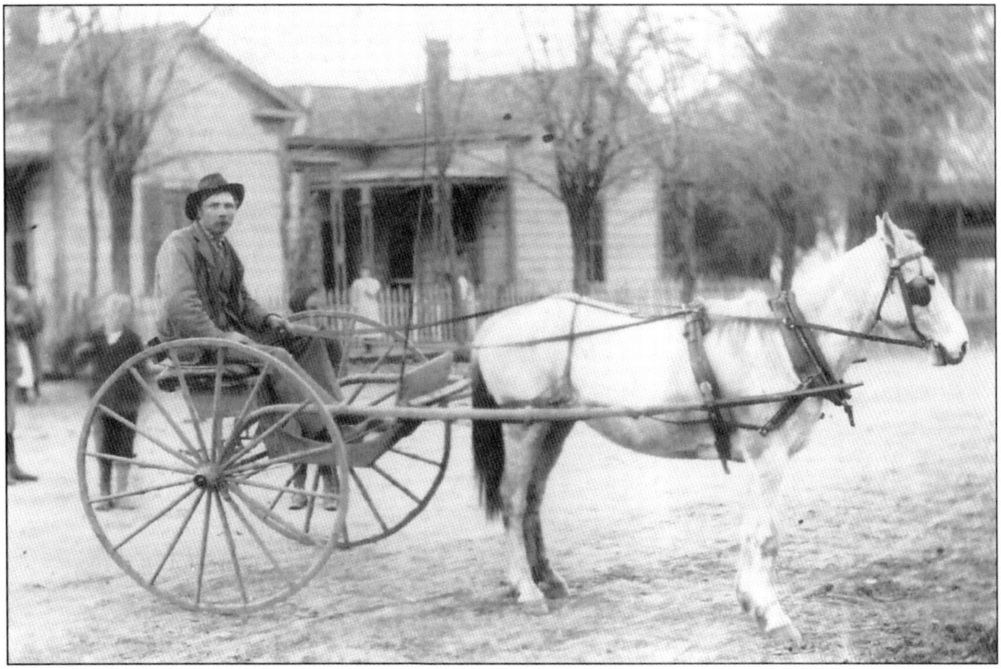

**Mixing Blood.** Andrew, known as "Charlie," and Ellen had nine children. Since Ellen was Indian and Andrew was English, their children were half quantum Native American. (Courtesy Herren family archives.)

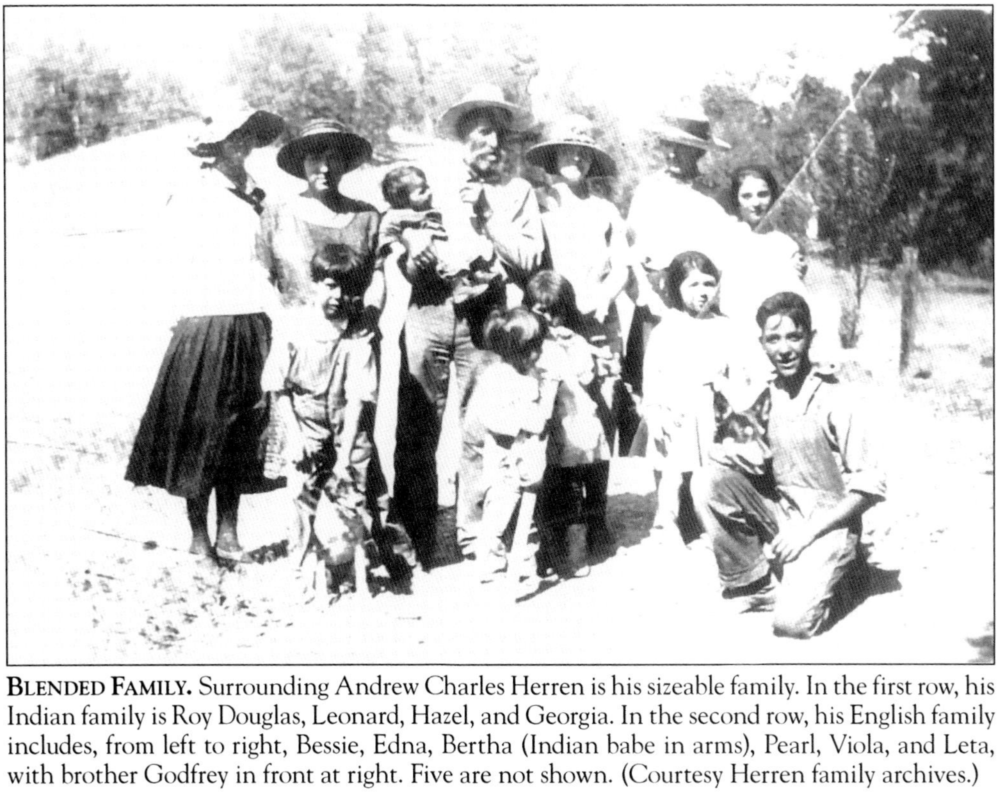

**Blended Family.** Surrounding Andrew Charles Herren is his sizeable family. In the first row, his Indian family is Roy Douglas, Leonard, Hazel, and Georgia. In the second row, his English family includes, from left to right, Bessie, Edna, Bertha (Indian babe in arms), Pearl, Viola, and Leta, with brother Godfrey in front at right. Five are not shown. (Courtesy Herren family archives.)

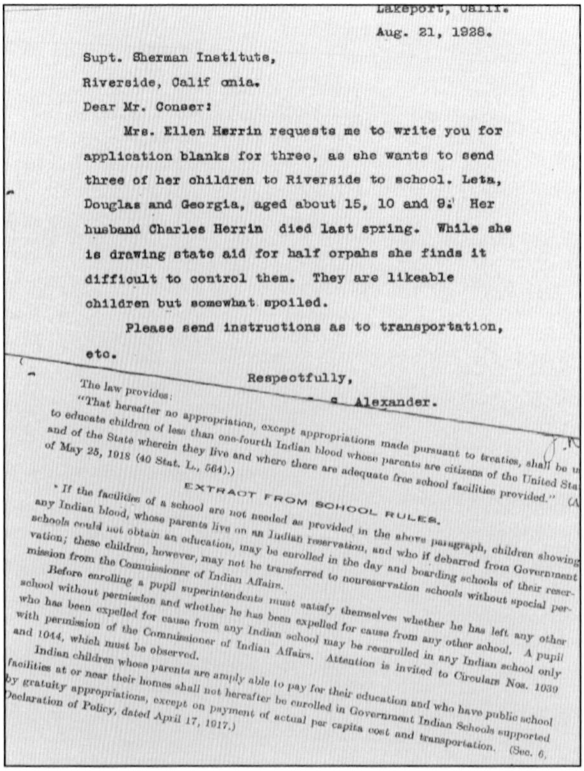

Lakeport, Calif.
Aug. 21, 1928.

Supt. Sherman Institute,
Riverside, Calif onia.

Dear Mr. Conser:

Mrs. Ellen Herrin requests me to write you for application blanks for three, as she wants to send three of her children to Riverside to school. Leta, Douglas and Georgia, aged about 15, 10 and 9. Her husband Charles Herrin died last spring. While she is drawing state aid for half orpahs she finds it difficult to control them. They are likeable children but somewhat spoiled.

Please send instructions as to transportation, etc.

Respectfully,
G. Alexander.

The law provides:

"That hereafter no appropriation, except appropriations made pursuant to treaties, shall be u[sed] to educate children of less than one-fourth Indian blood whose parents are citizens of the United Sta[tes] and of the State wherein they live and where there are adequate free school facilities provided." (A[ct] of May 25, 1918 (40 Stat. L., 564).)

EXTRACT FROM SCHOOL RULES.

If the facilities of a school are not needed as provided in the above paragraph, children showing any Indian blood, whose parents live on an Indian reservation, and who if debarred from Government schools could not obtain an education, may be enrolled in the day and boarding schools of their reservation; these children, however, may not be transferred to nonreservation schools without special permission from the Commissioner of Indian Affairs.

Before enrolling a pupil superintendents must satisfy themselves whether he has left any other school without permission and whether he has been expelled for cause from any other school. A pupil who has been expelled for cause from any Indian school may be reenrolled in any Indian school only with permission of the Commissioner of Indian Affairs. Attention is invited to Circulars Nos. 1039 and 1044, which must be observed.

Indian children whose parents are amply able to pay for their education and who have public school facilities at or near their homes shall not hereafter be enrolled in Government Indian Schools supported by gratuity appropriations, except on payment of actual per capita cost and transportation. (Sec. 6, Declaration of Policy, dated April 17, 1917.)

**SENT AWAY.** Charles and Ellen's son, Douglas Roy Herren was born in 1915. Mission Rancheria School and Indian Farm was abandoned in 1914, when the U.S. government established the Big Valley Rancheria. However, a small group of families moved to "the mini-rez" in Lakeport, where about 12 families lived on Martin or Armstrong Streets. Charley Herren died in the spring of 1928, and by late summer, Ellen applied to have her minor children, Leta (15), Douglas Roy (10), and Georgia (9), sent to Sherman Institute in Riverside for schooling. They were listed as Protestant, alternatively Berryessa or Digger tribes, and 1/4-degree blood. Though he repeatedly ran away and was captured and returned, Douglas was schooled in shoe and harness vocational training at Sherman, although automobiles were then in common use by 1929. (Courtesy Herren family archives.)

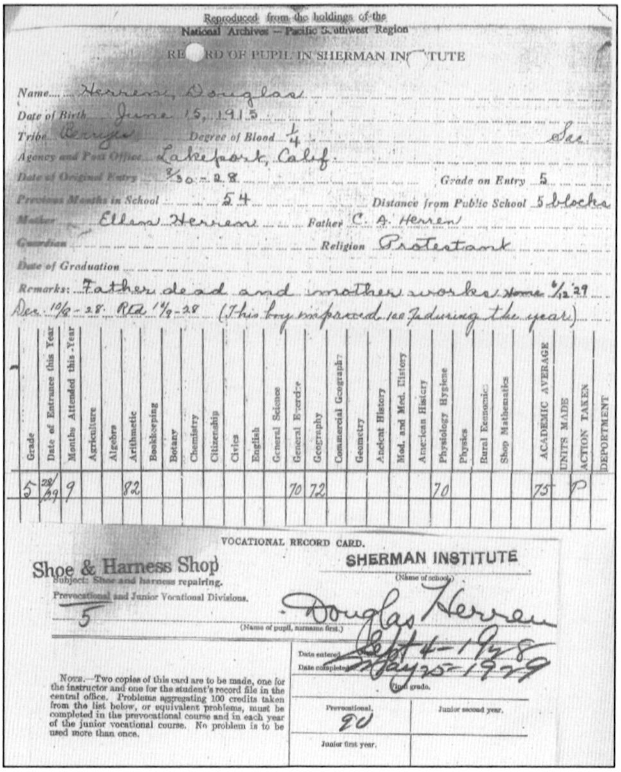

Reproduced from the holdings of the
National Archives — Pacific Southwest Region

RE RD OF PUPIL IN SHERMAN IN TUTE

Name Herren, Douglas
Date of Birth June 15, 1915
Tribe Berryessa Degree of Blood 1/4 Sex
Agency and Post Office Lakeport, Calif.
Date of Original Entry 8/30-28 Grade on Entry 5
Previous Months in School 54 Distance from Public School 5 blocks
Mother Ellen Herren Father C. A. Herren
Guardian Religion Protestant
Date of Graduation
Remarks: Father dead and mother works. Home 6/12/29
Des. 10/8-28. Rtd 11/9-28 (This boy improved 10% during the year)

| Grade | Date of Entrance this Year | Months Attended this Year | Agriculture | Algebra | Arithmetic | Bookkeeping | Botany | Chemistry | Citizenship | Civics | English | General Science | General Exercise | Geography | Commercial Geography | Geometry | Ancient History | Med. and Mod. History | American History | Physiology Hygiene | Physics | Rural Economics | Shop Mathematics | | Academic Average | Units Made | Action Taken | Deportment |
|---|---|---|---|---|---|---|---|---|---|---|---|---|---|---|---|---|---|---|---|---|---|---|---|---|---|---|---|---|
| 5 | 28/29 | 9 | | | 82 | | | | | | | | 70 | 72 | | | | | | 70 | | | | | 75 | | P | |

VOCATIONAL RECORD CARD.

Shoe & Harness Shop
Subject: Shoe and harness repairing.
Prevocational and Junior Vocational Divisions.
5

SHERMAN INSTITUTE
(Name of school)

Douglas Herren
(Name of pupil, surname first.)

Date entered Sept 4-1928
Date completed May 25-1929
Final grade.

Note.—Two copies of this card are to be made, one for the instructor and one for the student's record file in the central office. Problems aggregating 100 credits taken from the list below, or equivalent problems, must be completed in the prevocational course and in each year of the junior vocational course. No problem is to be used more than once.

Prevocational. 90
Junior second year.
Junior first year.

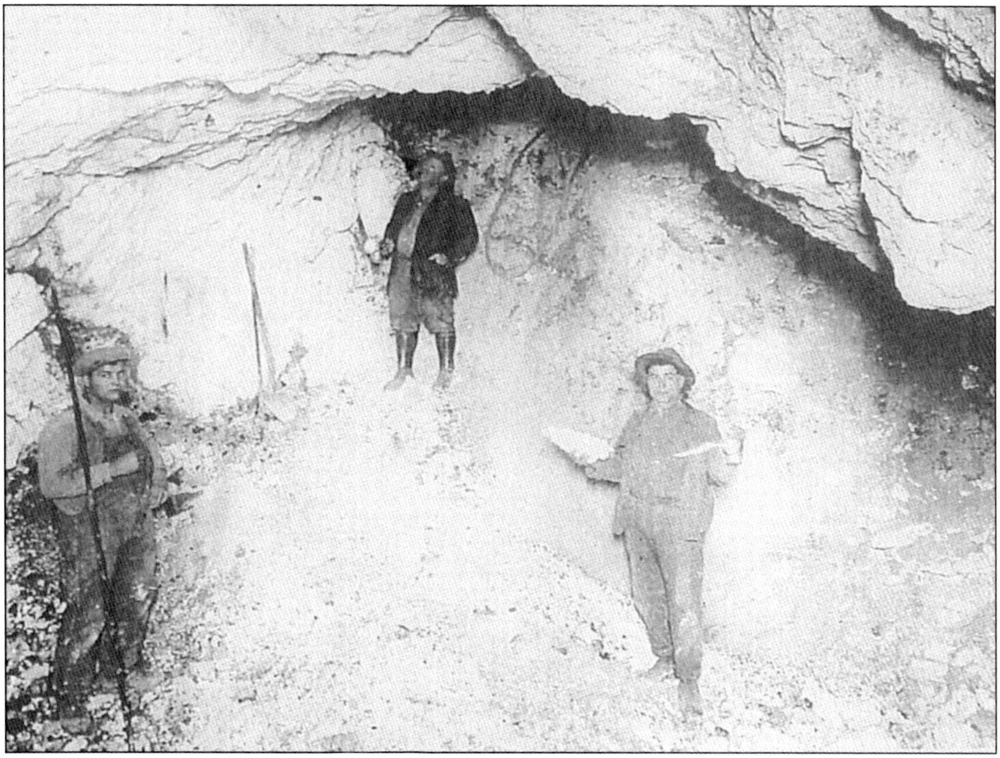

**FINDING WORK.** By the time Roy was 18, the institute gave up and no longer pursued him. He returned to Lake County, worked at Great Western Mine (above) near Middletown, married, opened a logging mill on Cobb Mountain, and ultimately gave it up to work for the County of Lake and a paid retirement. (Courtesy Lower Lake Historic Schoolhouse Museum.)

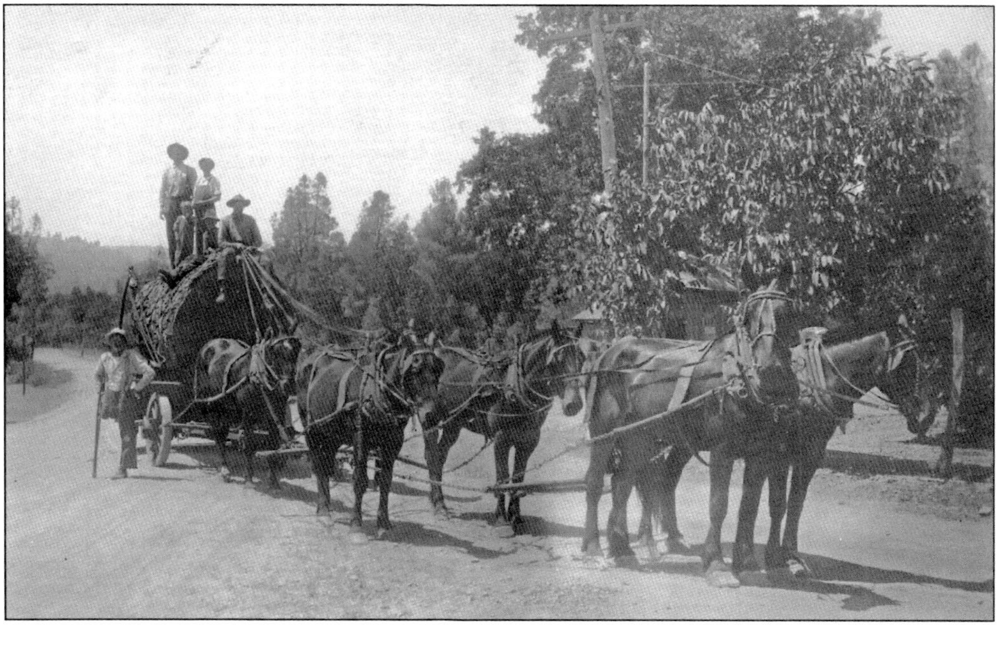

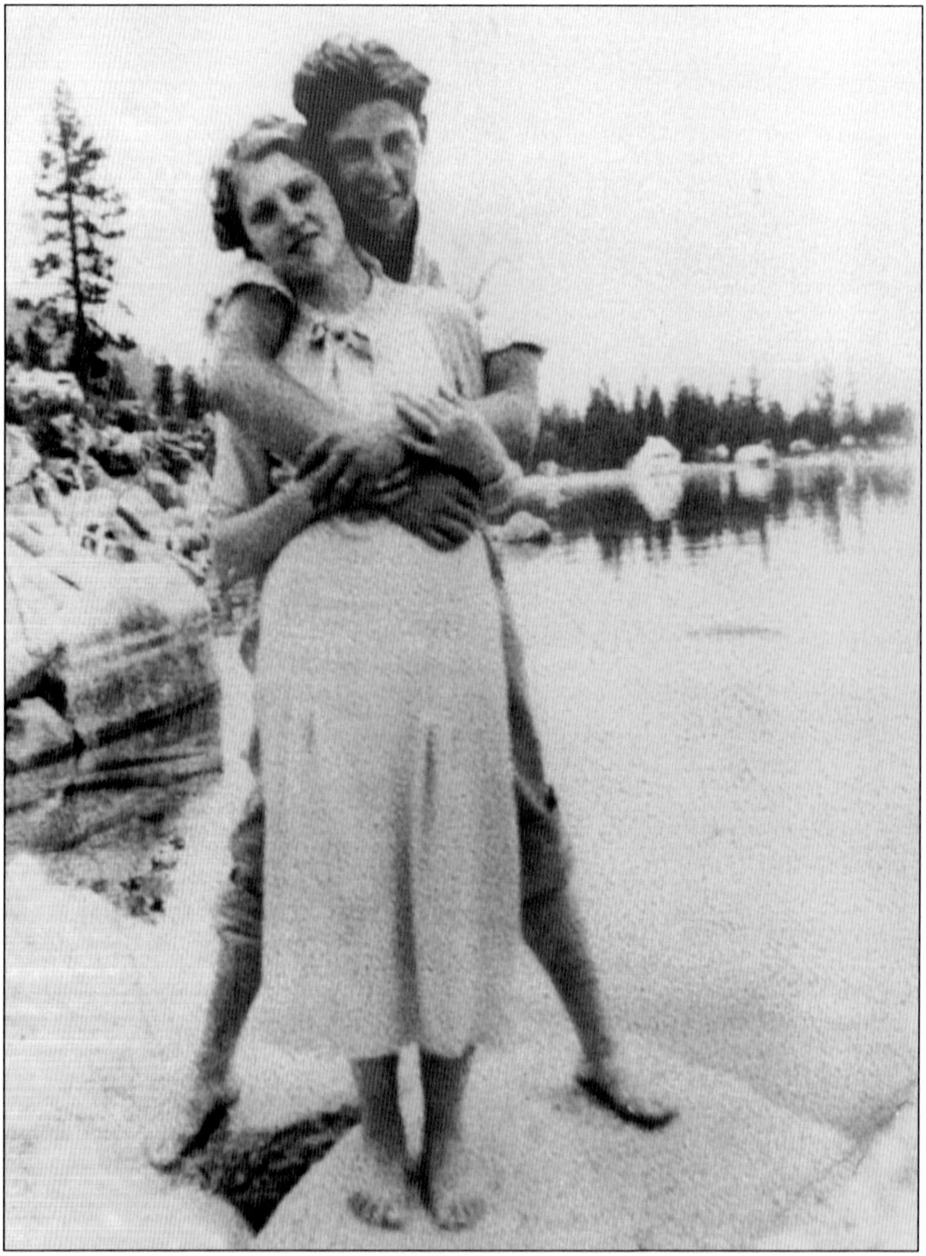

**Next Generation.** Roy married Cleora Van Dyke, daughter of a Dutch migrant farm-worker family. Donna Herren was born on August 1937 while the family lived on the "rez annex" in Lakeport. When they moved to Cobb, Donna walked some distance to classes at the one-room school. She remembers times the school-bus driver would laugh and wave and drive away without her; she was often late to class or absent. One day while teasing her about her attire, a classmate tore the sleeve off Donna's dress; the teacher made them trade dresses. The rest of the day young Donna preened in crisp, stylish clothes while her tormenter wore the objects of her scorn. Years later, when both women were married and living in other cities, the woman appeared at Donna's door just to apologize for her childhood actions, then disappeared again. (Courtesy Herren family archives.)

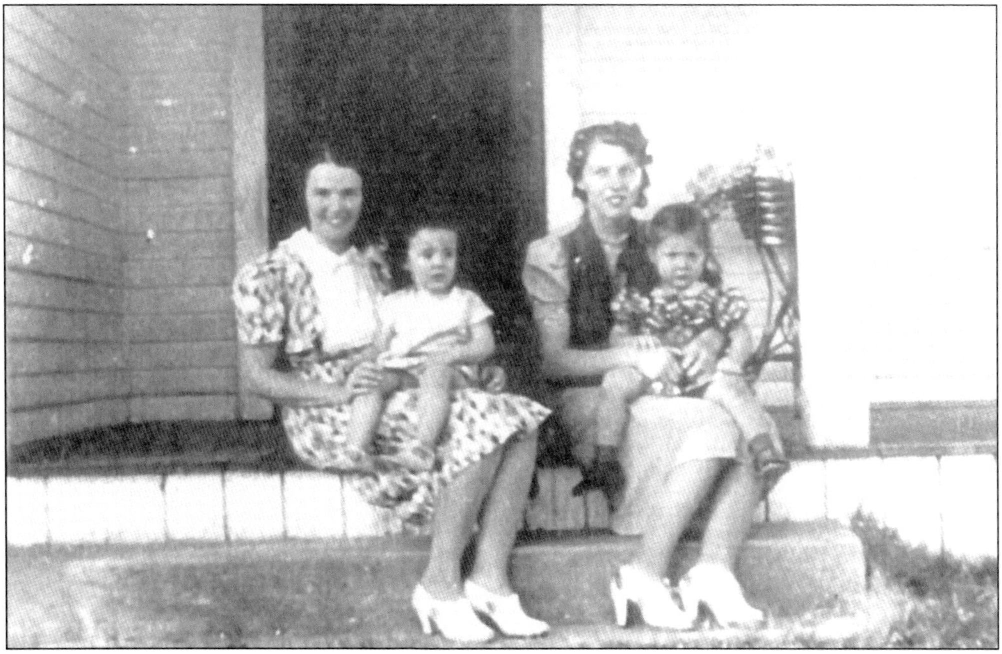

**Cousins.** Donna (right) and her pale-skinned cousin Mary-Ellen were close in age and family but also shared many differences. Donna attended elementary and high school in Lakeport, choosing to work in the cafeteria rather than accept "Indian-free" lunches. Others declined their Indian heritage, but Donna acknowledged hers, accompanying her father, and young brother and sister to the reservation for events and hiding out in the dance house (below) from children who threw rocks at them because they weren't 100-percent Indian. (Courtesy Herren family archives; courtesy Lake County Historic Courthouse Museum.)

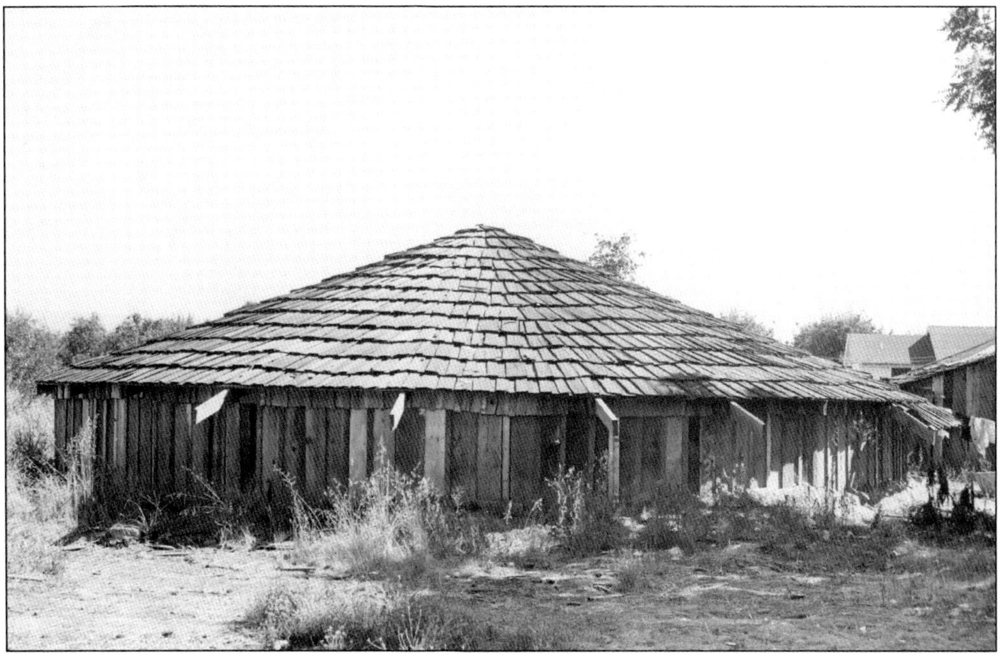

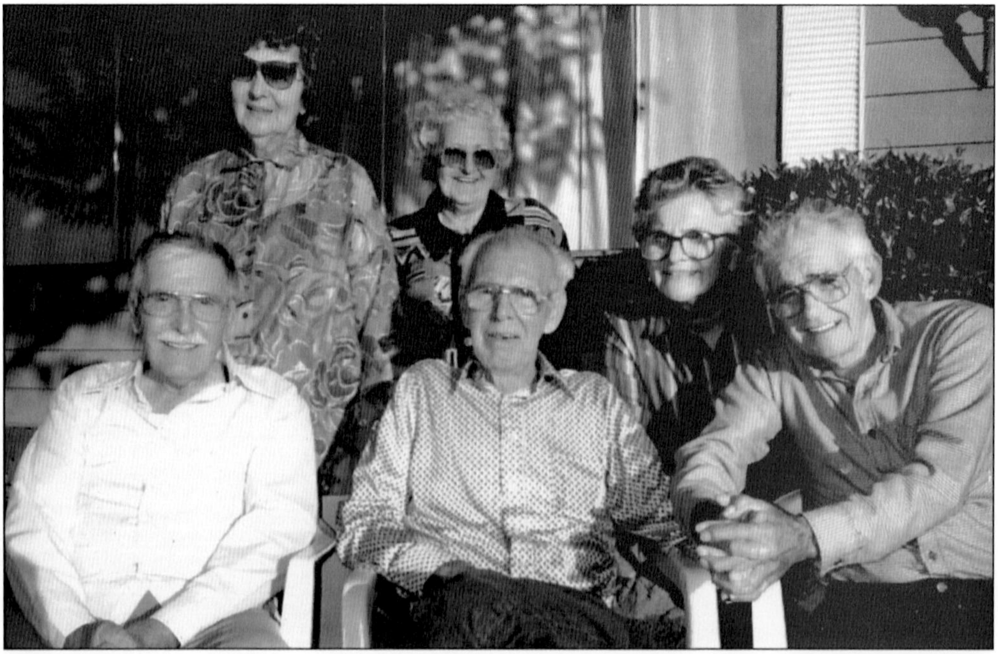

**FAMILY ELDERS.** In 1991, the remaining members of the senior blended Herren family reunited. From left to right are (first row) Godfrey Herren (84), Roy Herren (76), and Lloyd Herren (66); (second row) Leta Herren (79), Georgie Herren Giffells (74), and Bertha Herren Wright (70). (Courtesy Herren family archives.)

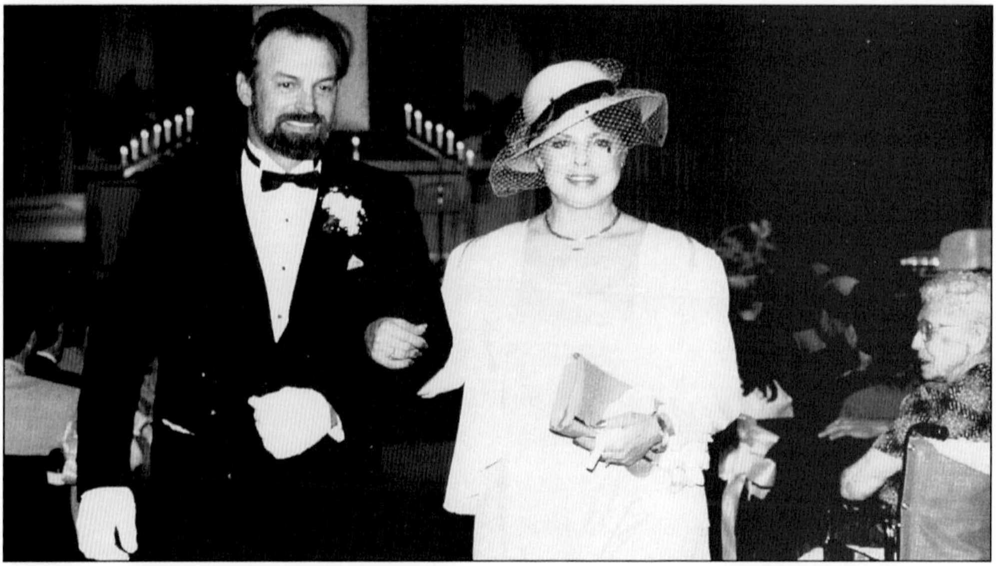

**ALMOST HAVING IT ALL.** Donna married Ken White, son of the Lakeport Elementary school nurse. They worked hard, saved, and raised two children. They are pictured at son Jim's wedding. Donna returned to Lake County to nurse each of their four parents. When Ken retired, he joined her at their home in Lakeport, where they live comfortably. Donna Herren White has survived because she is proud and sure of who she is. She is both American and Indian. And she is making sure her children and grandchildren know about it. (Courtesy Herren family archives.)

# *Eight*

# More Rancherias

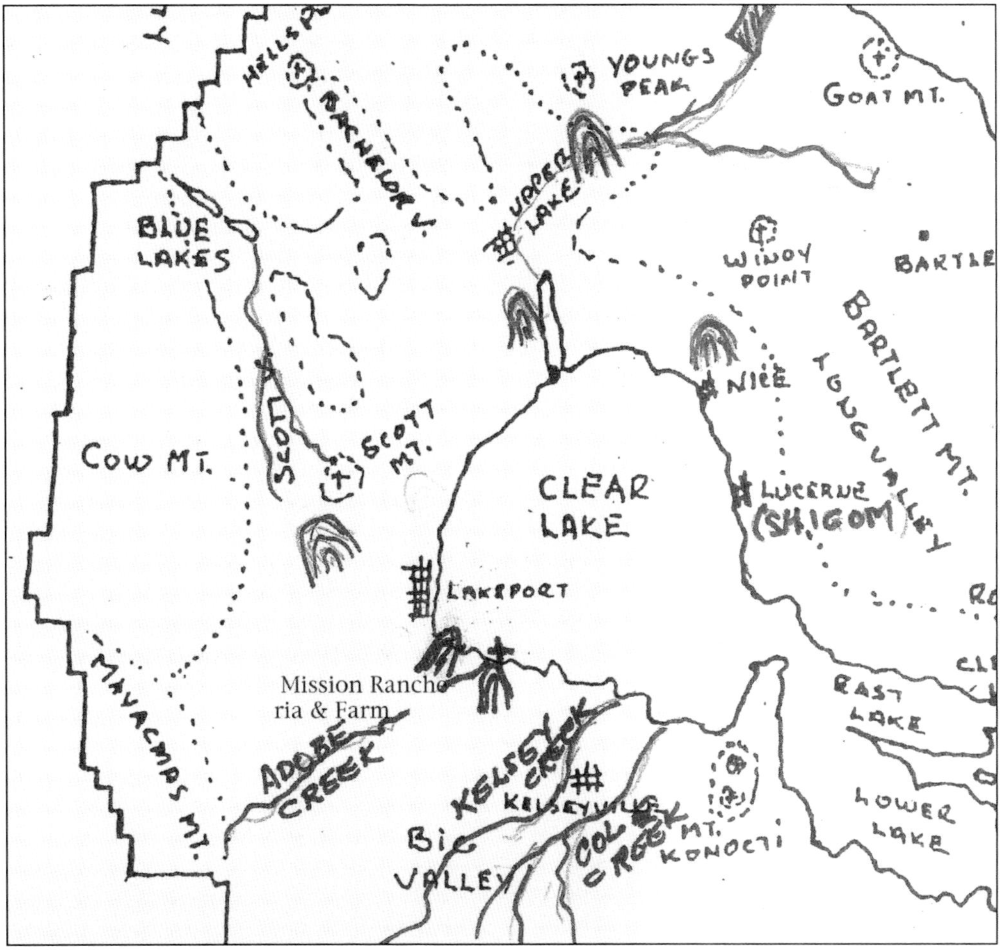


**Blessed Are the Poor.** When Fr. Luciano Osuna rode into Lake County on a burro in 1867 in a brown robe and sandals, he looked for all the world like his sainted Spanish idol, Fr. Junipero Serra, who in turn had emulated his idol, St. Francis of Assisi. Osuna had been called from his Guadalajara home by the archbishop of San Francisco, Joseph Sudoc Alemany, ordained, and sent by Bishop Eugene O'Connell of the diocese of Grass Valley to work with the Indians of Lake and Mendocino Counties. It is not astonishing that he named his St. Turibius Mission after a man beloved of the poor in Lima, Peru. Never was a man better suited to setting up a sort of United Nations for the homeless tribes among a babble of misunderstood languages. He welcomed and baptized them all, especially the disheartened, who had given up everything to await the end of the world and danced the *misha* ghost dance. For 47 years, the Mission and Indian Farm served as home until the Bureau of Indian Affairs took over and the site was abandoned in 1914.

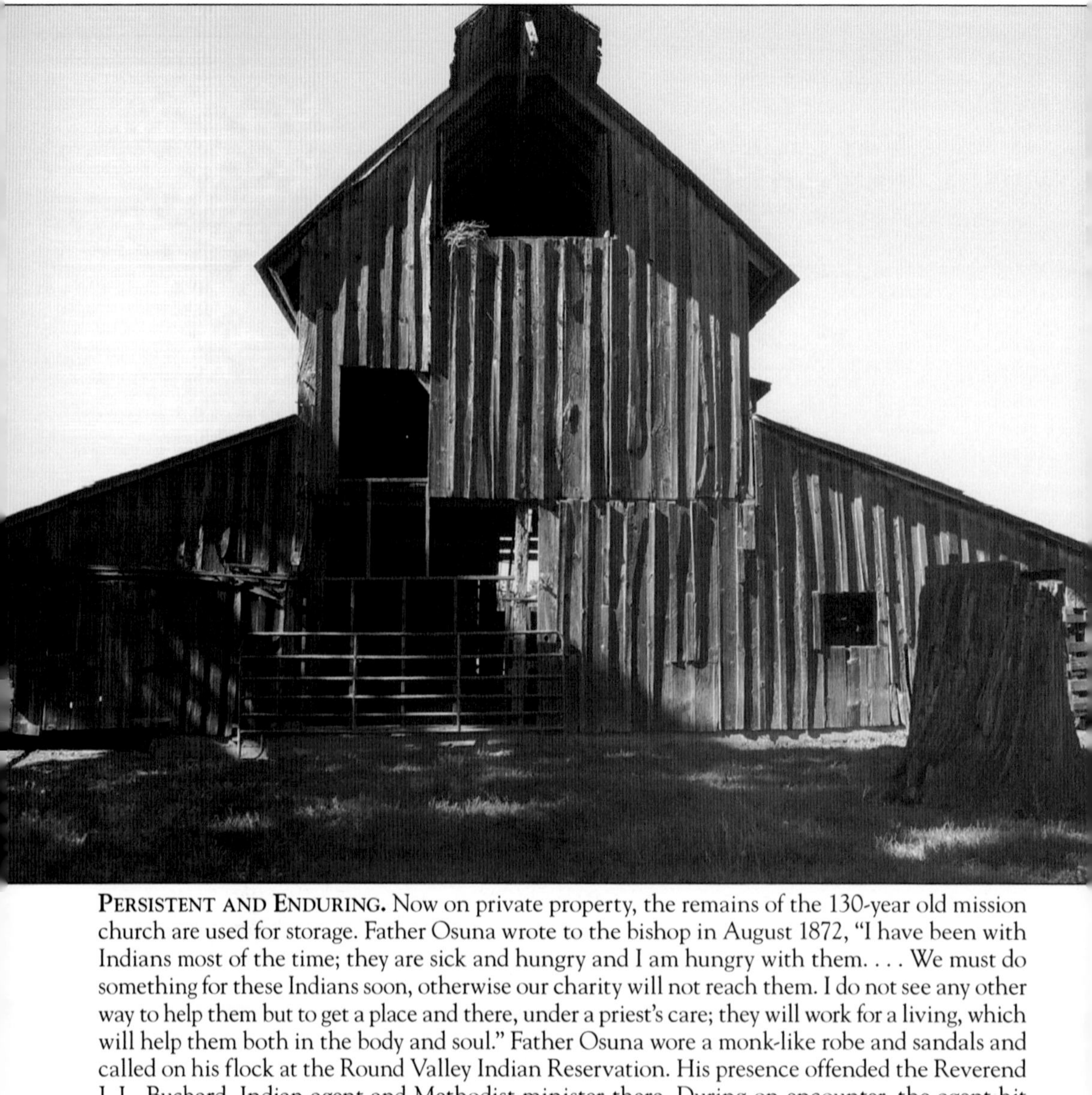

**PERSISTENT AND ENDURING.** Now on private property, the remains of the 130-year old mission church are used for storage. Father Osuna wrote to the bishop in August 1872, "I have been with Indians most of the time; they are sick and hungry and I am hungry with them. . . . We must do something for these Indians soon, otherwise our charity will not reach them. I do not see any other way to help them but to get a place and there, under a priest's care; they will work for a living, which will help them both in the body and soul." Father Osuna wore a monk-like robe and sandals and called on his flock at the Round Valley Indian Reservation. His presence offended the Reverend J. L. Buchard, Indian agent and Methodist minister there. During on encounter, the agent hit Father Osuna over the head with a cane and had him escorted off. Subsequently, the reverend charged the priest with insanity before a justice of the peace in Ukiah. Four prominent doctors found Father Osuna to be sane; he was well-known since he had built St. Mary's Catholic Church there in 1871. (Courtesy St. Mary Immaculate, *The Distant Bells of St. Turibius Mission*.)

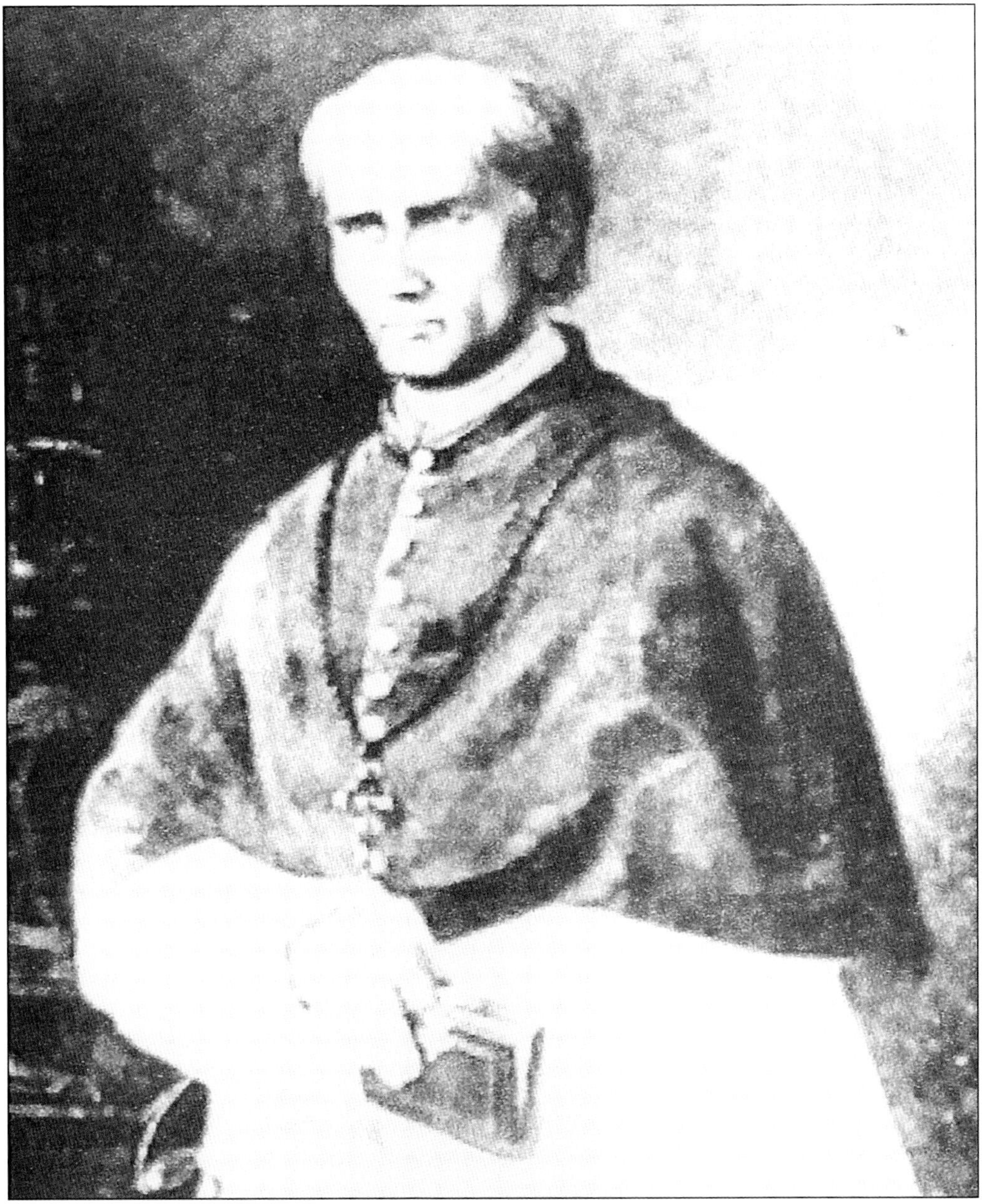

**Moved to Action.** Archbishop Alemany received Father Osuna, Peter B. Clark, and John Lynch, laymen who had built St. Peter's Catholic Church in Kelseyville in 1870, as they pleaded for land. They told how the government had issued orders for all Indians to be moved to the Round Valley Reservation, where they would be under the supervision of the Indian agent the Reverend Buchard. They asked for money to establish a Catholic mission and Indian farm, saying the government would cancel its orders if this were done. In October 1877, Father Osuna paid the $5,500 given to him from the archbishop's poor fund for 160 acres of lakeshore property. A formal statement said that it would provide a place for the Indians "where untrammeled by civil agencies, they may have a home and protector and spiritual guide to save their souls." (Portrait courtesy of Catholic Archdiocese archives.)

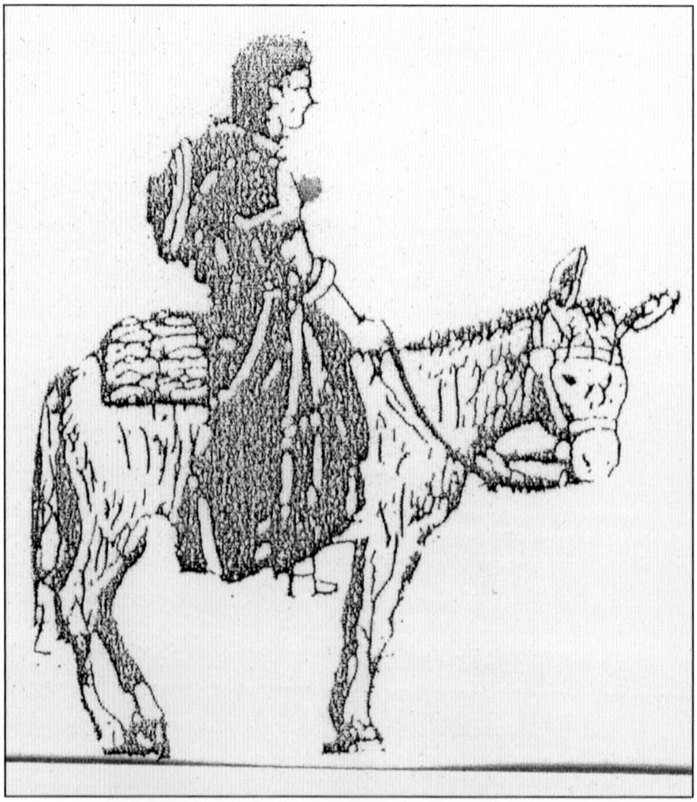

**Leaving His Image.** Father Osuna gradually purchased 175 more acres of swampland that were generously forested with tules and were home to fish and waterfowl. He built a large rough-board building to act as a school and a church or chapel. He also built a small cottage for himself but allowed the Indians their tule houses and located them in clusters of shared languages. Crops were planted and buildings added to house the people and the livestock. A burial site was set aside. Late in 1879, Father Osuna suddenly left the mission and returned to Mexico. (Woodcut from *The Distant Bells of St. Turibius Mission.*)

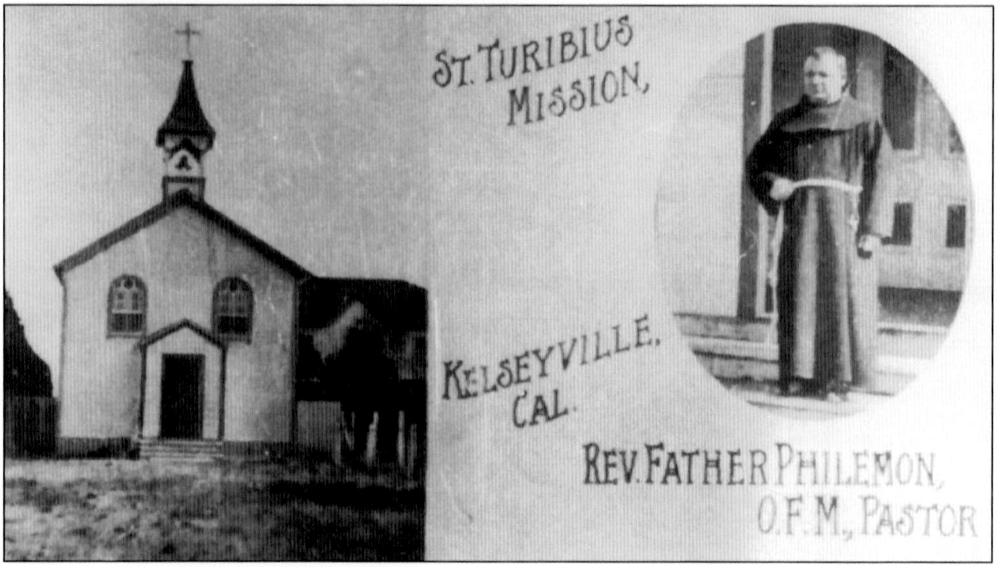


**Following in the Footsteps.** Father Osuna's missionary work was assumed by various orders until its abandonment in 1914. During 1912, the federal government bought 150 acres of property extending from Soda Bay Road to the lakefront for the Big Valley Rancheria, and residents of St. Turibius Mission and Indian Farm moved there as wards of the Bureau of Indian Affairs. Fr. Philomon Toefer moved the newly built chapel to the rancheria; it later burned. (Courtesy of Lake County Historical Society.)

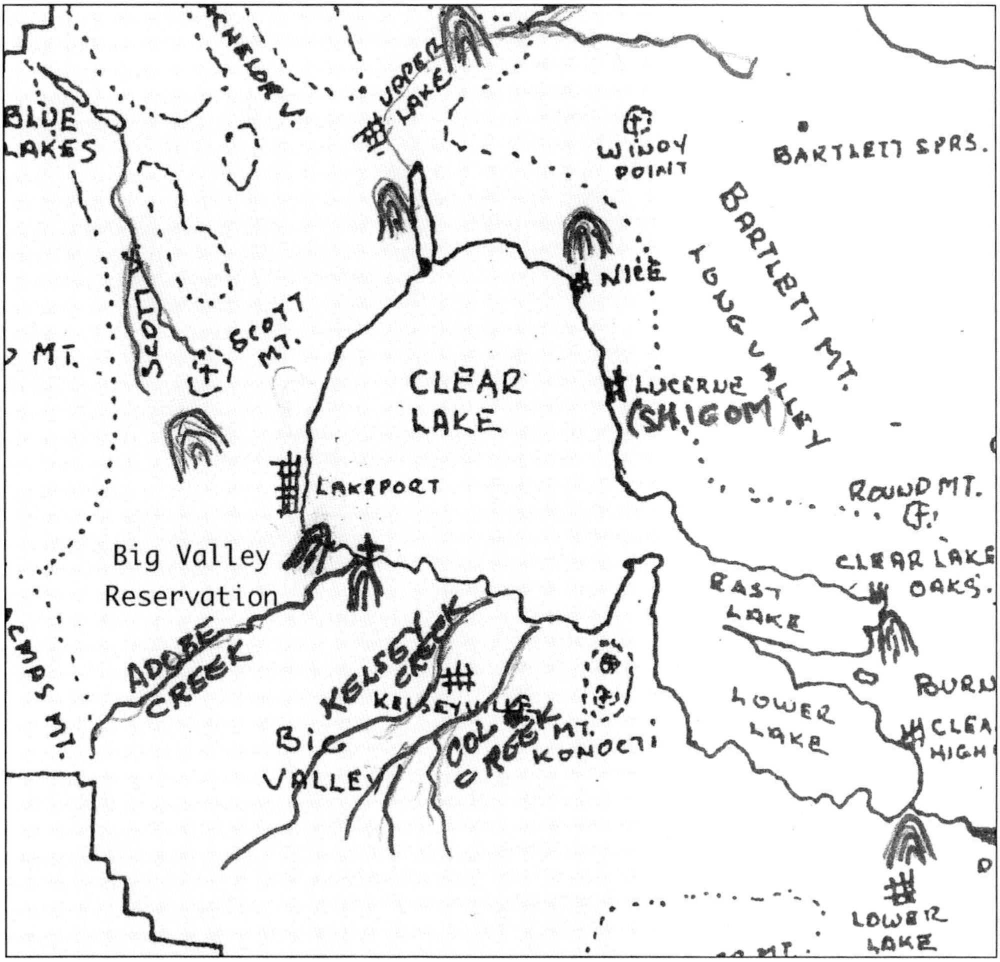


**RELOCATED THREE MILES NORTH.** The Big Valley Rancheria keeps "Mission" as part of its name because of the close historical connection with its former home.

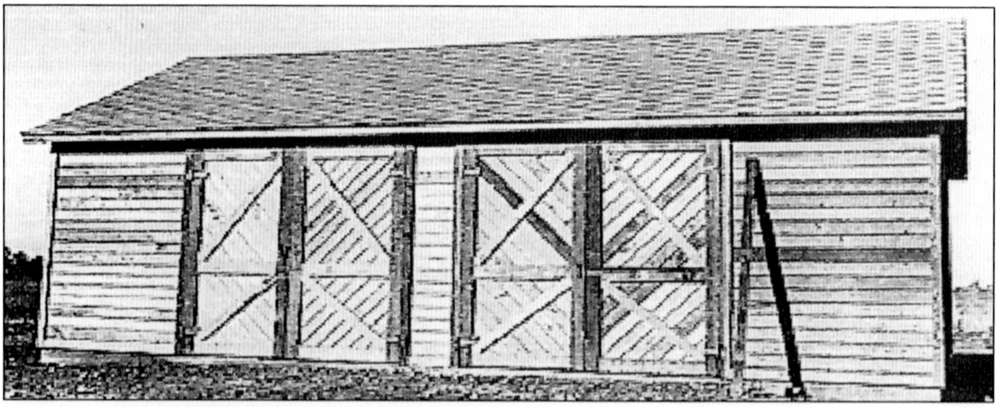

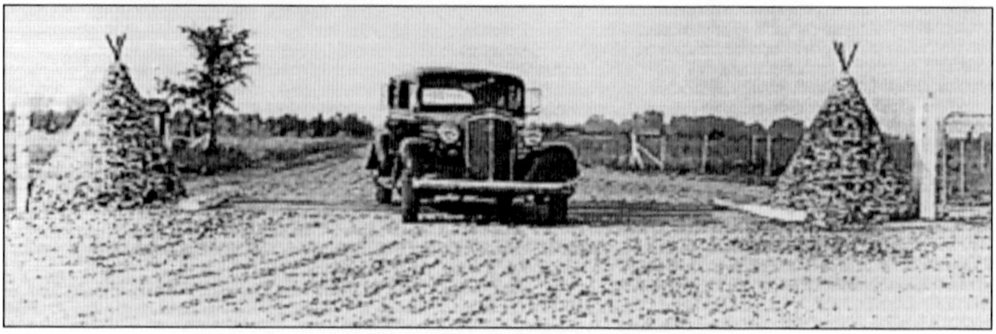

**Entrance to a Reservation.** This 1930s page from a BIA scrapbook shows the essential disconnect between the image of reservation builders and the real state of its dwellers. The obsidian teepees and cattle crossing mark the entrance on Mission Reservation Road, but Lake County Pomos never built teepees. While Indian Affairs boasted of the two-car garages they were building, the only automobile was the visiting Indian agent's shown in the photograph. The garages were useful as housing for homeless extended family members or as firewood. (Courtesy National Archives, Sacramento Region BIA.)

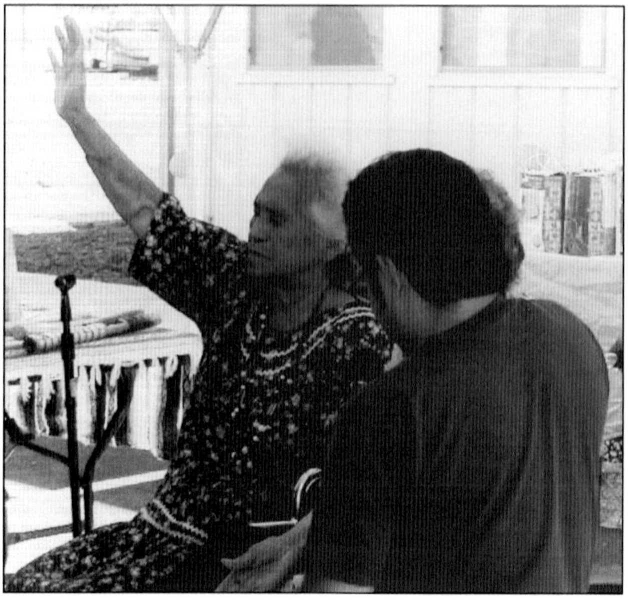

**Building a Community.** The government promised new housing, water, and sanitation facilities, as well as farmland for crops and orchards, but the natives were starting from scratch. The families tried to form a unity based on their common experiences of time spent at the mission and cultural similarities and ceremonies. They built an aboveground dance house, and Father Toefer moved his newly built church from the old mission site. Here Elvina (Elem/Big Valley) Brown offers a blessing on a ceremony at a later time. (Courtesy Brown family archives.)

**LINEAGES.** Mary (John) Posh learned basket making from her mother, Mary/Pauline John; her art is now displayed at the Grace Hudson Museum in Ukiah. She was born around 1880 in a native community in Big Valley. She died after the birth of her fifth child in 1911. Her son, Roger Posh, was chair of the Big Valley Community Council when it was ratified in 1934, and Lincoln Dennison (right) signed as secretary. (Courtesy Lake County Historic Courthouse Museum.)

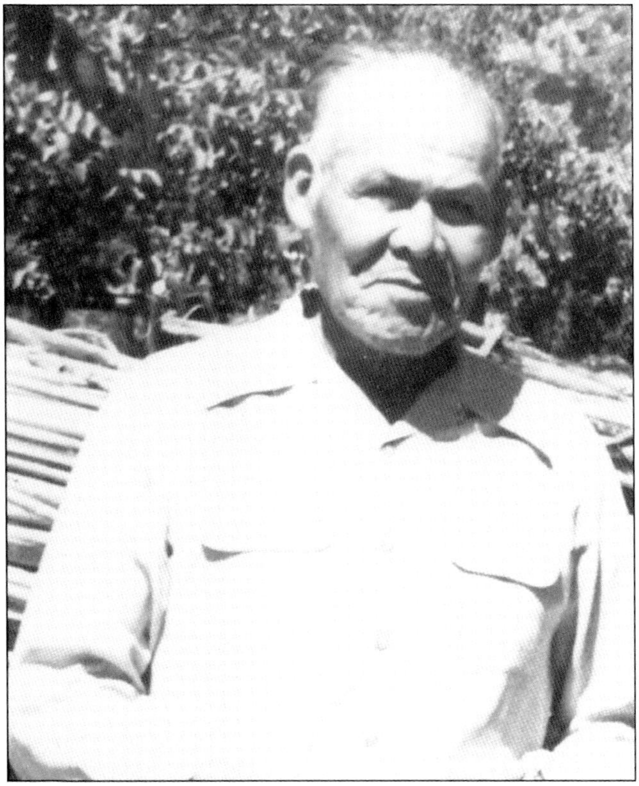

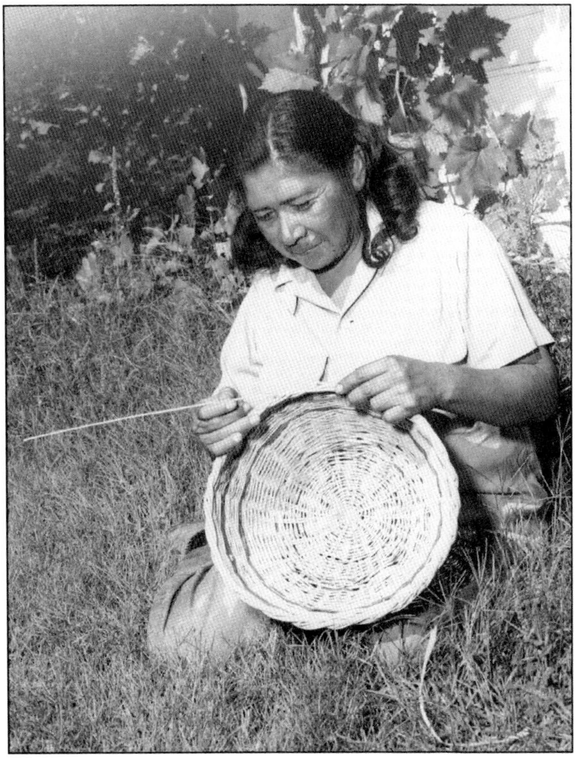

**DOWN THE LINE.** The basket-making facility continued with Frances Posh (later Dennison) and Vivian Posh, a skilled basket weaver seen in this photograph by Keith Dennison at Big Valley Rancheria. (Courtesy Lake County Historic Courthouse Museum.)

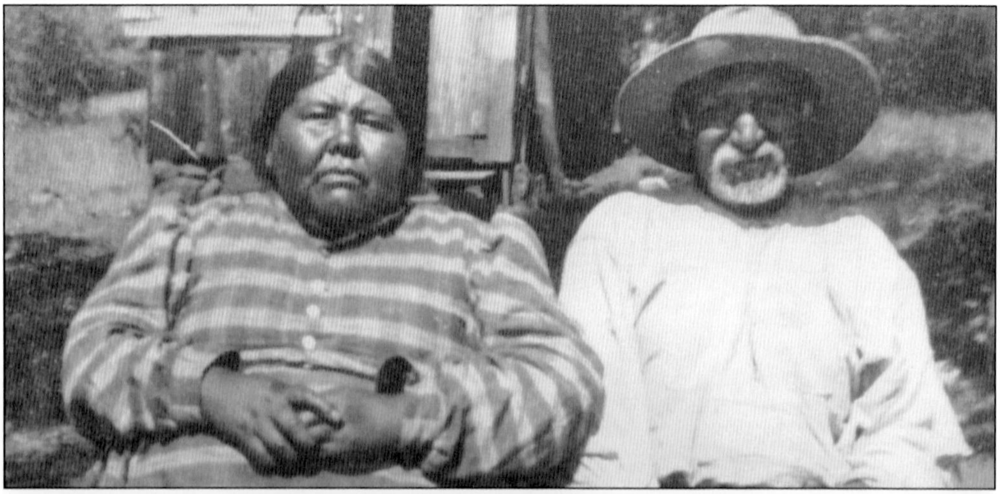

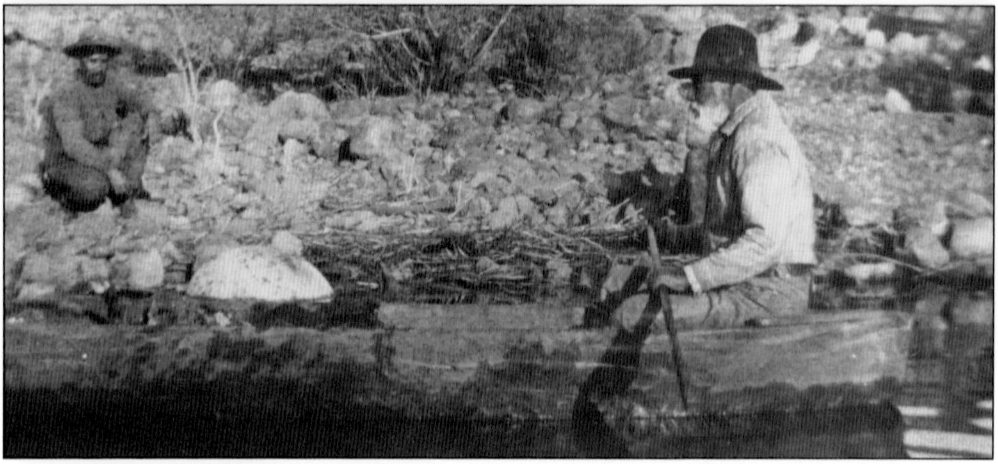

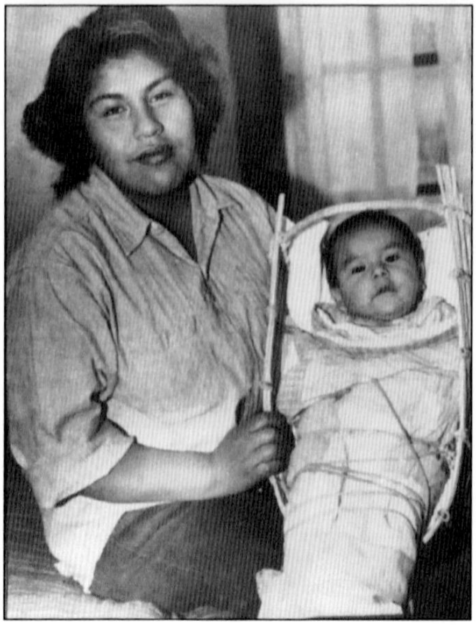

**DRAMATIC ORIGINS.** The murder of "Cherokee John" Holmes (top, right) for his Civil War pension and the lurid details of his body thrown into a pigpen led to one of the most inflammatory trials in Lake County legal history. His wife, Polly (top left), and her son Harris (center photograph) were from Sulphur Banks (Elem) but spent their lives at Big Valley. He became the preacher at the Assembly of God church on the rancheria and converted many. The council gave him space to build his church, which still stands but no longer holds services. His daughter, Ruth, is shown with her son, David Mitchell Jr., in a photograph by Keith Dennison. (Courtesy Lake County Historic Courthouse Museum.)

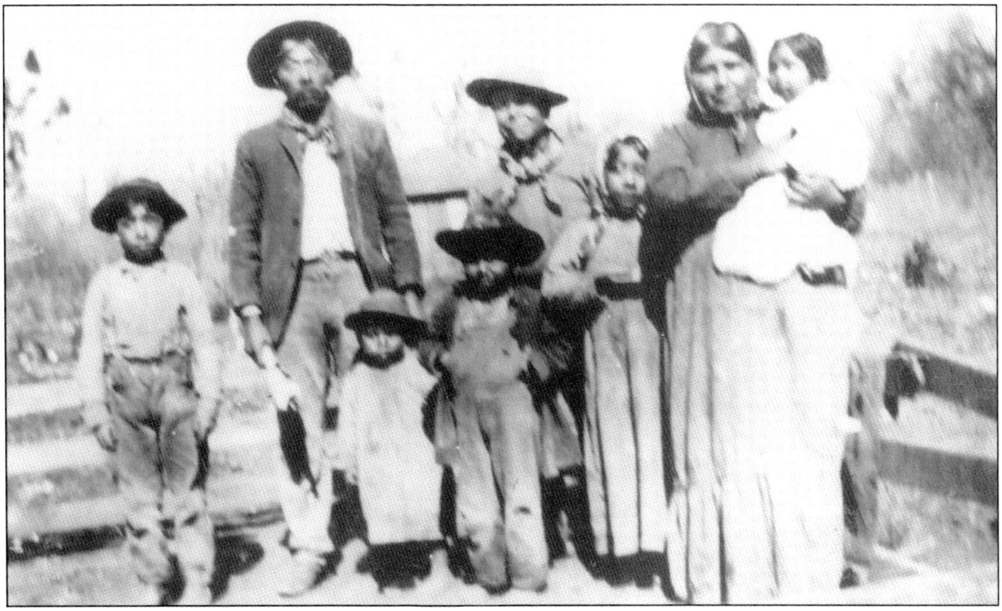

**Just Take Another Name.** Bob Fred Hogan (left and below, left), a full-blooded Pomo born in 1872, dropped his last name when an employer asked him to; he and his wife, Rose Gomez (right and below, right), became the Freds. Rose's brother Louis is at center above, and the boy to the left above is their eldest son, William. Family lore suggests Bob Fred was jealous of his wife's spiritual powers, so Rose denied her role as a spiritual leader. She was told in a dream that as a consequence, she would know great sorrow. She bore 13 children, and 10 died. Her three remaining children were William (called "Gerald") Fred, Vivian Fred, and Ramona (Fred) McCloud. (Courtesy Fred family archives.)

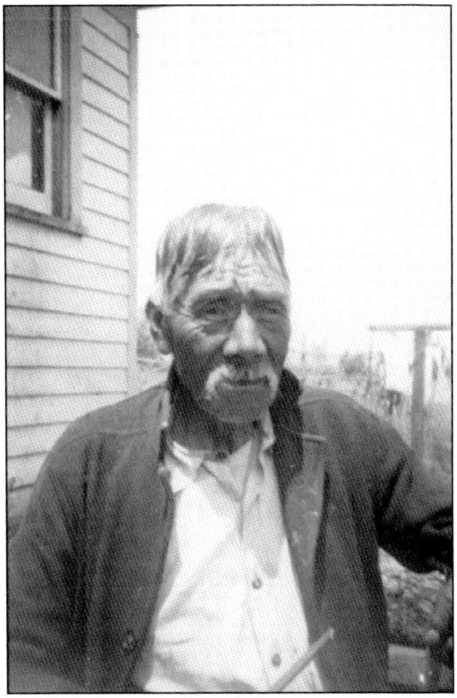

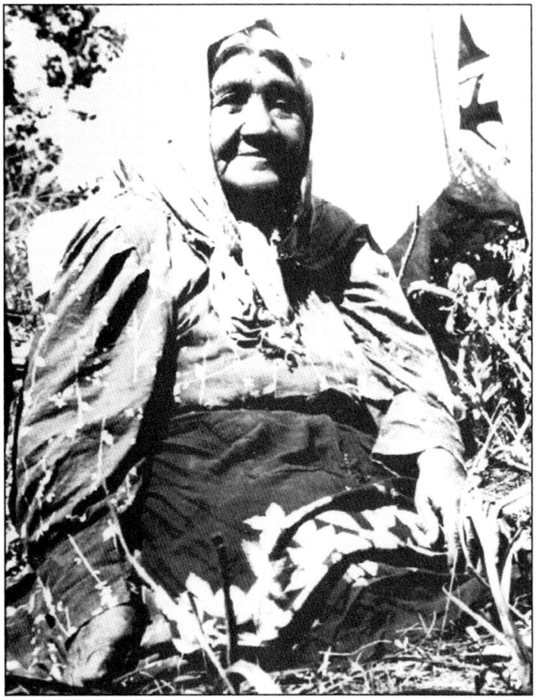

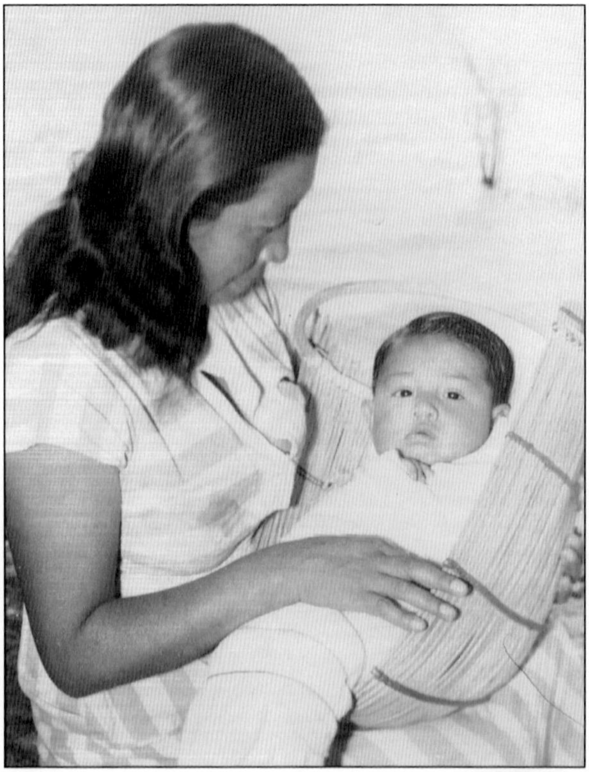

**A True Dreamer.** Vivian Fred (with her son Carl Freeman in a photograph by C. M. Davidson) was a *maru* dreamer, whose visions told exactly how the dance house ceremonies should be instituted at Big Valley Rancheria. From her dreams and with her family's support, she created the dancers' headpieces and regalia and the symbolic flags for the roundhouse ceremonies and instituted the ceremonial format. Eventually the work spread to other roundhouses. Dance regalia are part of a sacred ceremony and may not be sold or discarded. They must be destroyed. Historian Henry Mauldin acquired the dance regalia, secure in a display case at the Lake County Historic Courthouse Museum (below), when one dancer converted to Pentecostalism and did not follow the ritual destruction. (Courtesy Lake County Historic Courthouse Museum.)

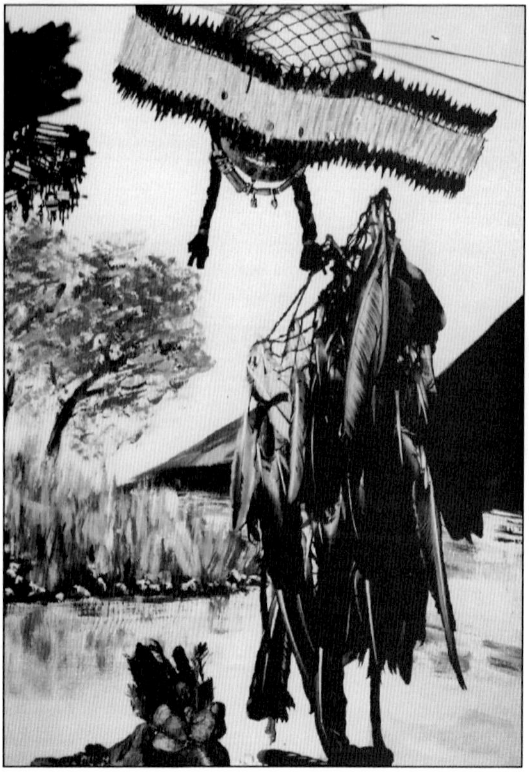

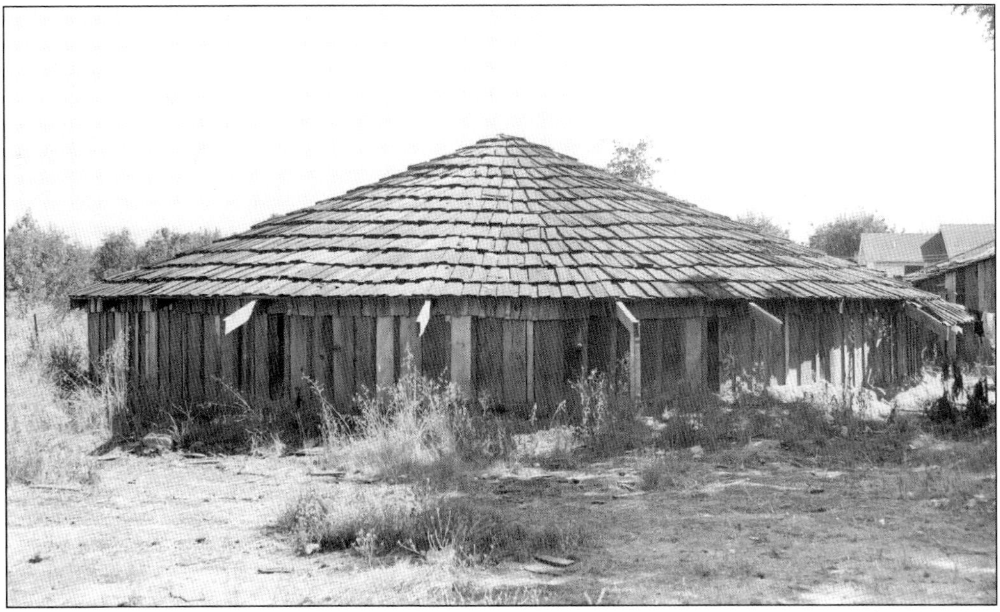

**A Circle.** Roundhouses were part of the earth. Modern ones are built aboveground with token excavations. Elders believe that roundhouses are destroyed as part of the earth's recycling of natural materials, and rebuilding is part of the next generation's education. This Big Valley roundhouse burned in the 1950s. The present roundhouse was built on the same site with entrance facing the same direction. (Photograph by Keith Dennison, courtesy Lake County Historic Courthouse Museum.)

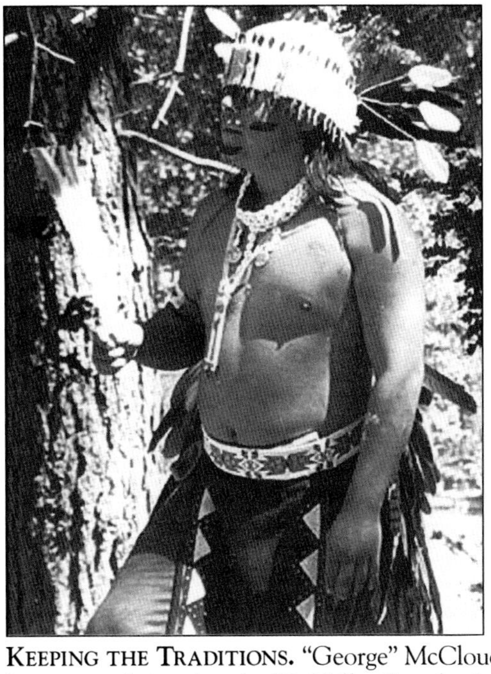

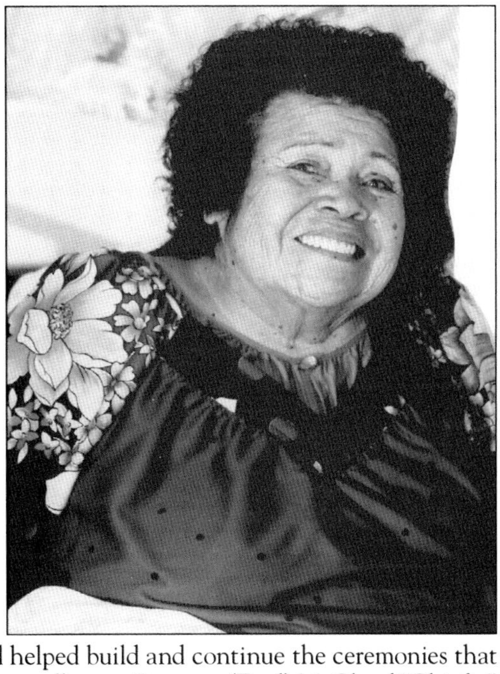

**Keeping the Traditions.** "George" McCloud helped build and continue the ceremonies that became traditional at the Big Valley Rancheria roundhouse. Ramona (Fred) McCloud "Chiefer" maintained the tradition of gathering materials and making fine baskets and teaching the children to carry it forward. (Courtesy McCloud family archives.)

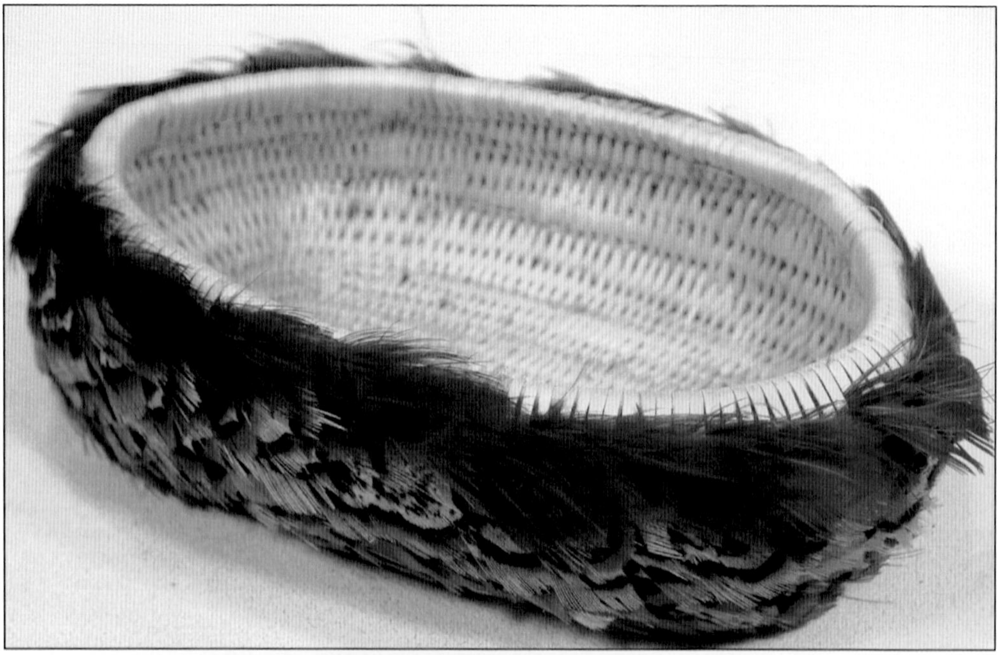

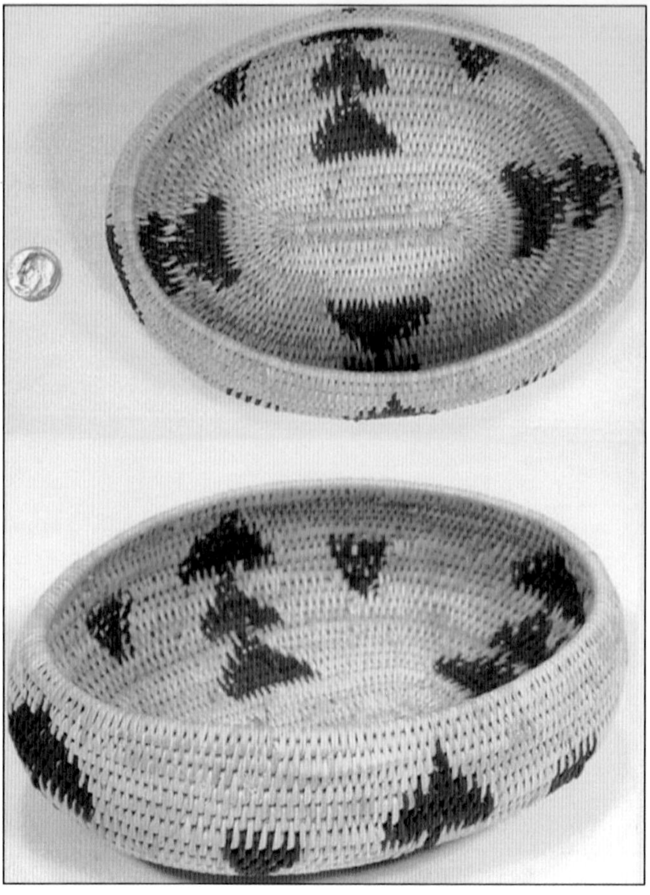

**Baskets on Display.** The miniature baskets made by Ramona McCloud and Joanne Lopez are on display in secure cases at the tribe's café inside the Konocti Vista Casino. (Photographs by Carol Dillenger, courtesy Big Valley Rancheria.)

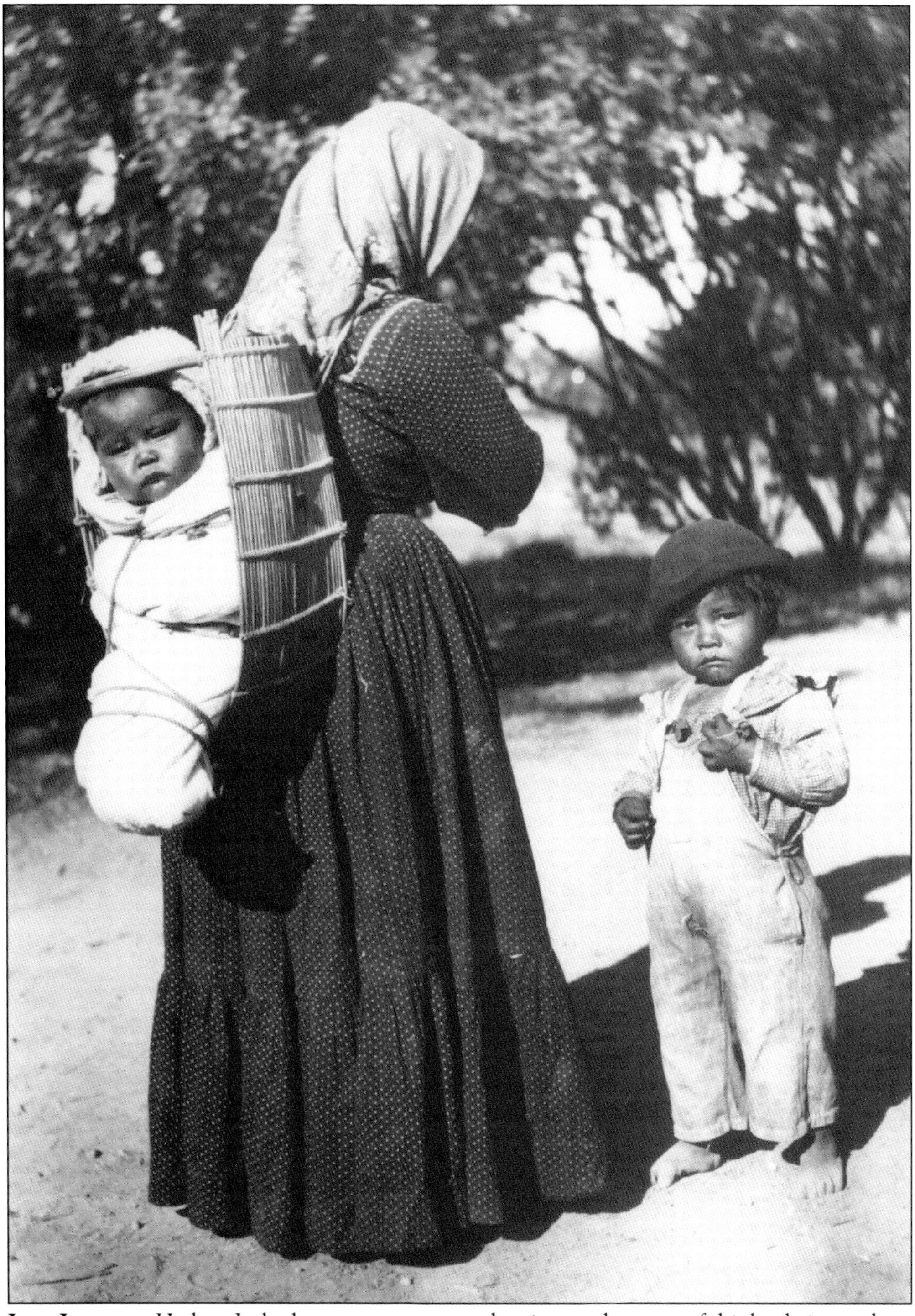

**Jack Lineage.** Hudson Jack, the mature man seen dancing on the cover of this book, is seen here in an earlier view. Rose Jack has her son Lawrence beside her and is carrying seven-month-old Hudson in his basket. In 1994, her grandson, Valentino Jack, as tribal leader brought the Konocti Vista Casino to Big Valley Rancheria. (Courtesy Lake County Historic Courthouse Museum.)

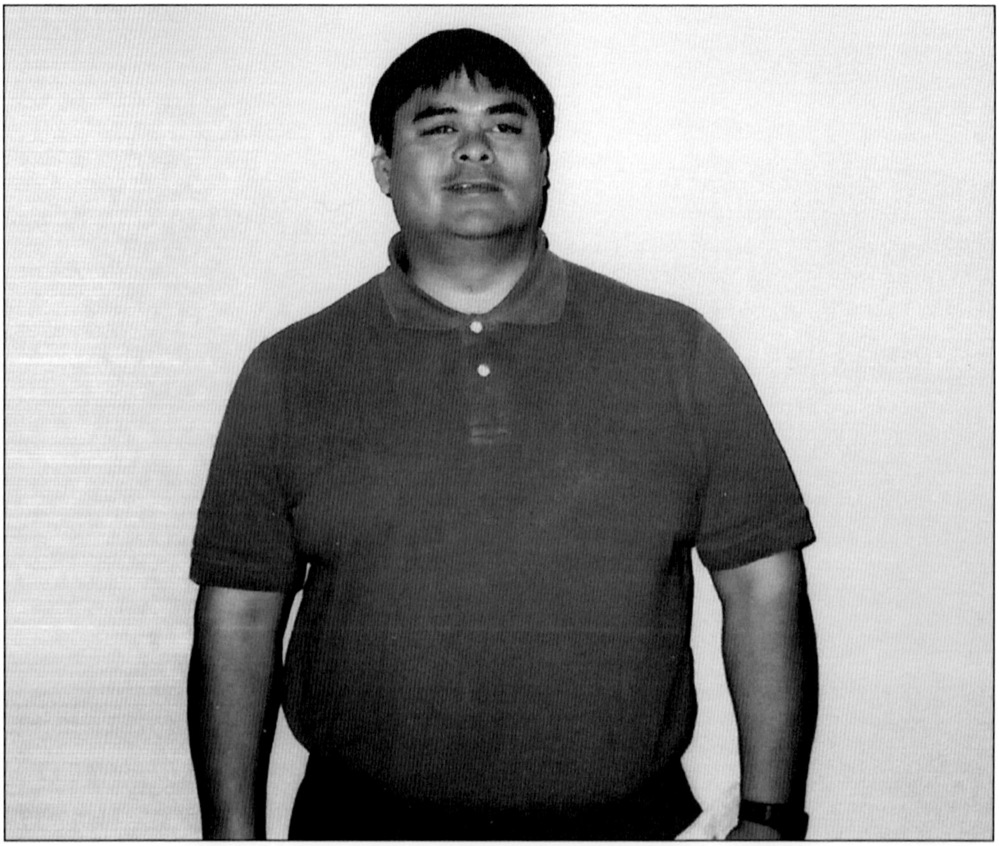

**WHO IS IN AND WHO IS OUT.** In 2000, Tribal Chair Anthony Jack explained the challenge of determining membership. "Many Indian Tribes are embroiled in deep divisions over the basic question of who is and who is not a tribal member. In California this question is more complex because of our interrupted history, of termination and then re-recognition. Here many tribes are comprised of only a few families where internal and petty family squabbles can contribute to an atmosphere of divisiveness. . . . The BIA uses the criteria of one-fourth-blood quantum. Critics feel that is a system with the explicit goal of eliminating tribes . . . [but] what criteria should be used? Our constitution states that you can be a tribal member only if your name appeared on the official census rolls of 1935 or [is] a child of a tribal member who was a resident of the Rancheria at the time of that child's birth. . . .The Big Valley Band of Pomo Indians is a weave of many strands. . . . Defining who can be a member of our tribe is our next challenge." (Courtesy Jack family collection.)

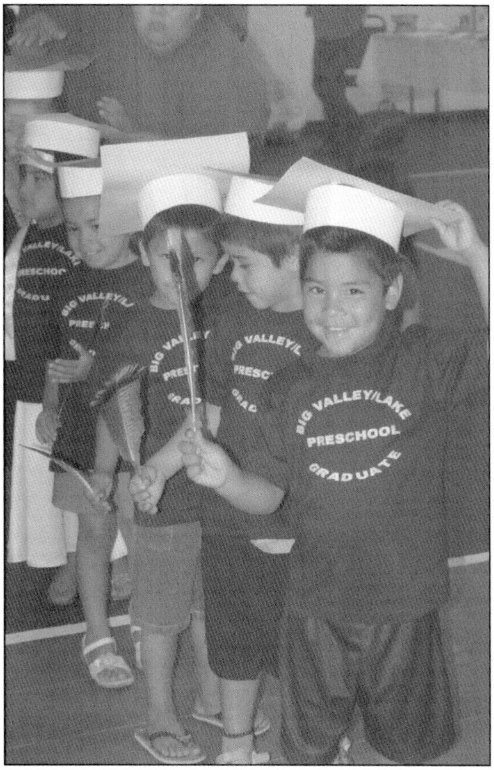


**TOMORROW'S EXTENDED FAMILIES.** There is no doubt that young Native Americans are full of hope at this age, in spite of everything. In all the diversity, there is one agreement: their future lies in a balance between maintaining tradition and educating for the future. At right, eager preschool graduates wear self-made mortarboards and clutch feathers. Below Lucille "JoJo" (Fred/McCloud) Gomez leads them to begin their traditional dance ceremonies of celebration. They will soon be ready for the roundhouse. (Photographs by Carol Dillenger, courtesy Big Valley Rancheria.)

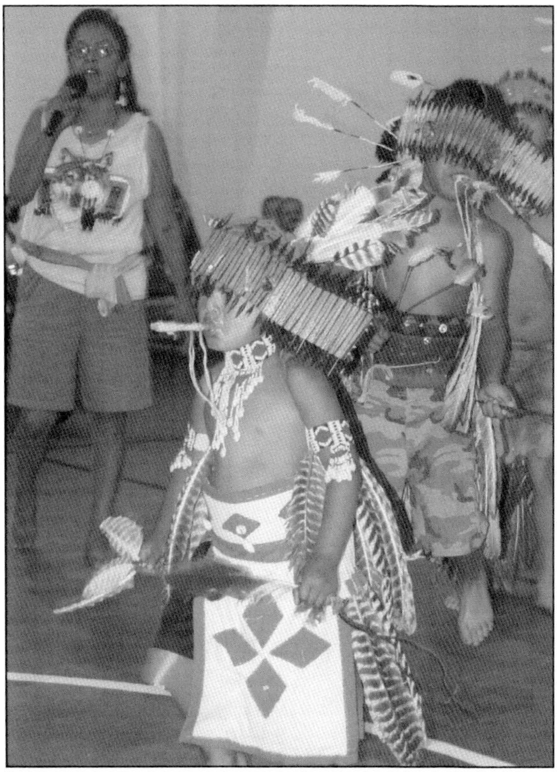

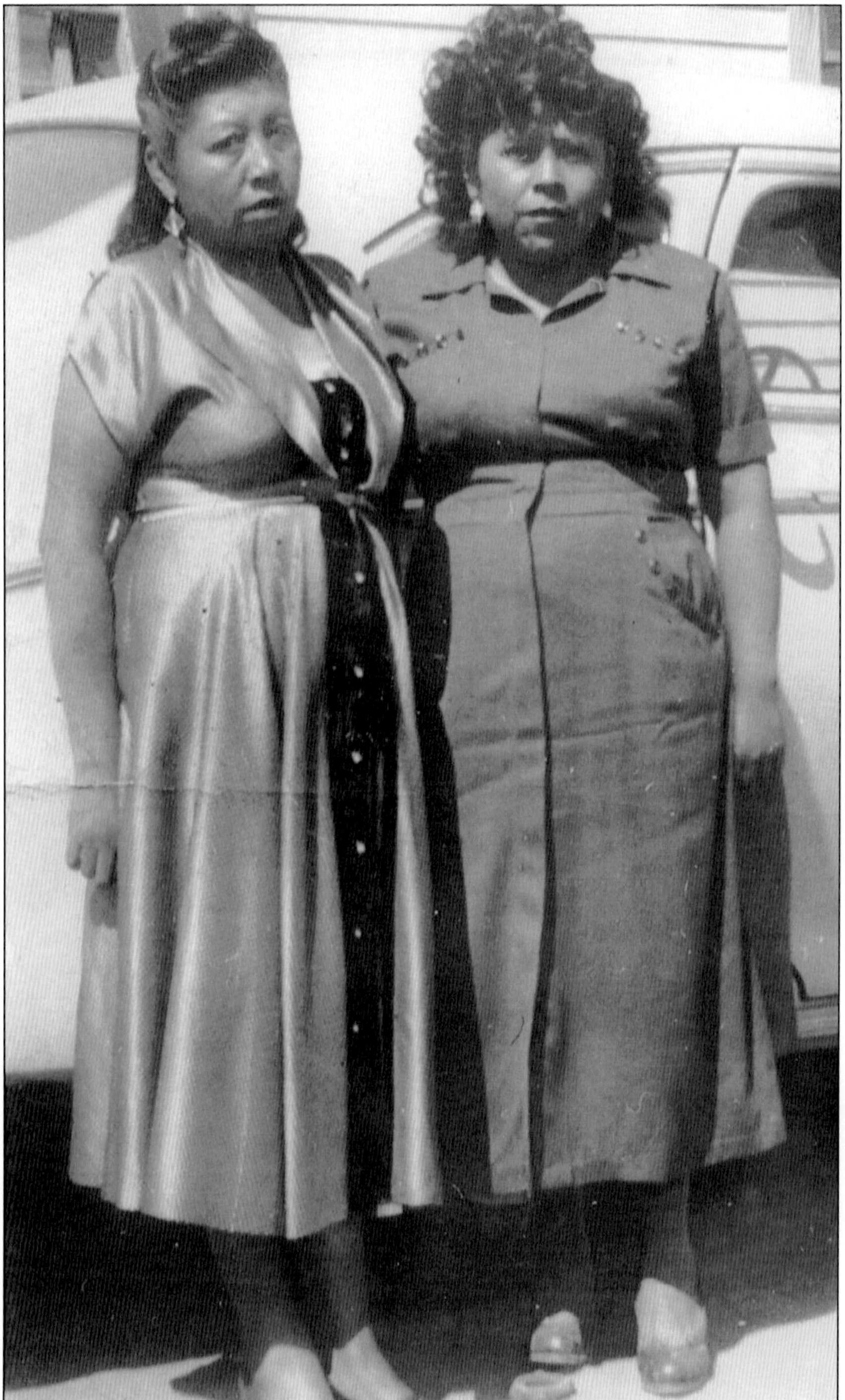

**BASKET MASTERS.** Vivian Fred and her sister Ramona (Fred) McCloud (right) and Joanne Lopez (not shown here), carried on their families' tradition of excellent basket weaving. The sale of artistic baskets to collectors often supported Native American families from the end of the 19th century up until the Great Depression. (Courtesy Fred family archives.)

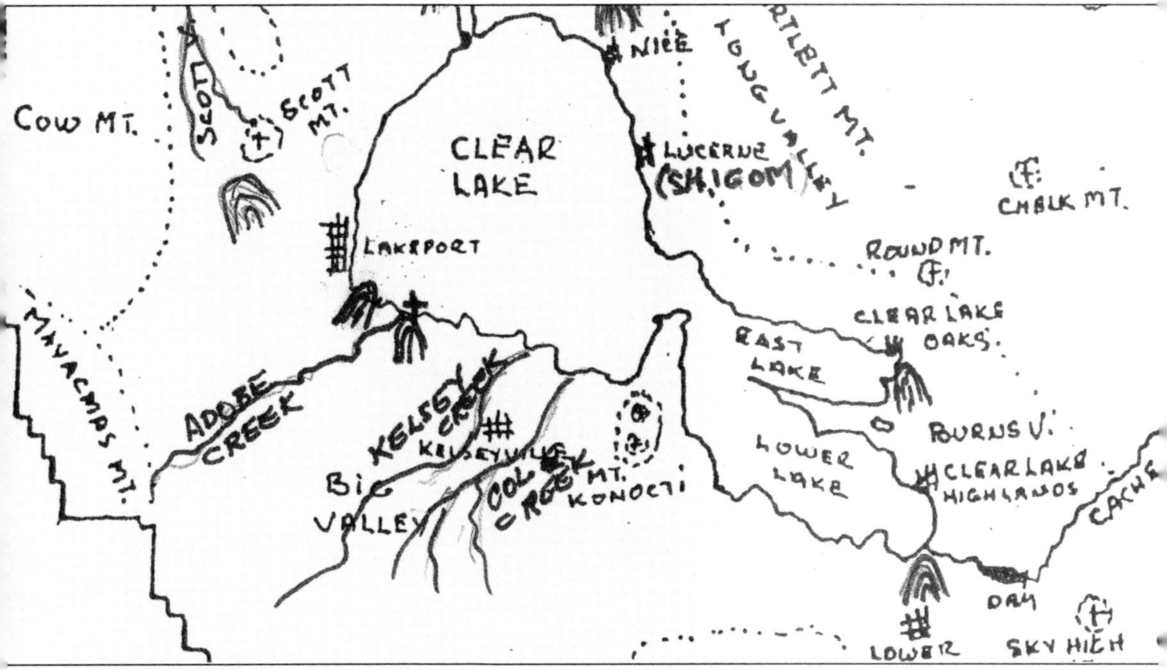


**ANCIENT ONES.** Elem is a Southeastern Pomo colony on Rattlesnake Island (Sulphur Bank Island) and the lakeshore mainland facing it at the eastern tip of the east arm of Clear Lake. Its early territory is said to have extended around East Lake through what is now Clearlake Oaks and overlapping or adjoining Koi and Kamdot territory, including the obsidian source. The language and customs are distinct from that of the Eastern Pomo, though they have been good neighbors time out of mind and share some ceremonials and a similar attachment to homeland. They are island people, and their story of first causes says that the world of their people began here and includes tales of Mount Konocti's eruptions.

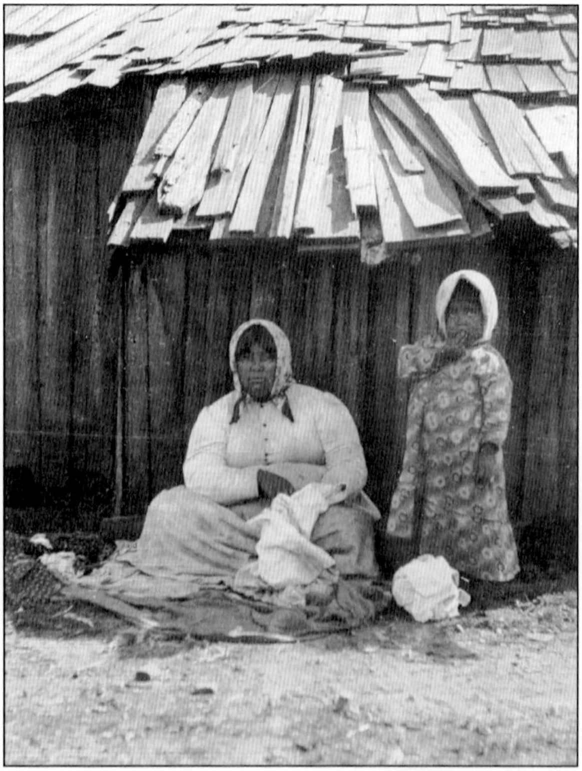

**Quickly Adaptive.** In the old ways, Ethel Bogus and her daughter sit outside the Sulphur Banks roundhouse, but they are already fully clothed in Anglo garments; note the buttons on Ethel's dress and the sawed planks of the building. (Photograph by John Hudson *c.* 1903, courtesy Grace Hudson Museum.)

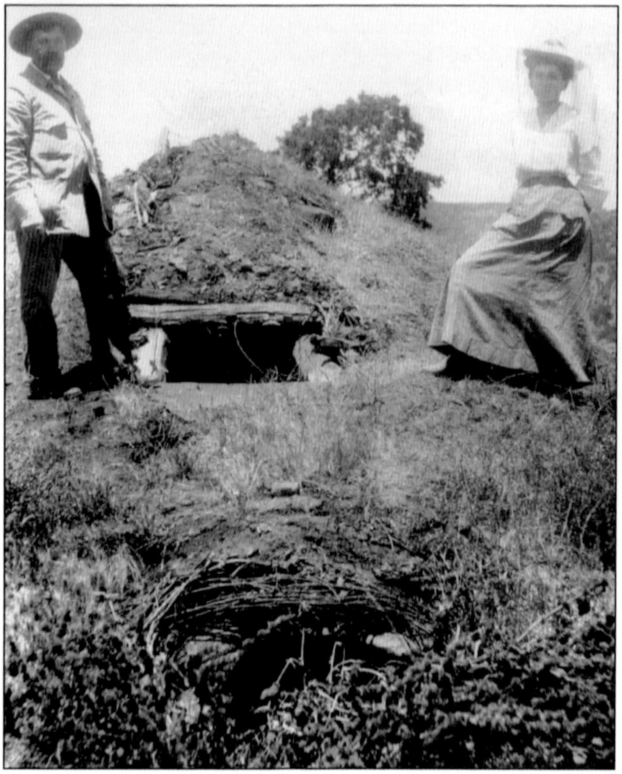

**Preventive Medicine.** The subterranean sweathouse (sudatorium), where men spent part of every day for health and cleanliness, has these 1906 visitors pointing out its entrance. The smoke hole is in the brambles in the foreground. These dirt-insulated sweathouses were used much like the modern-day sauna baths that are often followed by a cold dip in a nearby lake or stream. (Courtesy Lake County Historic Courthouse Museum.)

**GARDENERS, NOT FARMERS.** In 1912, the government designated 88 acres at Sulphur Banks for a reservation for the "Elem Band and other homeless Southeastern Pomo natives." Residents got horses and wagons no longer needed by the army, built barns and corrals, and learned to farm. Pomos had shepherded the natural vegetation with controlled burning, training roots and shoots for basketry, and spacing oak groves, but never grew crops. Traditionalists like Theresa Brown, right in 1982, still went to the Pacific to gather salt, seaweed, and shells. (Courtesy John Parker, Ph.D.)

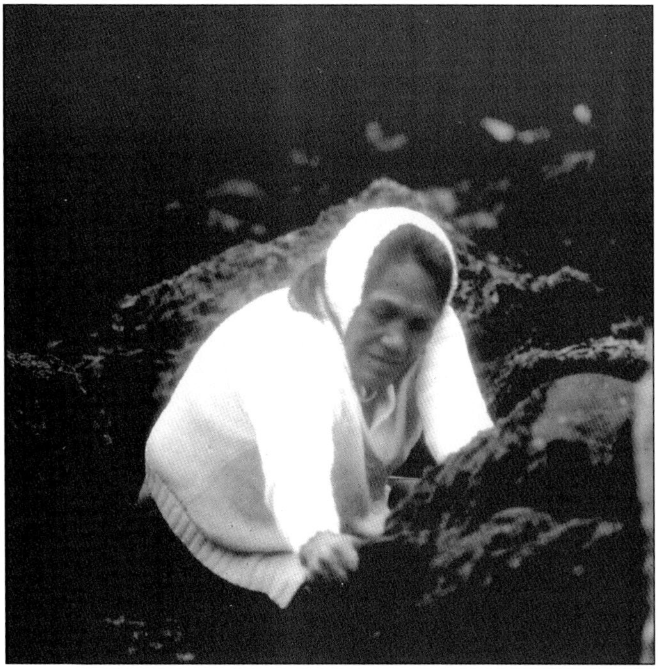

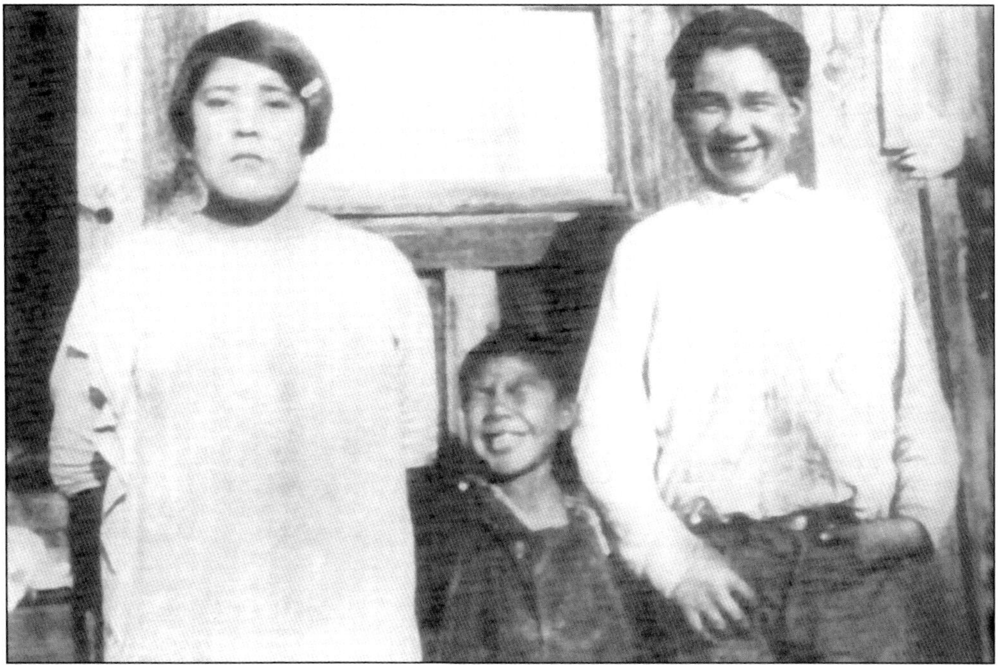

**READY TO GO TO SCHOOL.** They could not go to public school until 1934. Much of their learning was traditional. Pictured are Grace Elliott (later Barnes), Calvin Brown (center), and Houghton Brown. Elem had been made virtually uninhabitable by toxic mine tailings. Arsenic and mercury and runoff into Clear Lake have elevated it to a No. 1 Superfund site and, after 31 years, a clean-up by the Environmental Protection Agency in 2006. Tainted dirt was removed to the Bradley mine site. Modular houses replaced those demolished in the process, and new streets, curbs, and gutters were laid. (Courtesy of *Lake County Record-Bee*.)

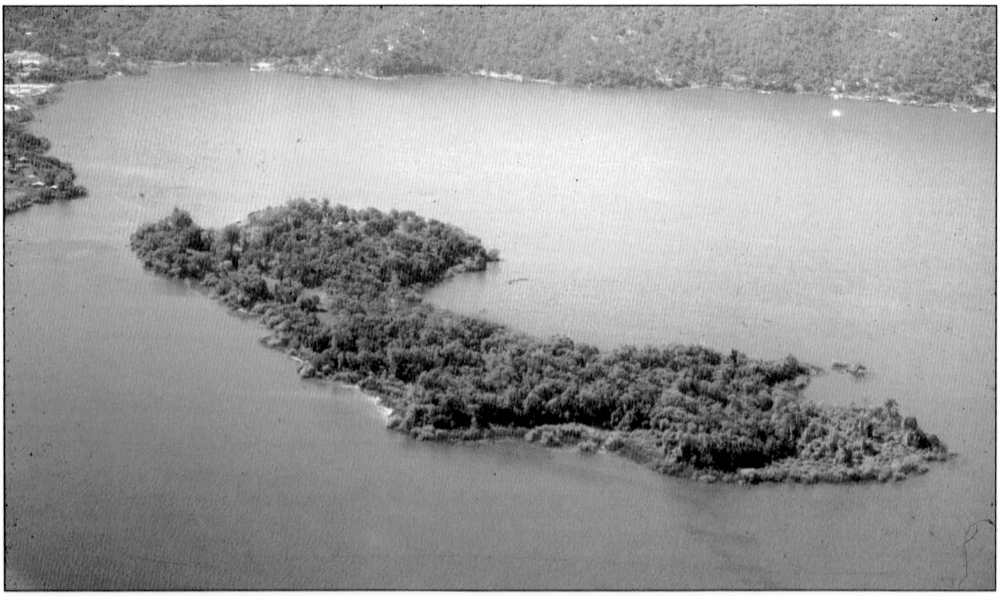

**YES, THERE WERE RATTLESNAKES** Rattlesnake Island (Hawina, Hisla) held one of the largest Indian populations in the county. No one lives there now, but there is evidence of recent occupancy, with house pits and a large old dance hole. On the north side is a village site, evidently long occupied but leaving behind no history or legend. On the island there are remains of at least five village sites, and Elem's territory is known to have extended beyond the island. Now privately owned, Elem Colony still considers the island its home. (Courtesy John Parker, Ph.D.)

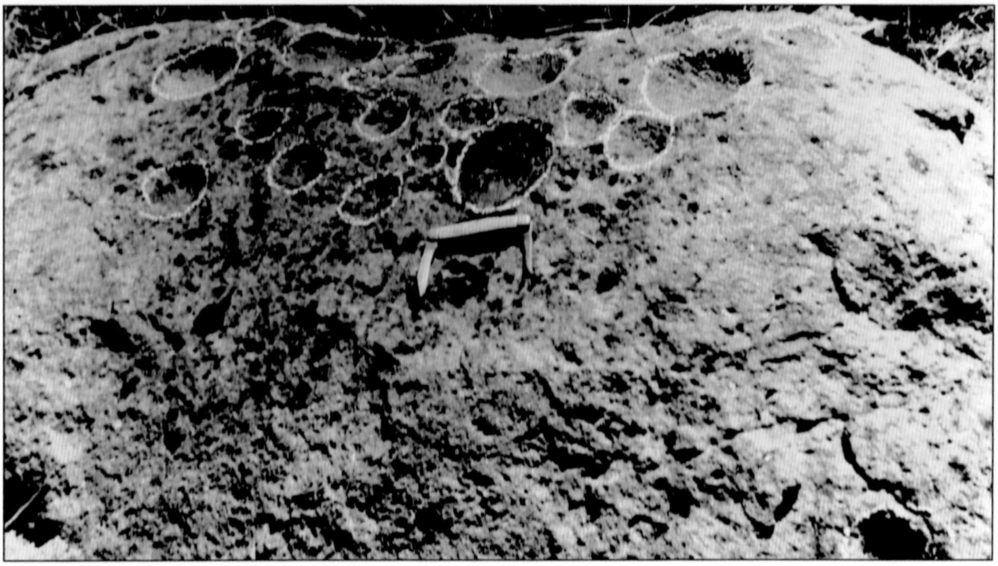

**MAYBE SACRED RAIN PITS.** Red Rock Island once held a large and well-used village where many pits may have been dug to produce rain or to stop it; other anthropologists think that they were conceiving cups made by women to encourage fertility. The Sulphur Banks mine used tailings from the mine to build two levees from the mainland to Red Rock, enclose Dollar Island (above site of these pits), fill the mineral springs, pump out the water, and make an irrigated pasture and levee to prevent runoff directly into the lake. (Photograph by Henry Mauldin, courtesy of Lake County Historical Society.)

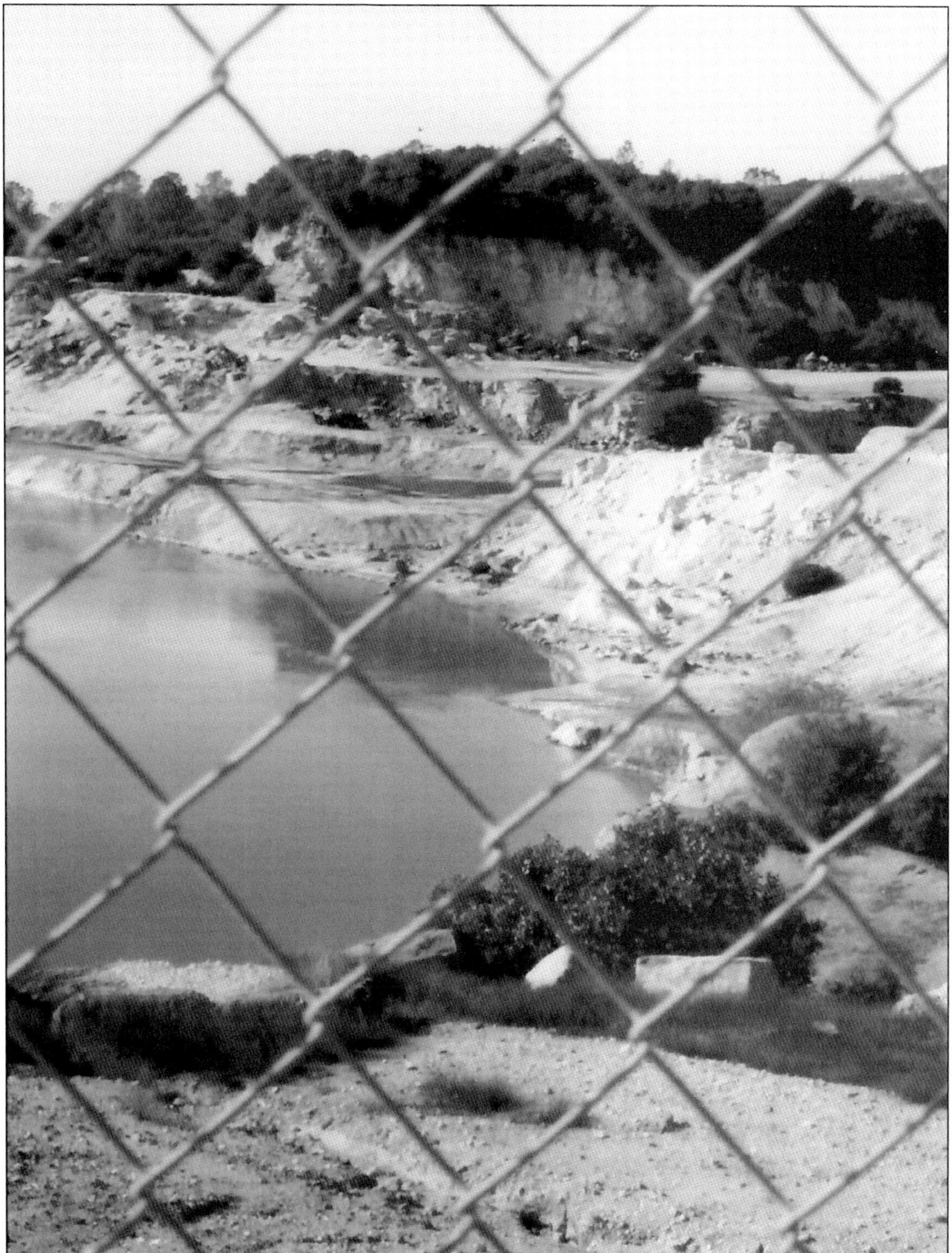

**WHY SULPHUR BANKS?** The huge mountain of sulfur was extracted and exported. The faint scent of sulfur, like rotten eggs, lingers in the air. In 1875, California Borax Company organized the Sulphur Banks Quicksilver Mine, and from beneath the layer of cinnabar, a fortune in quicksilver was extracted. Through the years, technology and markets evolved, and a shaft was sunk. Much later, with the advent of earth-moving equipment, a huge open-pit operation began. Herman Pit is the remaining dead lake held back from Clear Lake with an earthen dam. Its owners, Bradley Mining Company, abandoned the mine in 1957. (Courtesy private collection.)

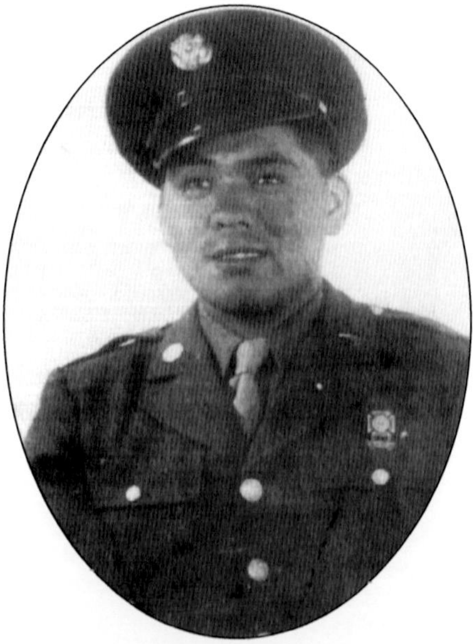

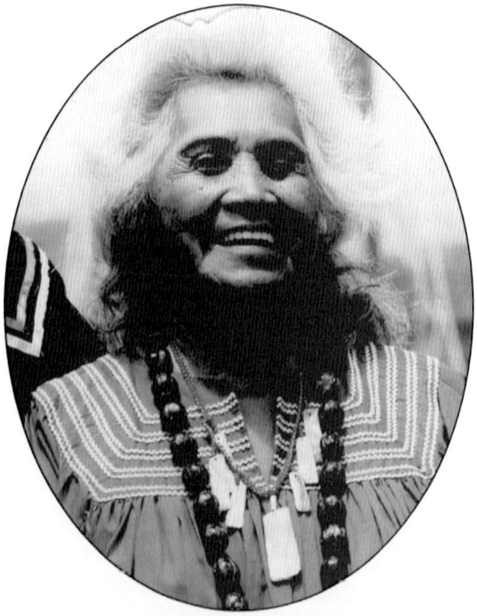

**An American at War.** "My father, [Jim Brown II] who was a war veteran and spiritual leader for our people, died young at age 59," Jim Brown III says. "For years he worked in that mine, and he had all of the symptoms. I believe he died because of the mercury, but in our tradition we do not perform autopsies, so we can't know for sure." Jim remembers his mother Elvina (right) and their family living at the mine foreman's house just before he went to kindergarten, when, after termination, they moved to Oakland to be urban Indians. (Courtesy Jim Brown family archives.)

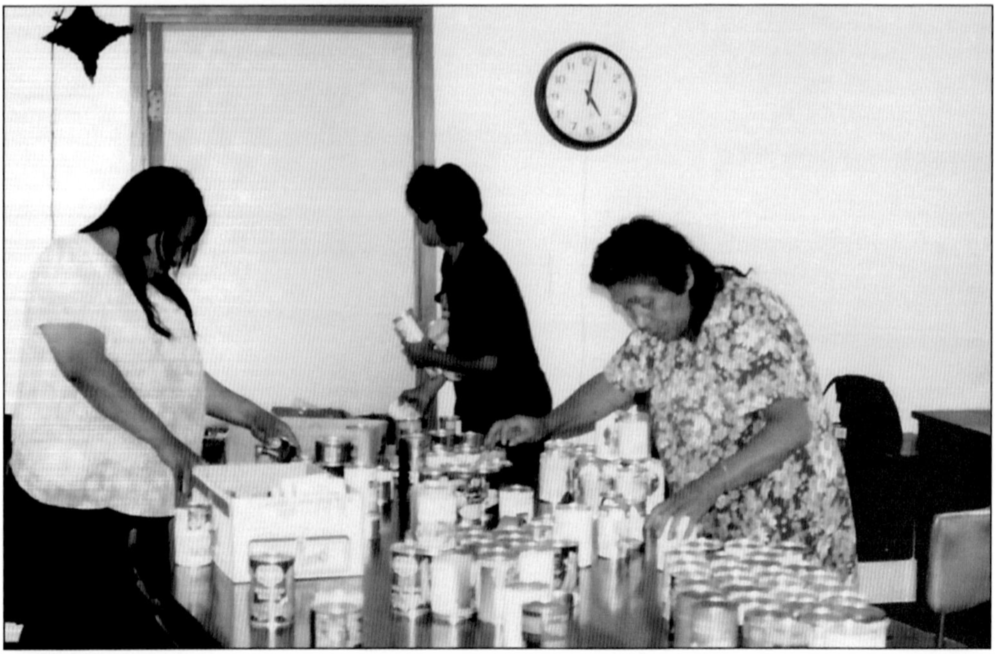

**Deposits at the Food Bank.** From left to right, Martha Morinda, her daughter, Koeya John, and her mother, Ermadine Geary sort donations from the Oak Hill Middle School food drive to restock the community food closet at Elem Colony's restored tribal office. (Courtesy Lake County Historic Courthouse Museum.)

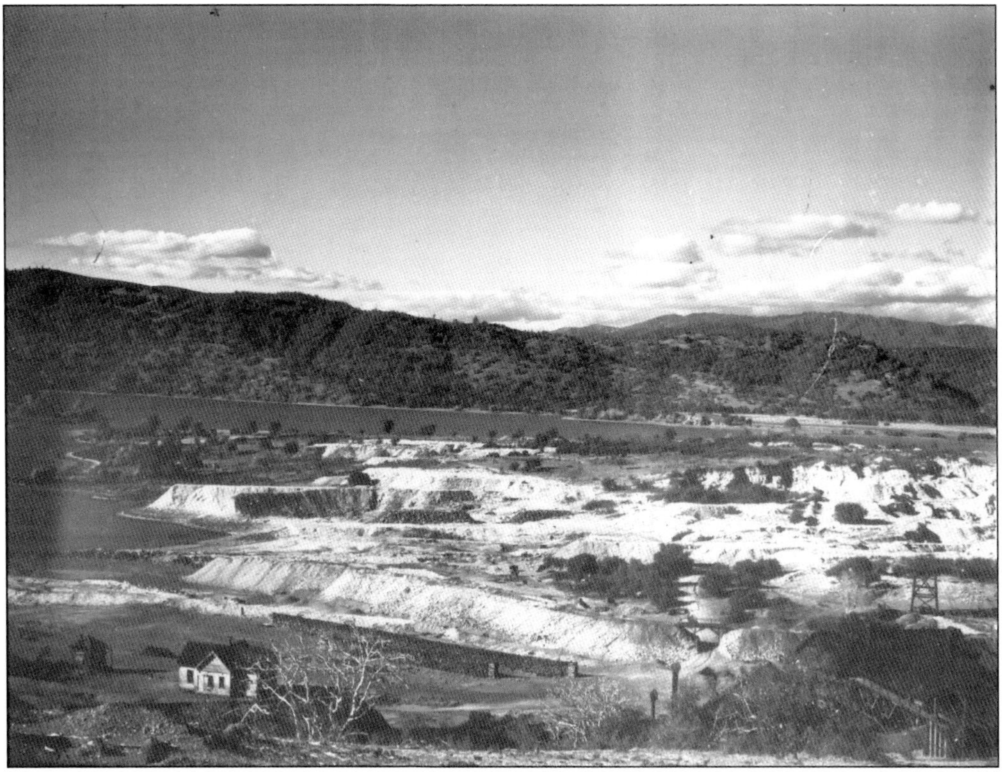

**THREE VIEWS.** In the 1960s, BIA was trying to fulfill promises of improving rancherias to health and sanitation code levels. "In the 1970s, the BIA bought leftover tailings from [mine-owner] Bradley," Jim Brown, an Elem Pomo leader (seen below left with archaeologist John Parker), told a reporter. "They used it as fill when they built our first houses in 1971. We don't know yet what the long-term effects of living on these tailings will be." "At the time, we didn't know the tailings were contaminated," Harold Bradford, BIA director for central California, was quoted as saying. "Who's to say the fish haven't always had mercury in them," Frederick Bradley, president of Bradley Mining Company, is quoted as saying in the same article. "Nature put it there, not me." (Courtesy Lake County Historic Courthouse Museum; courtesy private collection.)

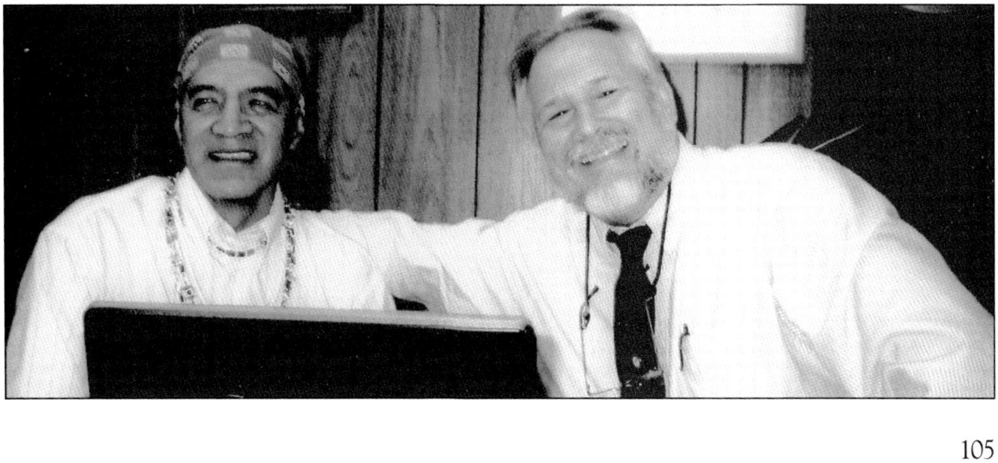

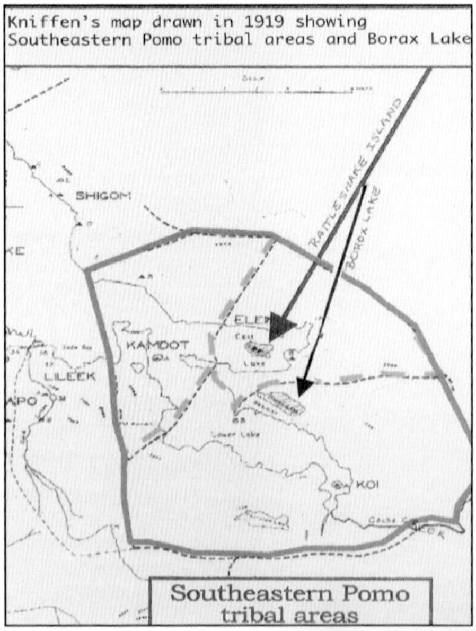


**Changing the Whole Field.** The Borax Lake site was placed on the National Register of Historic Places in October 2006 with these statements: "The Paleo-Indian deposits from the Borax Lake Site . . . demonstrate the geographic spread of the earliest human occupation into the Far West. Previously archeologists thought that the path of migration left the West Coast as a marginal region that was not settled until thousands of years after man's original entry into the New World. Borax Lake is the type site for Far West Paleo-Indaian period . . . dating from 12,000 to 10,000 years B. P. The property covers a 26-acre site that is owned by the Archaeological Conservancy. . . . Early man was drawn to the location's reliable freshwater source and abundant lithic materials for tools. Borax Lake site is considered the best representative of Paleo-Indian occupation of the Far West." (Courtesy National Register of Historic Places.)

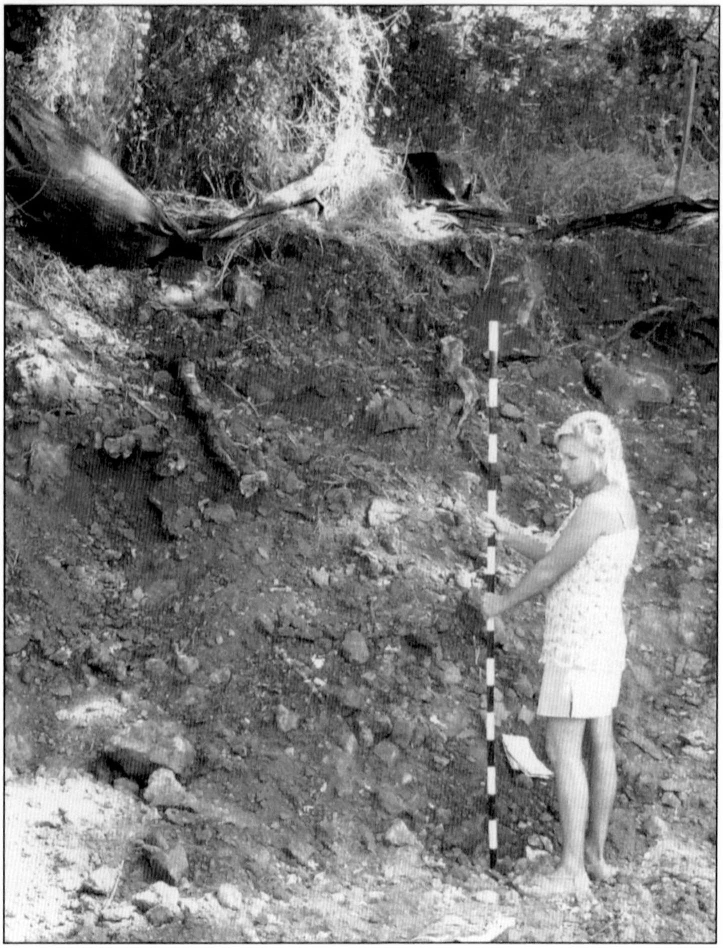

**It Cuts Deep.** The same month that the neighboring Borax Lake site went on the National Register, environmental contractors cleaning up the Superfund site at historic Elem Colony cut well into the heritage levels of soil in their removal of dangerous contaminants, as the photograph shows, and artifacts were destroyed. Intertribal violence and long-standing distrust between the Pomos and government officials, capped by a history of exploitation and genocidal policies, makes balancing the old values and modernism a sizeable challenge. (Courtesy John Parker, Ph.D.)

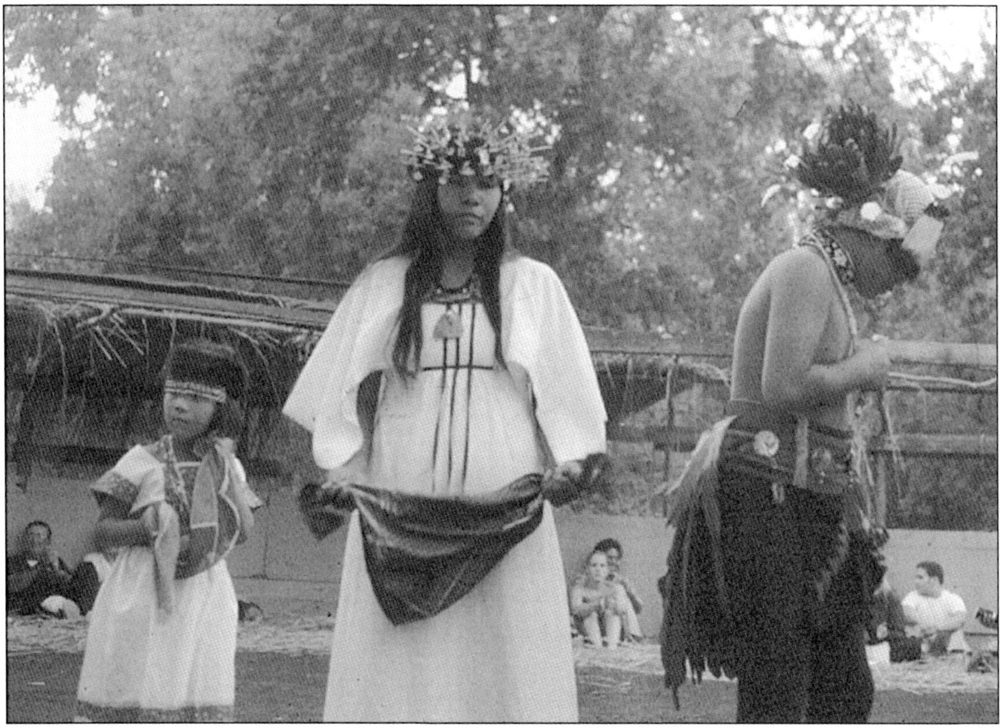

**WITH PRIDE AND REVERENCE.** After years of performing around the United States in the 1970s, the Elem Traditional Dancers were able to dance at their ancestral site on Rattlesnake Island. Women are Wah-ila Mota (left) and Gail Whiterock Brown; men are (from left to right below) Clifford Mota Jr., David Brown, and Gary Thomas. Gail designs and constructs the dance regalia. (Courtesy Jim Brown family dance archives.)

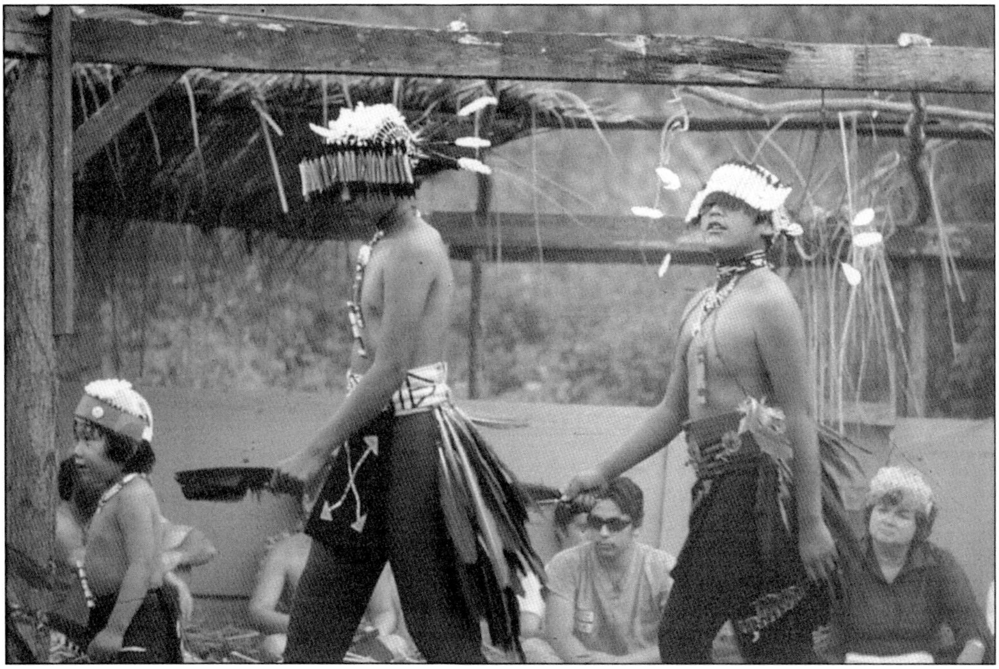

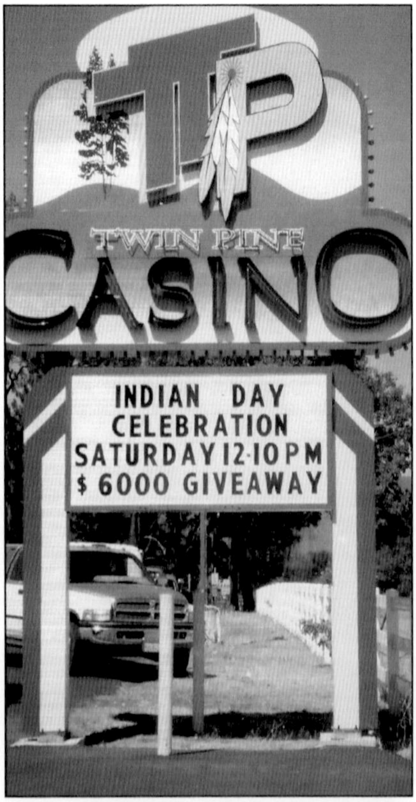


**More Bang for the Slots.** Lake County's three successful casinos are planning expansions and counting the blessings of Indian casino gaming. Jeff and Brad Knight from Middletown Rancheria reported that prior to the establishment of their modest-sized casino, 90 percent of the homes on the rancheria experienced at least one serious condition of alcoholism, drug abuse, or domestic violence. "In 2005," says Jeff, "that number has been reduced to about 20 percent. Gaming has given the people a job and a purpose and, more importantly, returned a sense of self-respect. Native sobriety has emerged from non-native gaming." Canadian news reports note more sober leaders in Indian communities and are seeing changes in political structure because they have healthier communities. A spokesman said they suspect health issues long ignored in Natives are really the root of problems such as alcohol, drug abuse, and violence. Lake County's four casino-less tribes are seeking ways to establish gaming. (Courtesy private collections.)

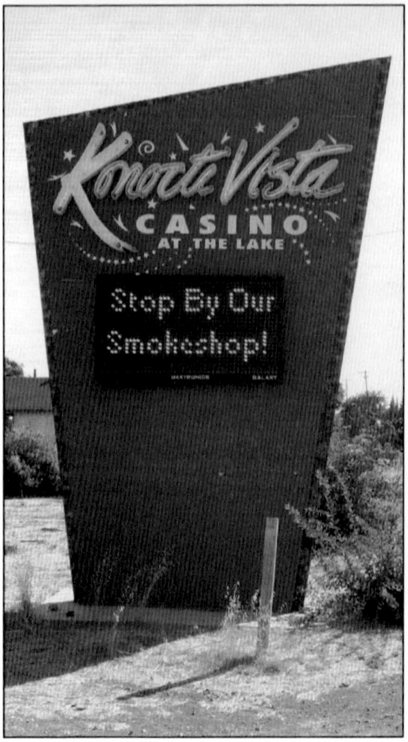


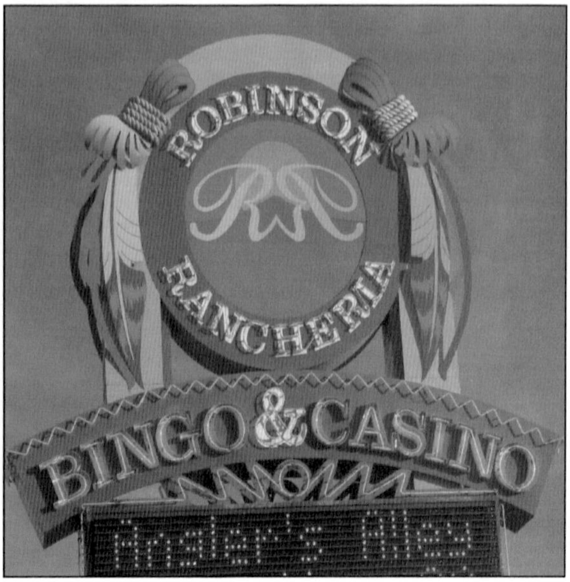

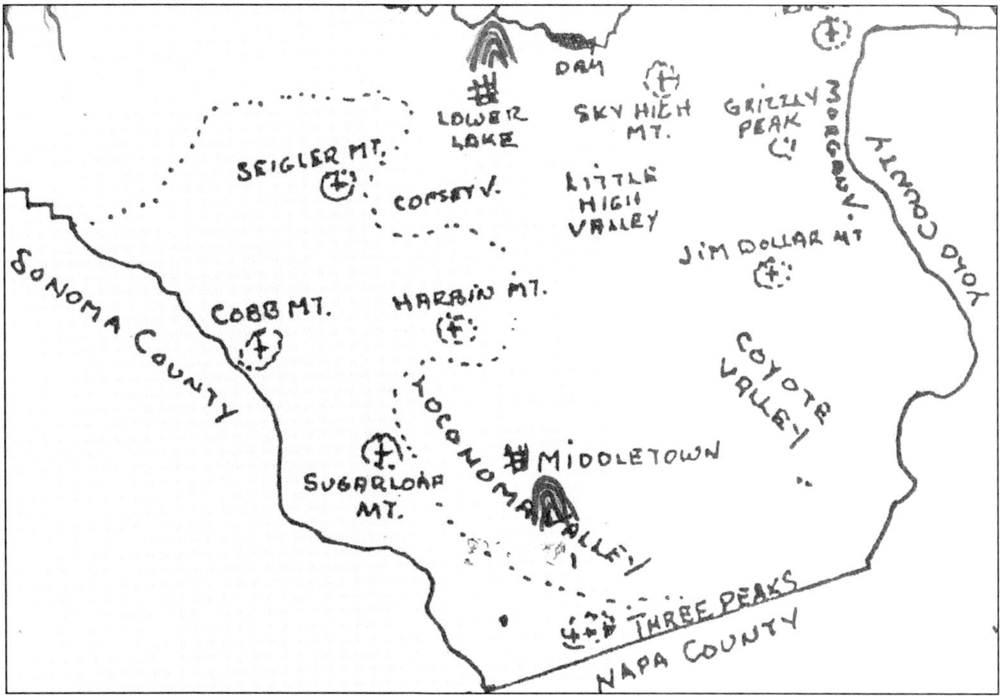


**It Is Halfway Either Way.** Middletown was a halfway stage stop between Calistoga and Lower Lake. Middletown Rancheria is the meeting point between the Lake Miwok Indian Nation and the Middletown Rancheria of Pomo Indians of California. Chinese intermarried and stayed because the federal immigration laws kept out their families. Some relatives moved there after the termination of the reservations at Cache Creek and Lower Lake. The rancheria is federally recognized as a California Indian tribe under Indian Reorganization Act of 1934, and the 100-acre rancheria owns and operates the Twin Pine Casino and the St. Helena Brewing Company.

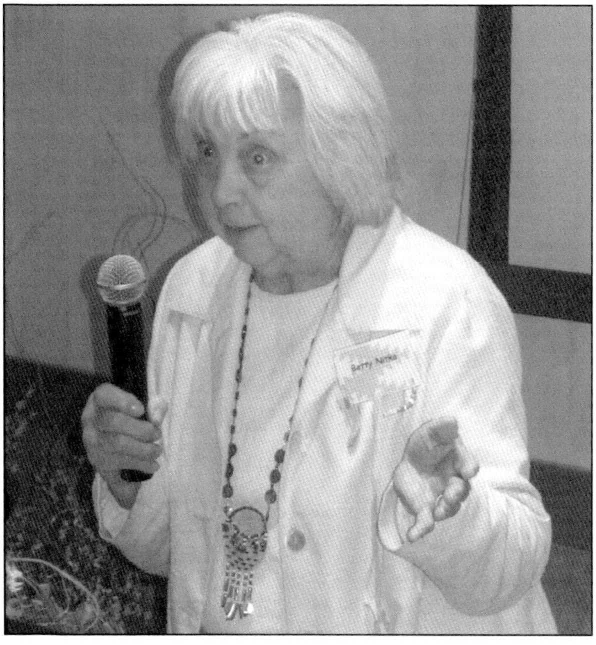

**Telling Stories.** Betty Nitka appeared at the Friends of the Museum's conference on Storytelling Through Pomo Basket Weaving in 2007. She is a tribal elder and a speaker of Lake Miwok. She told of the tribe's basket-making traditions and the triumph of the tribe's recent agreement with a vineyard that guaranteed rights to gather materials and to avoid spraying with pesticides. (Photograph by Trett Bishop, courtesy Friends of the Museum.)

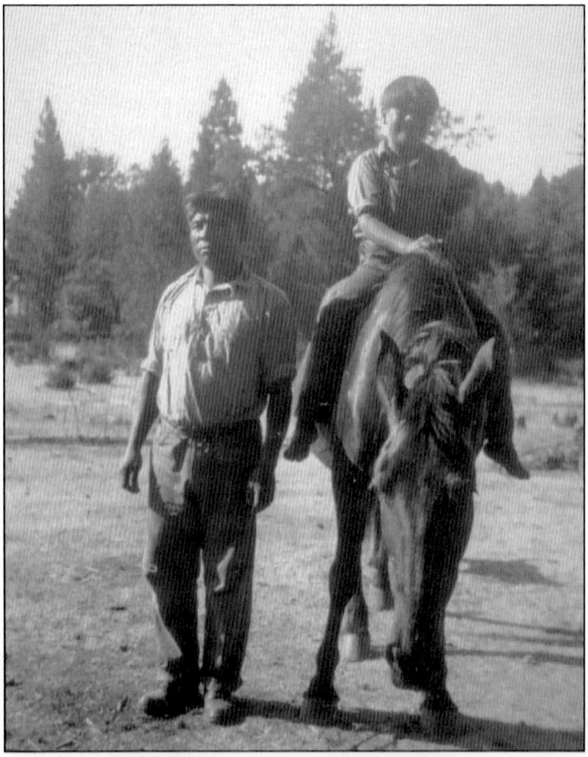

**MOVING IN.** In 1927, Henry Knight (left), his wife, Martha, and their sons lived on the Middletown Rancheria. Knight told historian Henry Mauldin in 1949 that he had worked hard to get this location, and that his family was the first of 35 to move there in 1912. Bradford and Jeff Knight, descendants and former members of the rancheria's tribal council, are remnants of three tribes: Pomo, Lake Miwok, and Wintun. Until recently, most thought they were Pomo, but a linguist from University of California Berkeley analyzed the language of one elder, and she was speaking Lake Miwok, a "lost" language completely distinct from Pomo. (Courtesy Lake County Historic Courthouse Museum.)

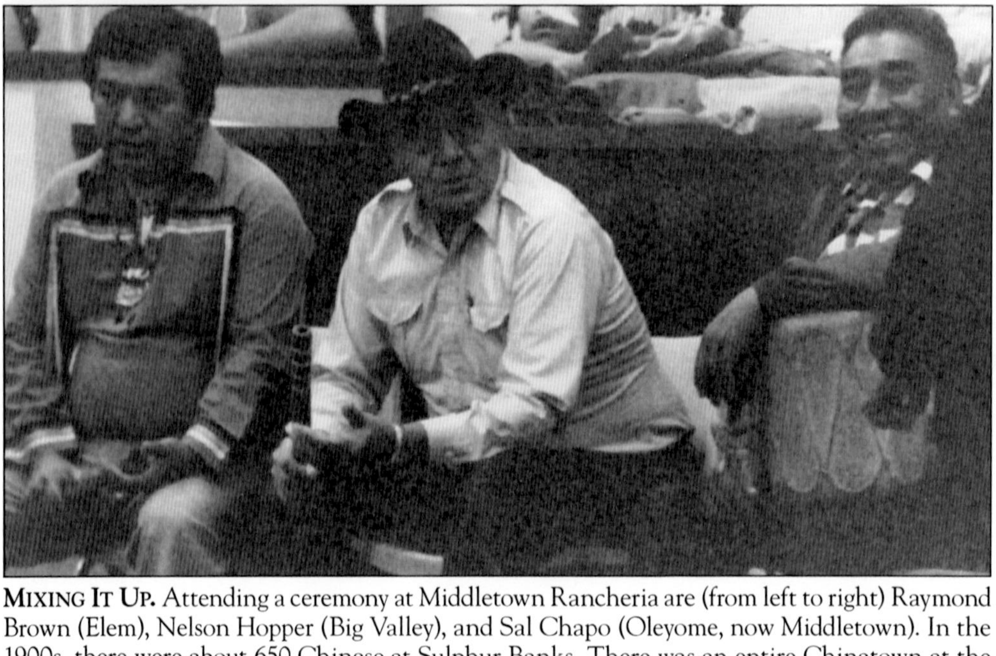

**MIXING IT UP.** Attending a ceremony at Middletown Rancheria are (from left to right) Raymond Brown (Elem), Nelson Hopper (Big Valley), and Sal Chapo (Oleyome, now Middletown). In the 1900s, there were about 650 Chinese at Sulphur Banks. There was an entire Chinatown at the Great Western Mine near Middletown. Chinese built many early toll roads and worked at Borax Lake. In the 1870s, a Chinese man hit another with a shovel at Johnson's brick kiln. On learning of this, the Lower Lake citizens made the 24–30 Chinese "put their belongings on their backs and walk to Calistoga." Middletown was halfway. (Courtesy Brown family archives.)

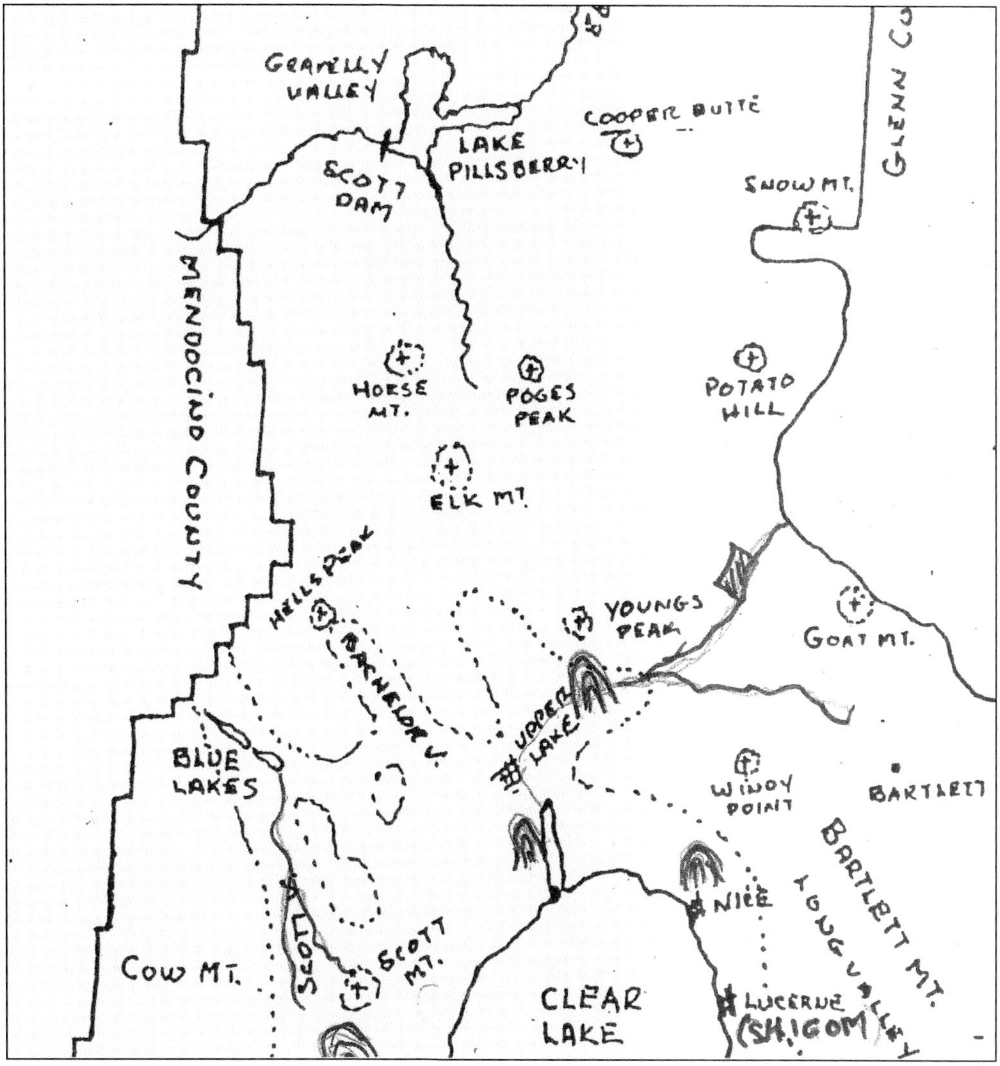


**OLD AND NEW.** Robinson Rancheria has two locations. In 1908, the government purchased 88 acres just south of Tule Lake at the old village of Danoxa and formally established the Robinson Rancheria. Its residents were primarily the former inhabitants of the community of Shigom, which had been abandoned in 1871, and their descendants. In the 1920s, an additional 80 acres was acquired, which expanded the rancheria's land base to 168 acres. Like 41 others, Robinson Rancheria was terminated under the terms of the California Rancheria Act of 1958. The land, with the exception of the old 6.4 acres at the tip of the lake was lost.

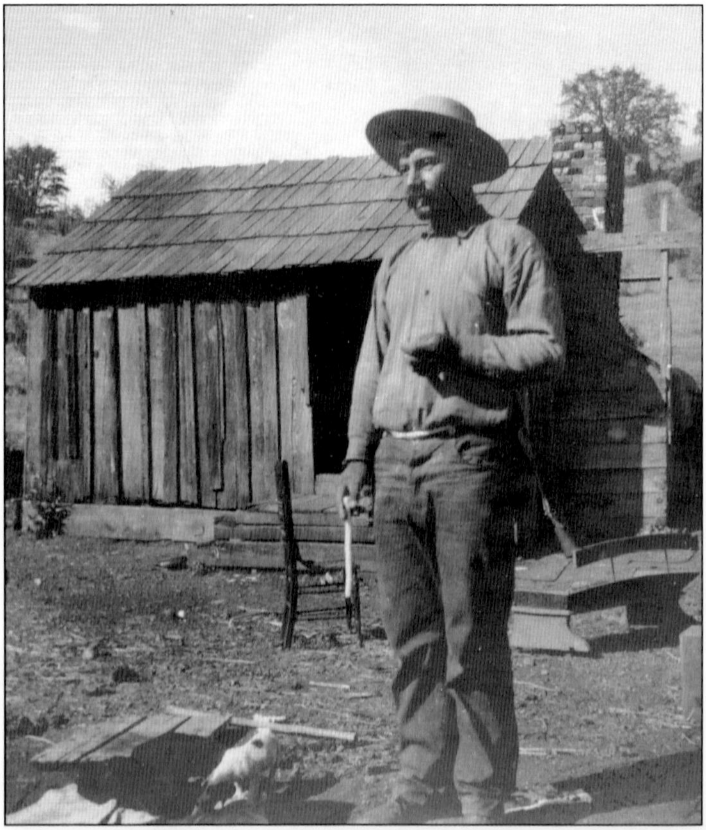

**Challenging Termination.** Often called the last chief of Shigom, Charley Gunter (sometimes spelled Gunther) led a group to a site near Lower Lake until Robinson Rancheria was founded. His father, a white man, started the Utopia mine in the 1890s but later abandoned his Indian wife. In 1975, as a result of a lawsuit filed by tribal member Mabel Duncan, the termination of Robinson was reversed. In 1982, the tribe, with a federal grant, purchased 107 acres to re-establish a community near Nice. This created two tribal land sites. (Photograph by John Hudson, courtesy Grace Hudson Museum.)

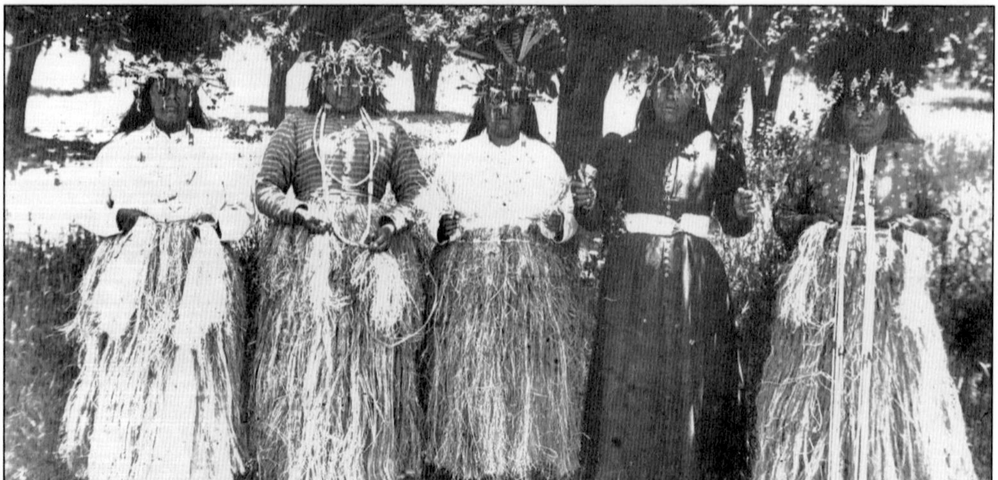

**A Native American Salad.** Through the centuries, there has been much immigration and intermarriage between those speaking Pomo languages other than Eastern. Now that almost everyone speaks American English, most of the Native languages are in disuse. Following the Spanish-American War in 1898, Filipinos moved to California, working beside Lake County's Native American agricultural workers, adding a dash of Spanish and Tagalog to the language. Either for a ceremonial or a social occasion, these traditional women stand ready for a dance *c.* 1915. (Courtesy Lake County Historic Courthouse Museum.)

**FIGHTING FOR THE VOTE.** Ethan Anderson, an Eastern Pomo, attempted to register to vote with the county clerk in 1915 and was denied. He and several members of his increasingly outspoken group (Arthur Treppa from Upper Lake and Stephen Knight from Ukiah) worked for two years to raise money to take his case to court. A state court ruled in his favor in 1917. It received little notice, but in 1922, fifty Hoopa Indians voted in the general election. The Anderson decision applied only to non-reservation Native Americans. Anderson and his wife, Clara (McCall), sold her traditional baskets, which were well known for their craftsmanship. Examples of her work are found at the Hearst Museum and the Smithsonian Institution. That revenue helped fund their poultry business. Below, Clara occupies a different role, one of mother to young Rose. (Contributed by Evaline Jordan, courtesy Lake County Historic Courthouse Museum; courtesy *Lake County Bee*, c. 1937.)

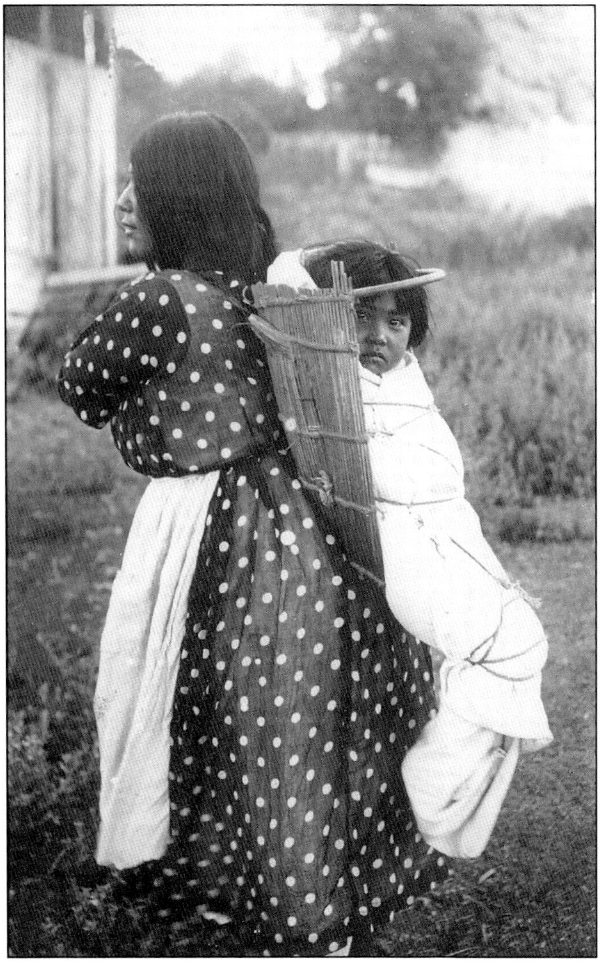

## ETHAN ANDERSON INDIAN LEADER, HOLDS HIGH RANK

Ethan Anderson, Indian delegate, was asked to submit his accomplishments in Indian welfare work. His statement follows:

I was born in Scotts valley, September 13, 1886. My early education was at the St. Turibius mission in Big valley. In 1910-11 I was a liquor suppression officer in the U. S. Indian service. I went to Carlisle, Pa. for more education. There I became a member of the Carlisle Invincible debating society. Then I was selected on the honor roll of the Society of American Indians. In 1912 I won second place in the literary contest which was held all over the United States in Indian schools (see Indian office records, Washington, D. C.) In 1916 I won in the test case (Anderson vs. Shafter Mathews) establishing the legal status of the California Indians. The State Supreme Court of California rendered its decision in my favor.

I have been active in helping F. G. Collett to have the Indian children admitted to the public schools.

I was elected secretary of the Indian board of cooperation in 1915 during the Panama Pacific Exposition. I had helped to form this organization which is now known as the Indians of California, Inc.

On July 2, 1934 I was elected to meet the senate investigation committee in San Francisco and saved the life of the organization. At present I am a member of the advisory committee of California Indians, Inc., demanding compensation for all Indians in California concering the lost treaties of 1851-52.

I am opposed to the Indian Reorganization Act. There is no liberty, no confidence and hardly any progress for the Indians but heavy debts that will be hard to pay.

There is plenty of complaint about it since the bill became a law.

I believe the Indians should be given a chance to exercise their constitutional rights like other American citizens and that is what our intelligent Indians desire.

ETHAN T. ANDERSON,

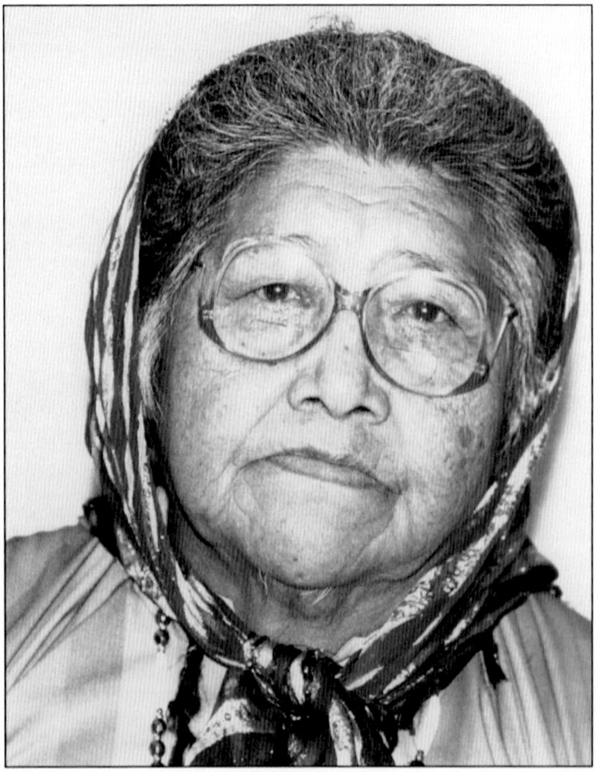

**TALENT PASSED DOWN.** Rose Anderson carried on the basket-making tradition, and her work, too, is in the homes and halls of private collectors as well as museums. Her health in later years kept her from weaving. (Photograph by Cheryl Adams, courtesy Lake County Historic Courthouse Museum.)

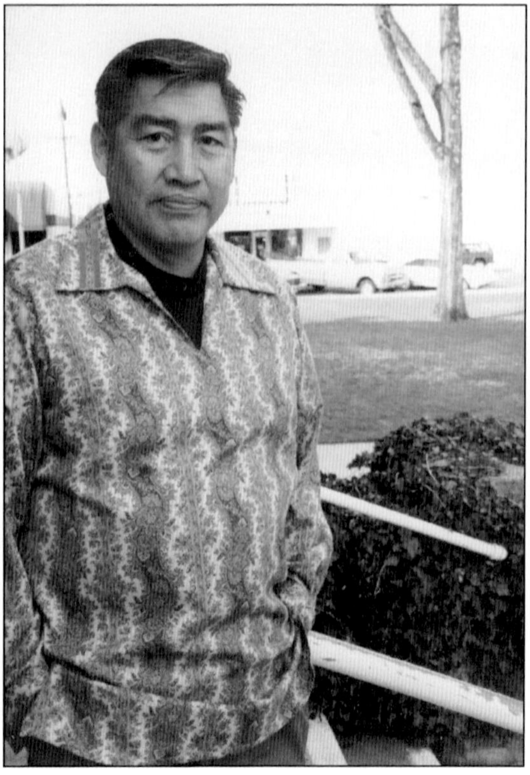

**GIVING BACK.** A graduate of Clear Lake Union High School in 1957, Marcus Anderson (1939–2000) spent at least half his boyhood with his grandfather. He pursued a career in the U.S. Air Force and spent much time in Europe. He returned and served as tribal chair at Robinson Rancheria during its initial tribal gaming discussions. (Photograph and shirt design by Donna Howard, courtesy Lake County Historic Courthouse Museum.)

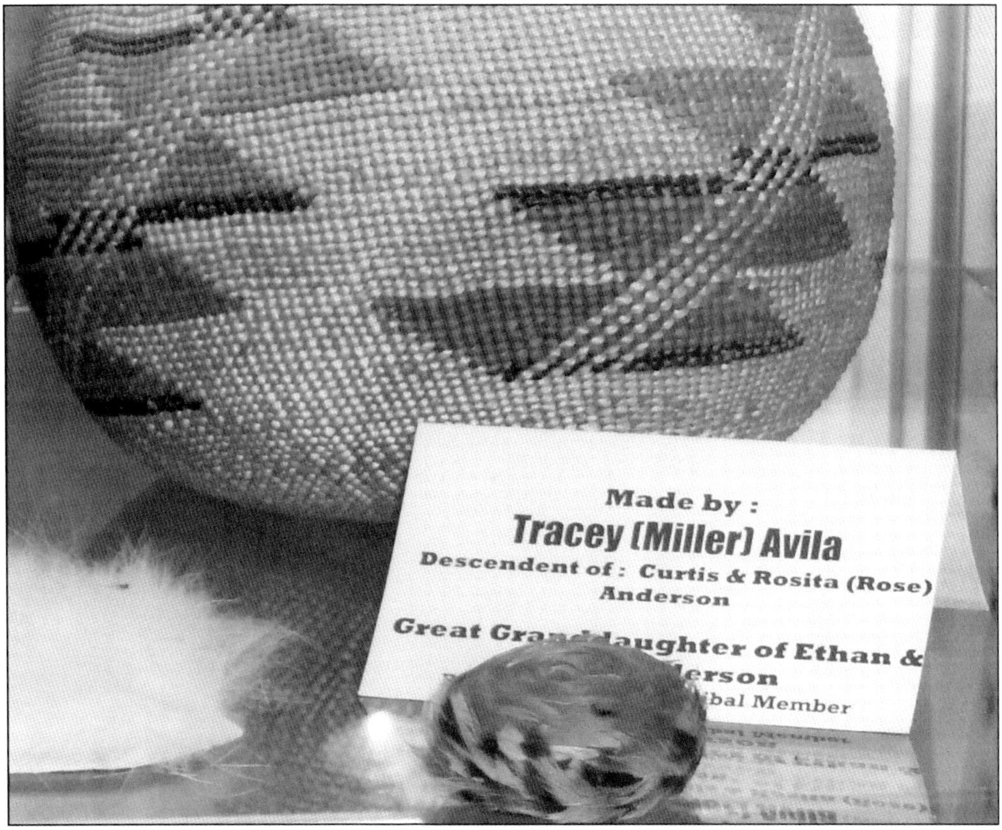


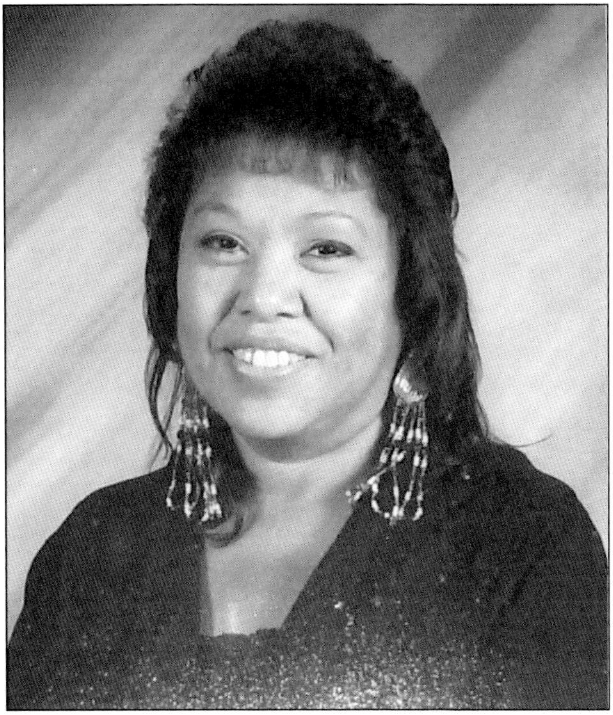

STILL THE ANDERSON LINE. Tracey (Miller) Avila continues the Anderson family tradition with her delicate baskets on display at the Robinson Rancheria Conference Center. Her portrait as tribal chairwoman hangs there too. Behind Tracey's miniature basket is an impressive traditional basket by Maude Bateman Boggs. (Courtesy private collection.)

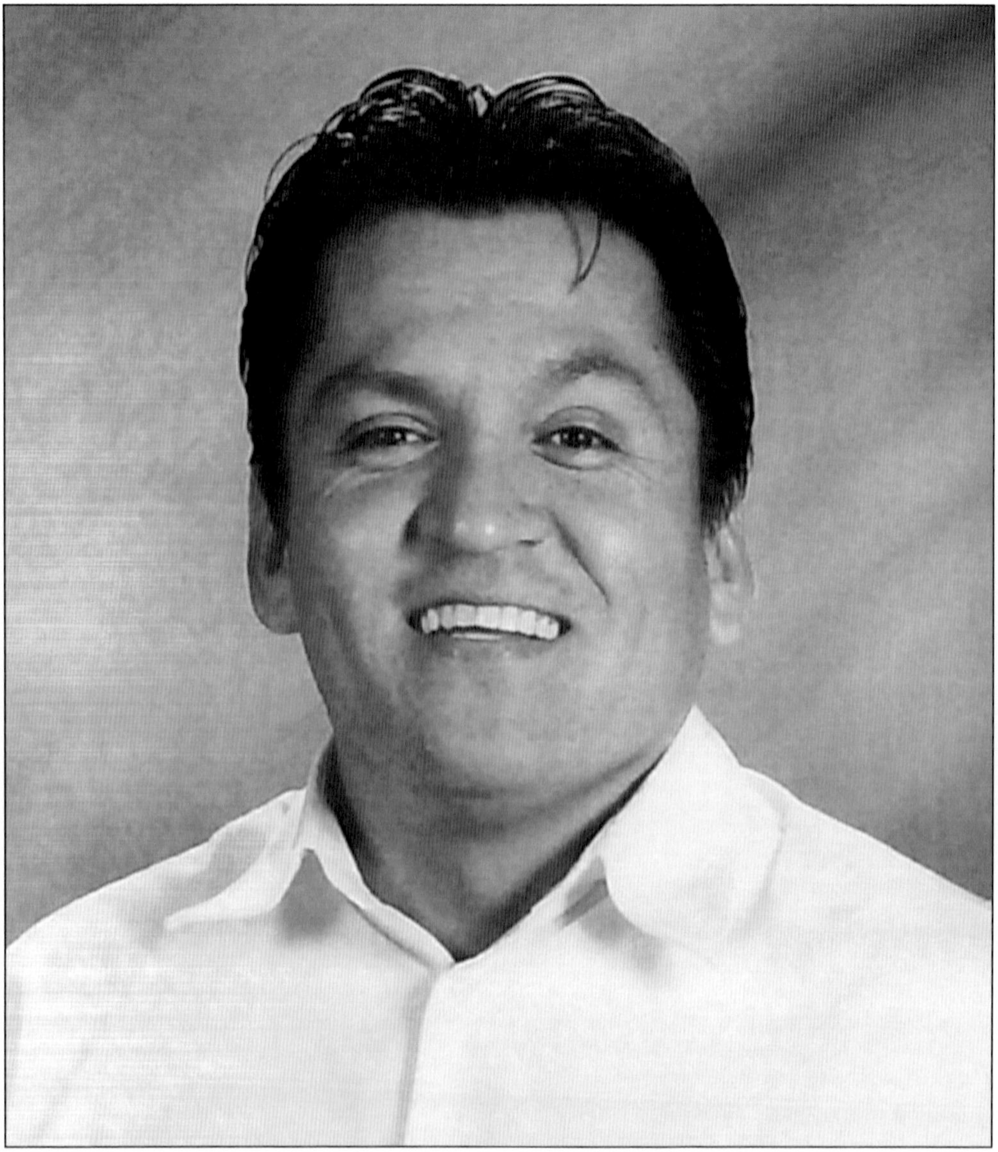

**ANOTHER LINE.** Harry and Maude Bateman Boggs are followed in tribal responsibility by son Nathan Boggs and grandson Jaime Boggs. Since 1982, several buildings have been constructed: an education/recreation facility with a half-court gymnasium, a community center, and a destination resort that includes a gaming casino, conference center, restaurant, and hotel. The tribe has also constructed an environmental center and a living community on this site with more than 40 new homes. (Courtesy private collection.)

**Both Sides Everyday.** Activist Clayton Duncan reminds people of injustice every May 15 at memorials to honor those slain at Bloody Island. On one side of the lake is State Historical Landmark 426, which commemorates the first adobe home in Lake County, (built not by Stone and Kelsey but by the forced labor of 400 or so Indians starved, abused, humiliated, and pushed to murder). Twenty minutes away is State Historical Landmark 427, which marks the indiscriminate massacre by soldiers of several hundred people who probably had nothing to do with Kelsey or Stone and were working their annual fish run. (Courtesy private collection.)

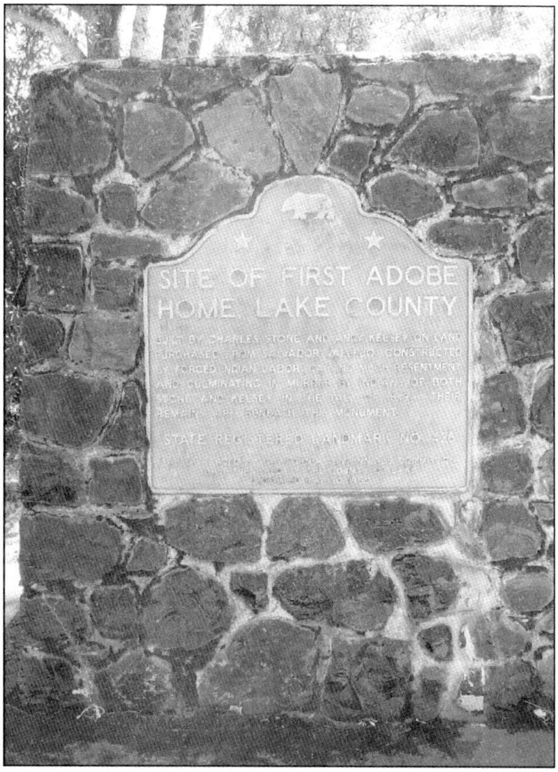


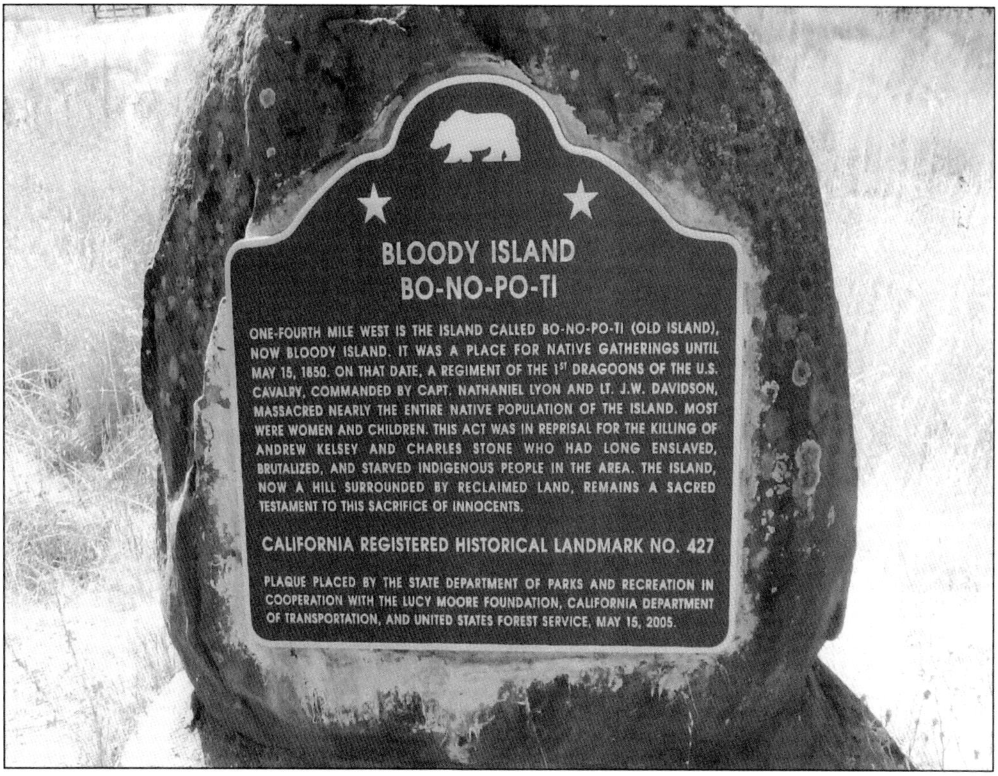

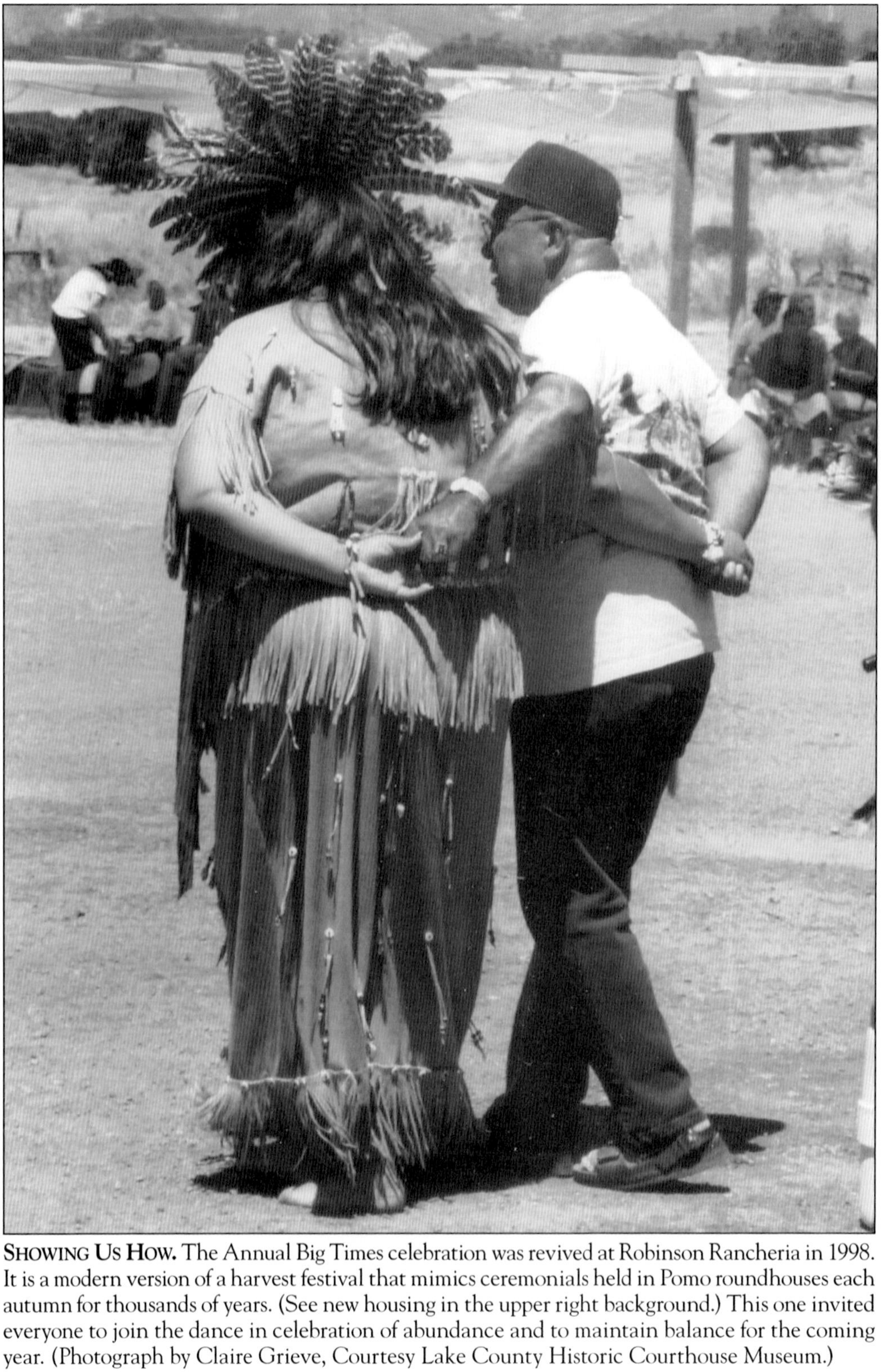

**Showing Us How.** The Annual Big Times celebration was revived at Robinson Rancheria in 1998. It is a modern version of a harvest festival that mimics ceremonials held in Pomo roundhouses each autumn for thousands of years. (See new housing in the upper right background.) This one invited everyone to join the dance in celebration of abundance and to maintain balance for the coming year. (Photograph by Claire Grieve, Courtesy Lake County Historic Courthouse Museum.)

# *Nine*

# POMO ARTS

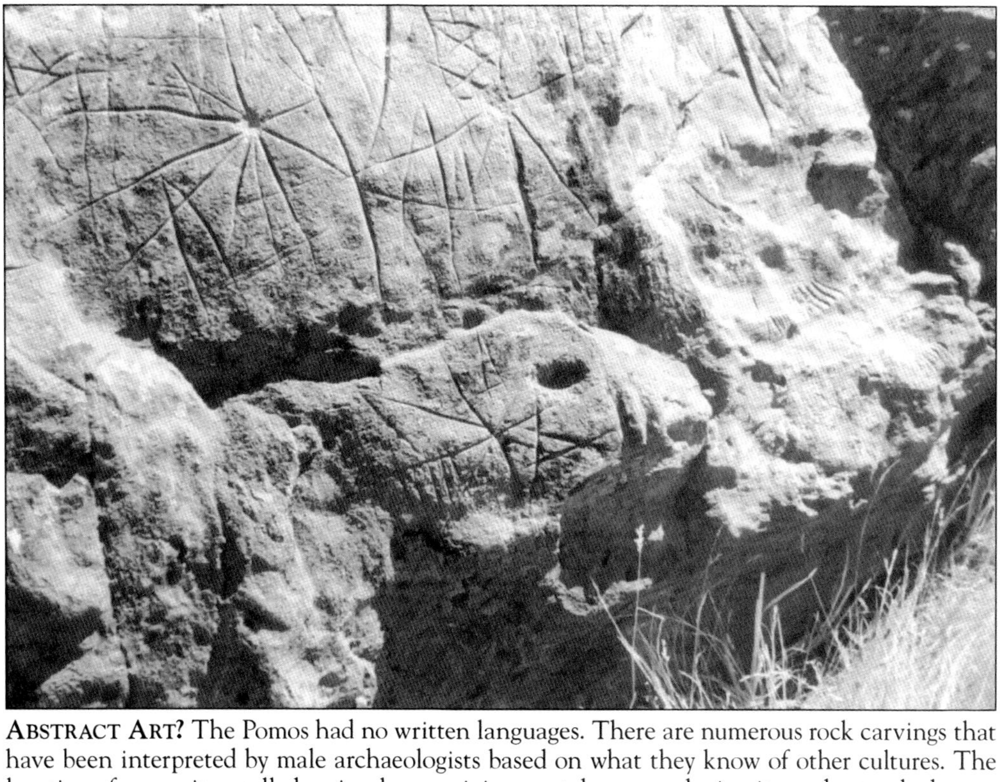

ABSTRACT ART? The Pomos had no written languages. There are numerous rock carvings that have been interpreted by male archaeologists based on what they know of other cultures. The location of many sites, called variously conceiving scratches, sacred rain pits, and petroglyphs, are kept quiet to avoid defacing by vandals. These conceiving scratches, photographed in Bachelor Valley in 1950, were marked with chalk to improve the photograph. A vocabulary of petroglyphs is displayed at Anderson Marsh State Historic Park near Lower Lake but no one has yet broken the code or identified who made them. Some can be seen on the ranger's tour, but others are left to the rattlesnakes. Visitors should ask. (Photograph by Henry Mauldin, courtesy Lake County Historic Courthouse Museum.)

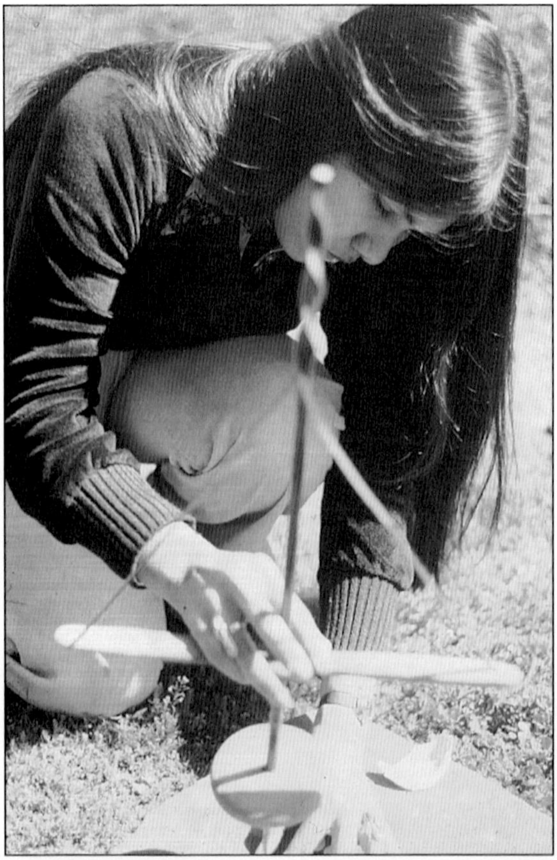

**COINAGE.** Tribes went to the ocean not only to collect salt, but also to bring back clamshells that would be ground into washer-like disks, drilled with a small hole, and strung in lengths indicating their value. The pump drill was invented a short time before contact; then metal drill points replaced bone. Gail Whiterock Brown works with a traditional drill; in modern times, shell disks are used as designs on presentation baskets or in decorative jewelry. (Courtesy John Parker, Ph.D.)

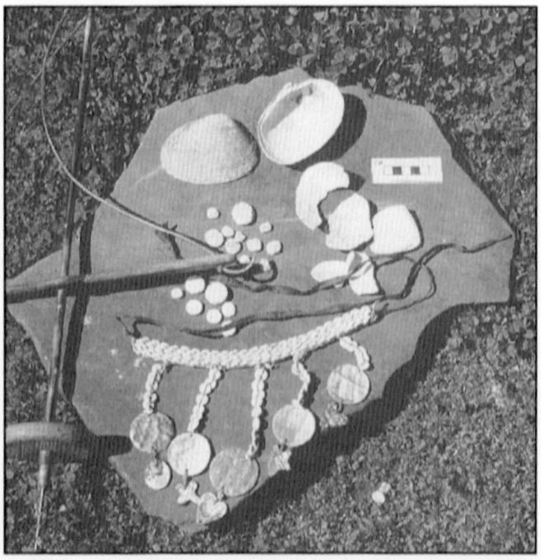

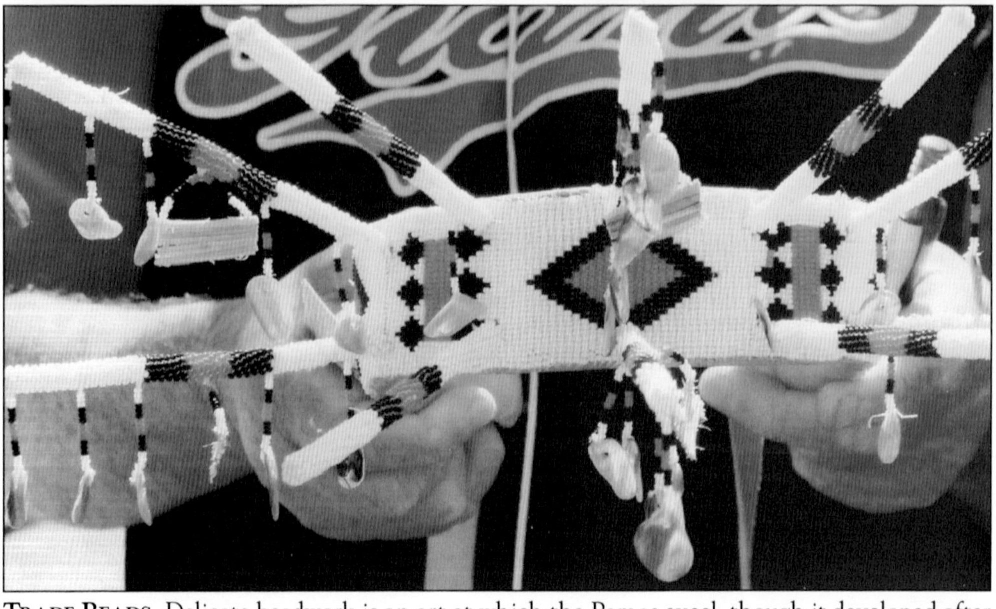

**TRADE BEADS.** Delicate beadwork is an art at which the Pomos excel, though it developed after Russian glass beads were available. Here is an example of a delicately beaded woman dancer's headpiece made by a man from the Pomo tribe in Point Arena. (Courtesy private collection.)

**FOLLOW THE LEADER.** Men and women learn to dance by dancing from the earliest age, training their muscle memory to follow and to express within traditional boundaries. Young women learn to hold their upper arms close to the body and move the lower arms back and forth, sometimes with a sash or cloth in hand. Their feet stamp a discrete, calf-numbing rhythm. Traditional drums were shaped logs played with the feet. (Photograph by Carol Dillinger, courtesy Big Valley Rancheria.)

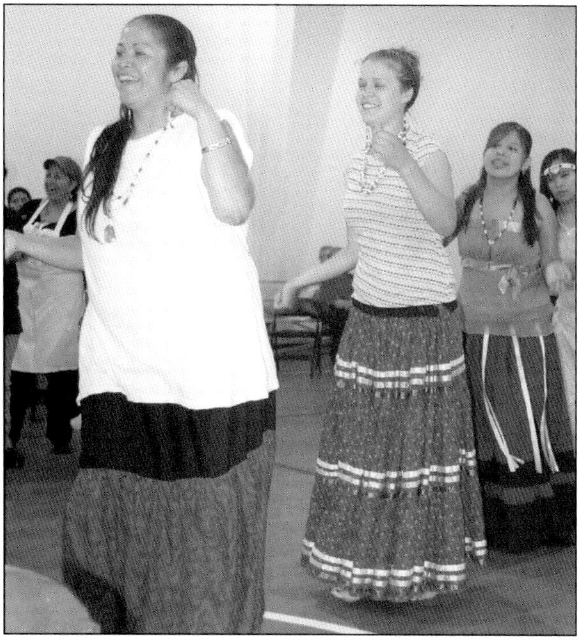

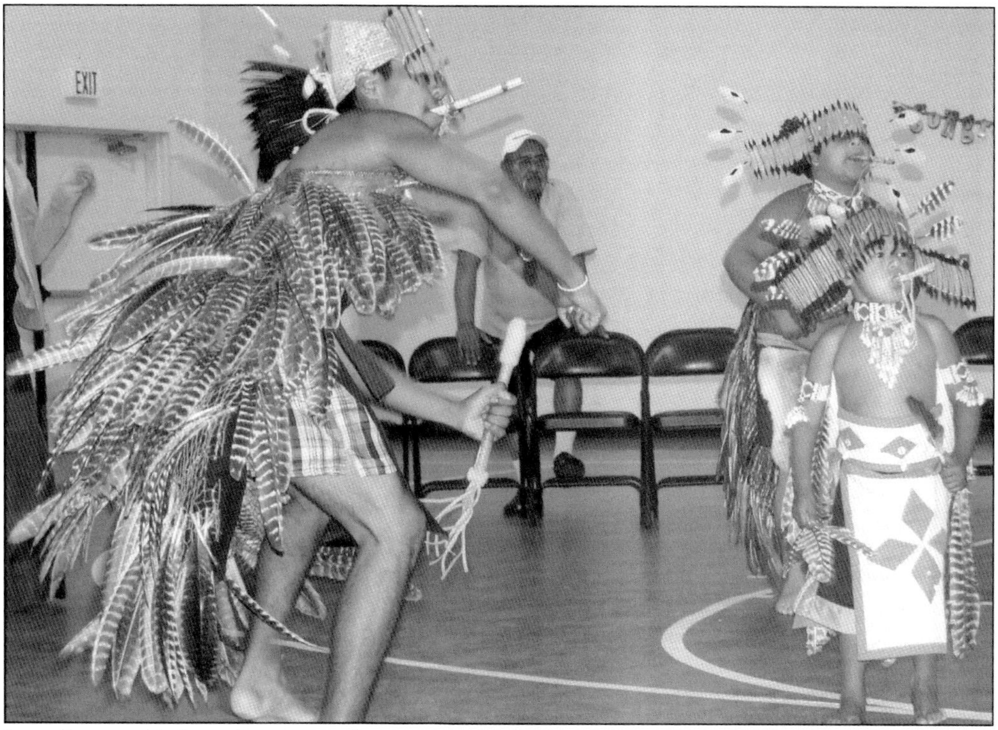


**JUST DANCE.** Robert Gomez coaches youngsters dancing in regalia, including the flicker-feather (yellow hammer) headdress, turkey feather mantles, and bone whistles in their mouths. Feathers are now gathered with difficulty, since federal laws prohibit killing many birds. Dancers perform with singers of traditional songs, percussionists, and a ceremonial dance director or captain. Dancers are trained in traditional placement, but the movement reflects each dancer's unique spirit. (Photograph by Carol Dillenger, courtesy Big Valley Rancheria)

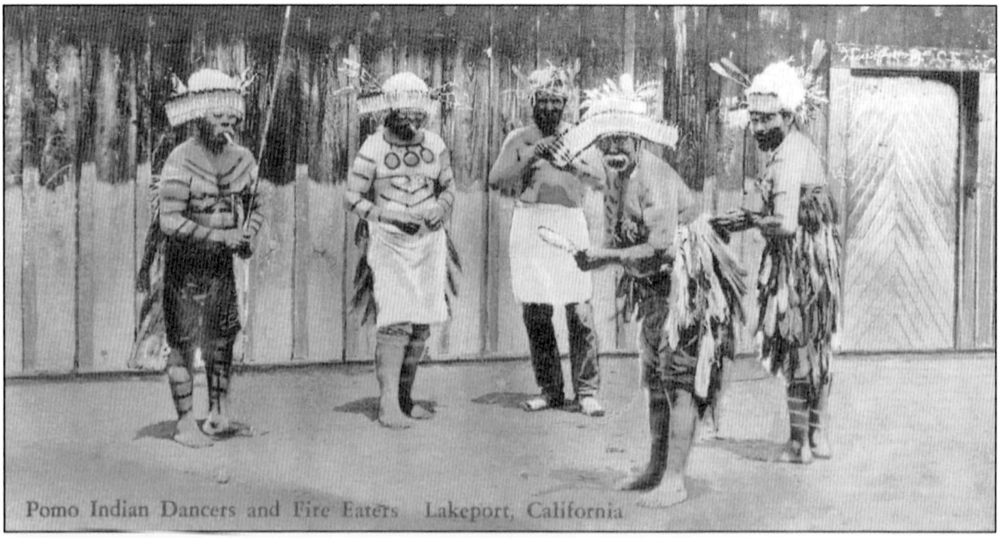


**FIRE-BREATHING DANCERS.** This 1906 postcard reproduced from a photograph by O. F. Meddaugh shows men painted, costumed, and ready for ceremonies that were rarely witnessed even then. Each man (tentatively identified) assumes a role for the Upper Lake roundhouse performance that is said to be religious in nature: (from left to right) Jim Rickabaugh, Johnny Bull (a fire eater and chief of Shigom), Dick Green (Whiskey Head), "Snap" Bucknell (best dancer), and Charles Rickabaugh (a fire eater). (Courtesy Lake County Historic Courthouse Museum.)

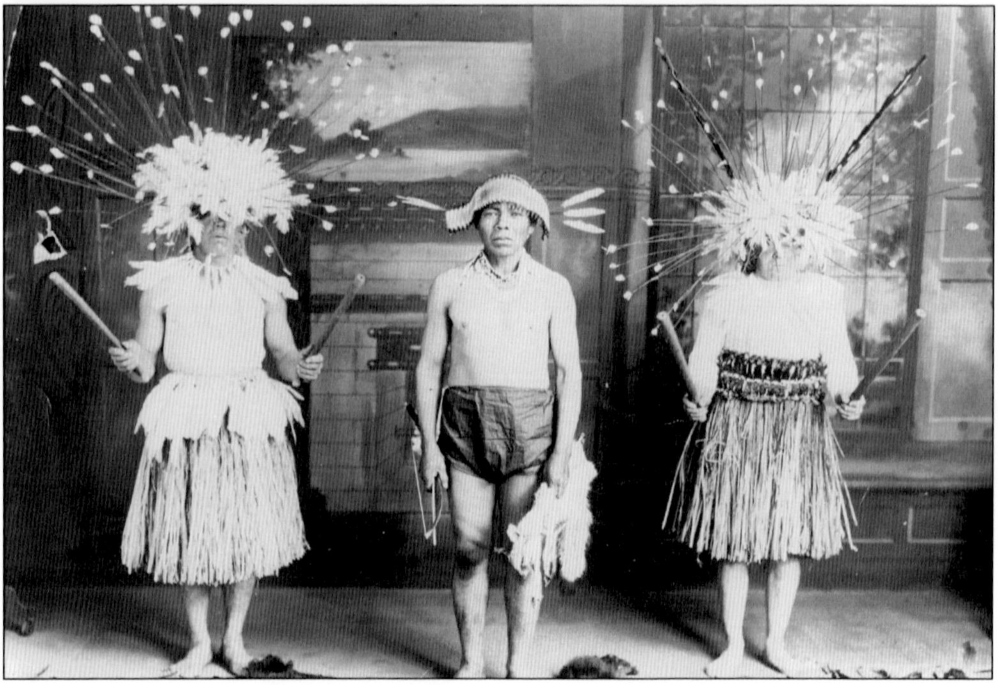

**LARGER THAN LIFE.** Big-head dancers perform in the roundhouse for special ceremonials since they represent particular characters or characteristics. As populations decreased, it was necessary to draw them from ever-broader areas in order to get a full cast. The above dancers came from Chico in 1923: Herby Young, George Nye, and Dewey Conway. (Courtesy Lake County Historic Courthouse Museum.)

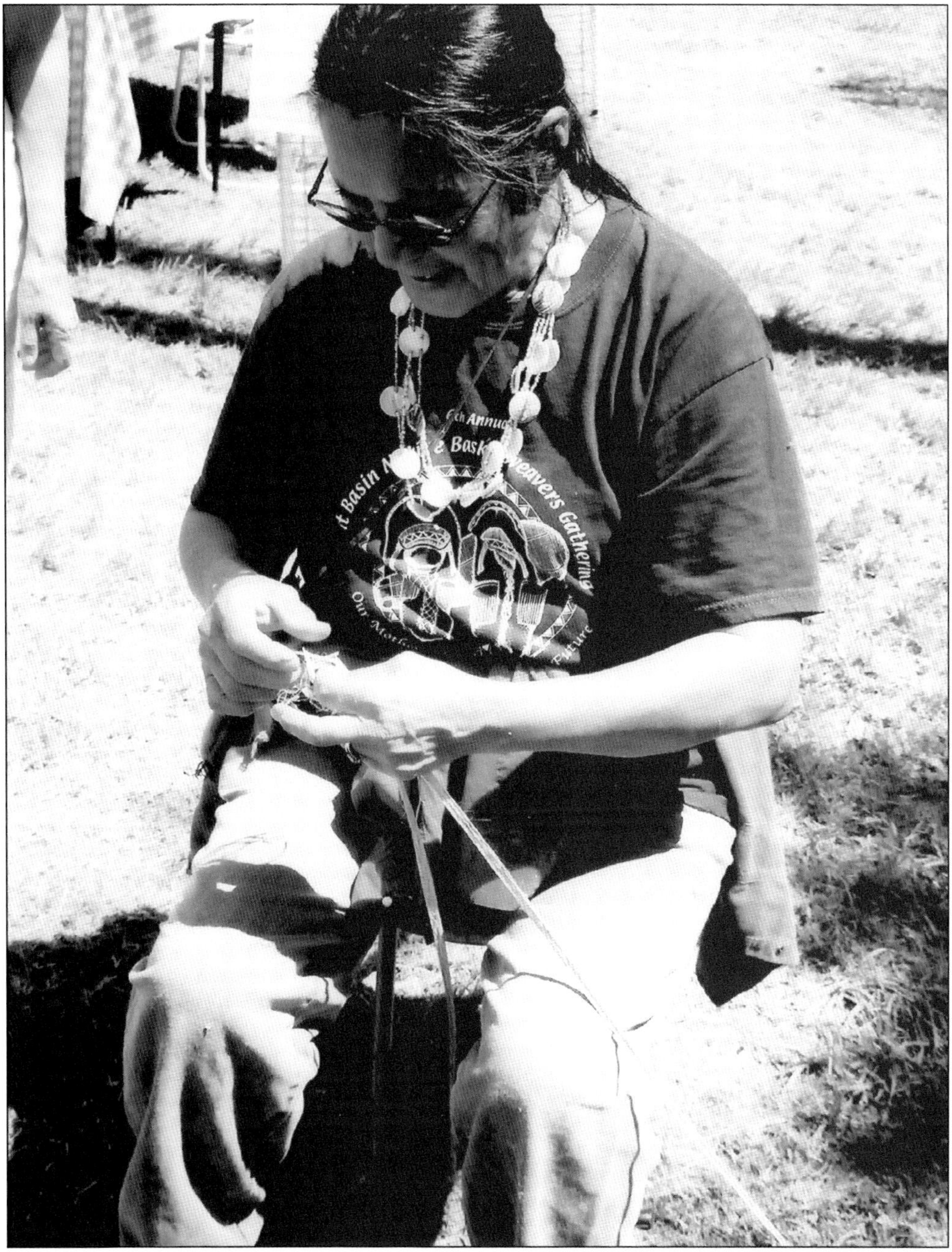

**LUWANA QUITIQUIT TEACHES THE CRAFT OF CORDING.** The quality of Pomo Indian baskets has never been equaled. According to Sherri Smith-Ferri, an expert on Pomo baskets, there were 22 distinct types, each with its own name and use. She says it took seven different types to prepare acorn mush, a dietary staple of the natives. Most of these can only be seen in ethnographic museums, since materials and mastery are no longer available. In the early 1900s, there was demand for basketry when the emphasis had shifted from utilitarian tools to artistic decorations, and the money was good. Later the demand fell off, and people found other work. Modern pesticides and fertilizers make basket materials inaccessible and poisoned. (Courtesy private collection.)

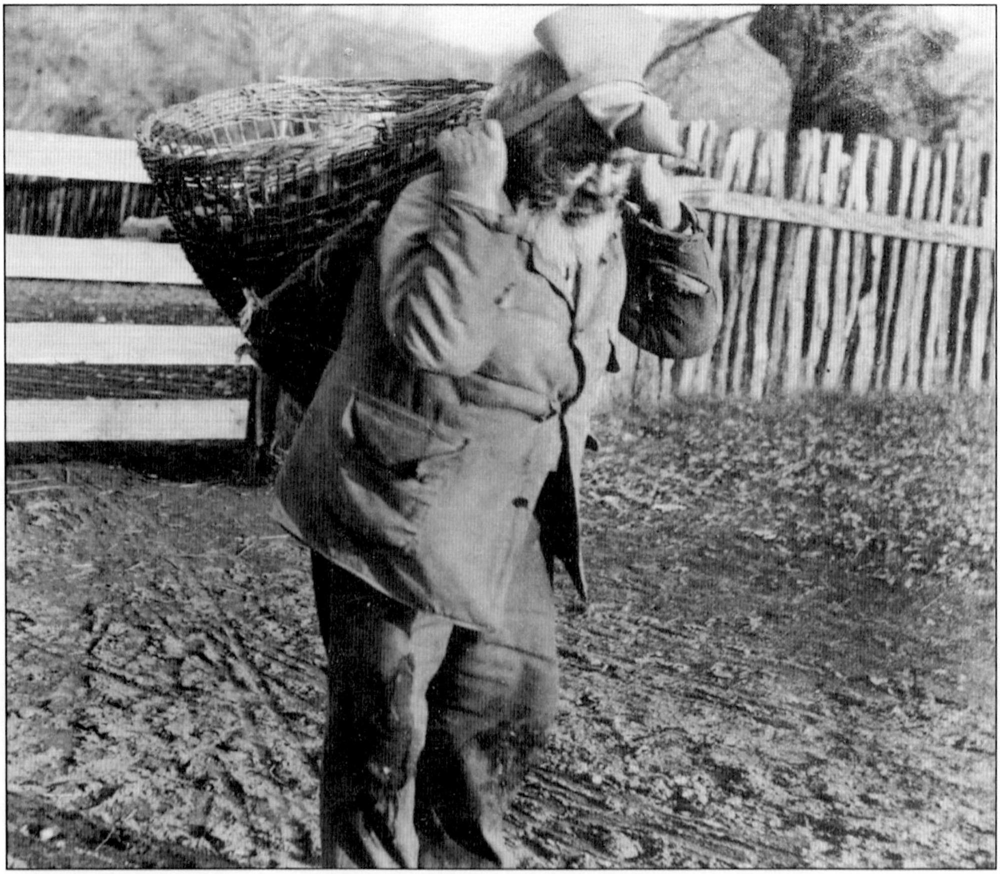

**WHERE TO LOOK?** Today there are only two kinds of baskets being made by those few craftsmen who work to keep their culture alive and lively. Twining is more like weaving, and coiling is more like sewing; these are the two types of basketry that contemporary basket makers work, and then often in miniature. Go to a museum or cultural center to see the fine wickerwork of items like Old Tom's burden basket (Scott's Valley *c.* 1910), or see the expertly devised fish traps at the Courthouse Museum's Pomo gallery. (Robert J. Lee Collection [Nevin], courtesy Lake County Historic Courthouse Museum; courtesy private collection.)

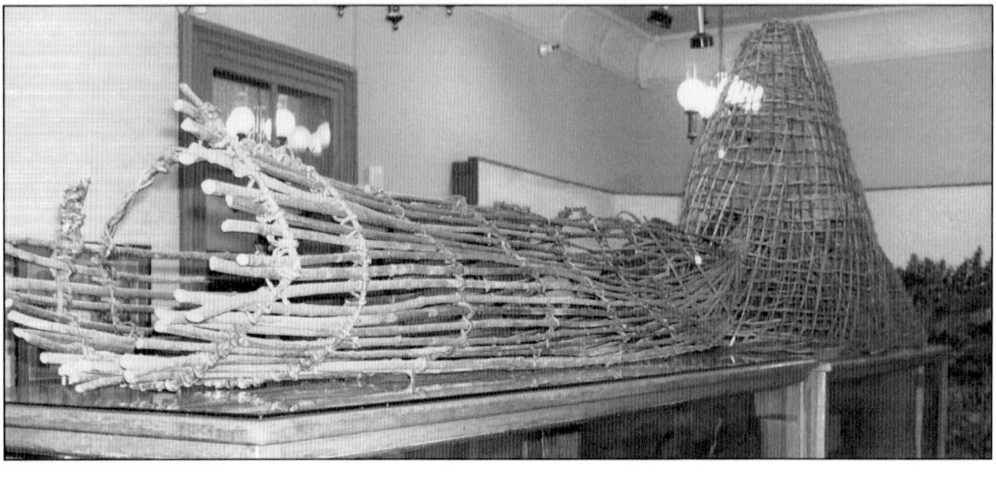

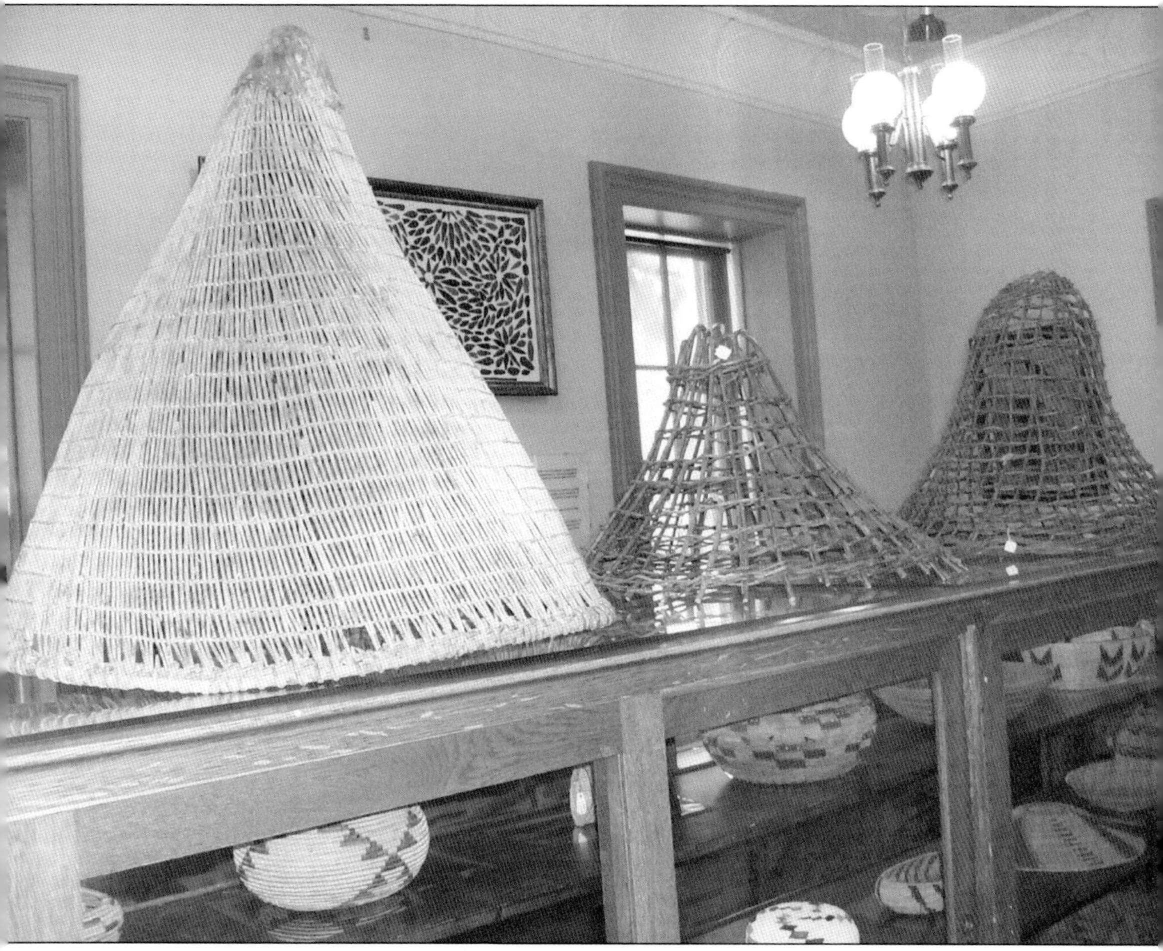

**CULTURAL RECORD AND ART.** More than 200 Pomo baskets have been acquired by Lake County's museums since the 1930s, a cultural record of the finest basket makers in the world. Not all of them are on display at the same time. A well-trained corps of docents gives school and adult tours. (Courtesy Lake County Historic Courthouse Museum.)

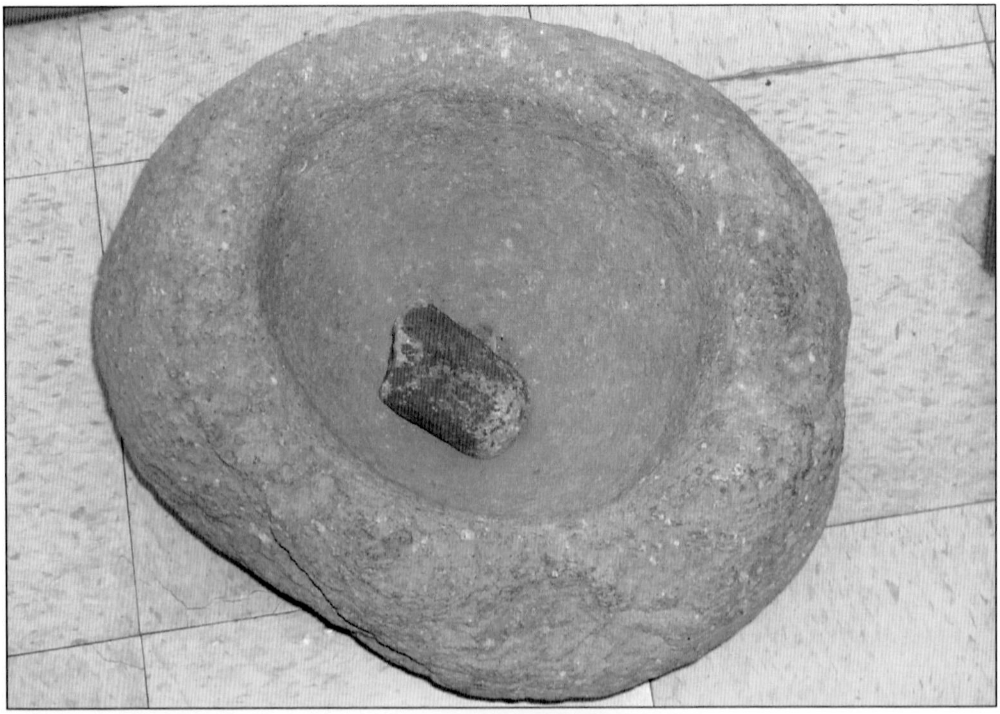

**WHAT'S IN YOUR BACKYARD?** One mortar was found while excavating for a building in the 1970s (top). The others are on display in the Courthouse Museum. If either artifact were found today, it would be subject to California Environmental Quality Act (CEQUA) regulations that require authorities to determine whether it is from an archaeological site, and if so, how it can be recorded. Such artifacts tell stories of historical significance and perhaps keys to survival as conditions change. (Courtesy private collections.)

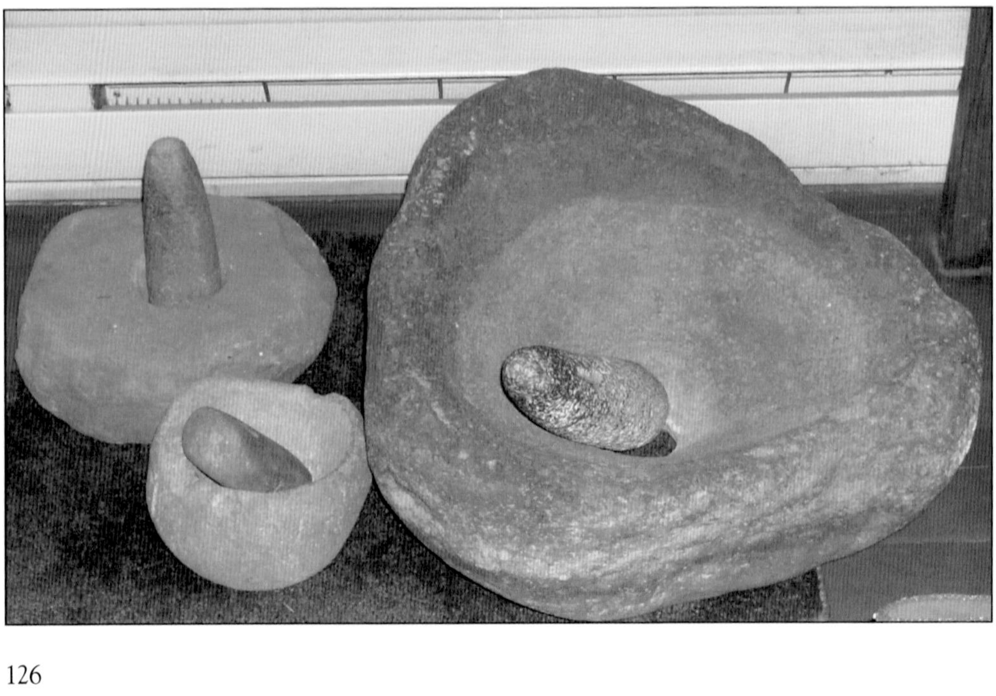

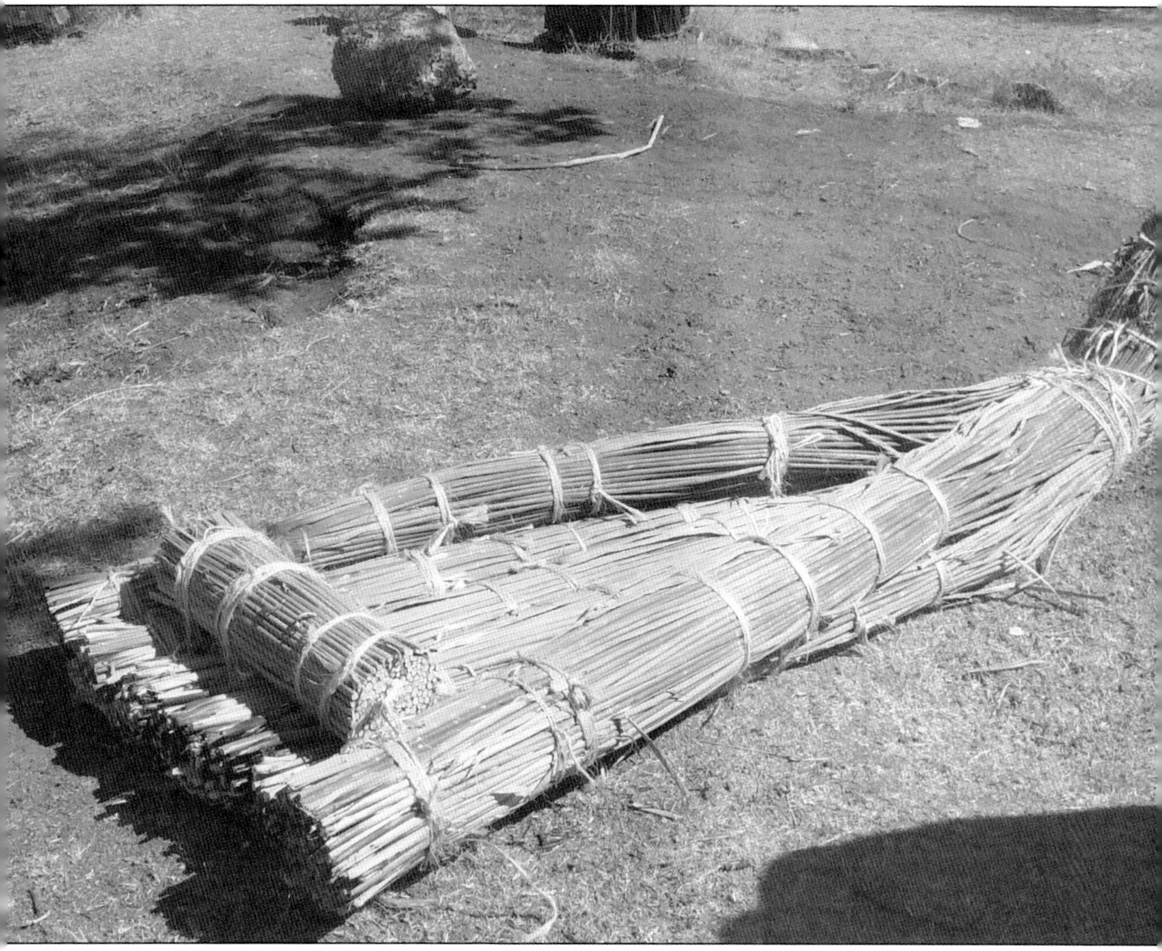

**WOVEN WATERCRAFT.** Tule rushes are still in great supply, and mats and carrying implements are easily made. The Tule Boat Races and Festival on Clear Lake have reinvigorated efforts at reed boat building for fun and cultural esteem. A recent issue of *News from Native California* featured a Pomo tule boat on San Francisco Bay sailing out to meet an arriving Maori vessel from Australia. (Courtesy Big Valley Rancheria.)